Church, Sacrament, and American Democracy

"This is a first rate work by a young emerging scholar. Borneman offers a refreshing new take on John Williamson Nevin's social thought in its theological context. Long neglected by historians of religion, Nevin has recently been the subject of renewed interest by theologians and historians alike. Situated in the middle of the tumultuous ante-bellum period, Nevin's work is neither easily caricatured nor categorized. Borneman does a masterful job in locating the significance of Nevin's thought in relation to the Jacksonian revolution in American democracy and the resurgence of revivalism of the Second Great Awakening. Borneman's analysis is both political and theologically sophisticated, a rare combination in the scholarly literature on Nevin. Borneman also understands the difficulty of lining Nevin up on the classic conservative/liberal religious spectrum. Nevin does not easily fit into those categories and Borneman offers a refreshing new angle on why this is so. As Borneman persuasively argues, Nevin's social thought is driven by his theological convictions about the nature of the Incarnation of Christ. His social convictions derive from his theology and therefore stand separate from religiously liberal progressives and from religiously conservative traditionalists. Borneman captures nicely the uniqueness of Nevin's voice and encourages us to hear that voice in prophetic ways in our own day by putting it into conversation with other significant and unique socio-political traditions. This is a work that will deeply impact the way historians and theologians understand John Williamson Nevin in the years ahead."

—Richard Lints
Andrew Mutch Distinguished Professor of Theology
Gordon-Cownell Theological Seminary

"Recent years have seen an increase of attention given to John Williamson Nevin and the Mercersburg theology. This interest is not merely nostalgic, as Nevin and company were well ahead of their time and have a bevy of insights to offer us today. Nevin was among the most philosophically sophisticated orthodox theologians of his day and thus speaks as much to our current controversies and questions as he did to those of his own era. Nevin lived in period of great intellectuals, perhaps the high point of American intellectual history; time and again he proved himself not only a worthy conversation partner, but a towering and important figure whose legacy demands respect and careful study.

Adam Borneman's unique and important monograph addresses the sociological and political aspects of Nevin's theology, areas which have been largely neglected in the spate of recent studies. As Borneman delves into this relatively unexplored terrain, he examines Nevin within his broader social and cultural context, giving us a better understanding of a crucial era of American history and the genius of Nevin's wide-ranging, largely counter-cultural work. By focusing on his sociopolitical theology, Borneman also uncovers many contemporary applications of Nevin's thought to today's ecclesial and social conditions; in other words, Borneman demonstrates that Nevin continues to be a vital conversation partner even from the grave. Borneman's work is sure to magnify contemporary appreciation of Nevin by showing that this nineteenth century mastermind offers a coherent, integrated, Christocentric view of the cosmos, history, and culture. Nevin challenged many viewpoints that most Americans, including most American theologians, have long taken for granted; Borneman brings that challenge to us afresh in this profound new book."

—Rich Lusk
author of *Paedofaith*

"Adam Borneman's work on the sociopolitical dimensions of John W. Nevin's theology provides a valuable and unique addition to the expanding landscape of Mercersburg studies. The "Eucharistic wholeness" for which Nevin contended throughout his career has dramatic ramifications for both the Christian church and larger human society. As Borneman ably demonstrates in his erudite study, there has been lacking to date a presentation of Nevin's thought that adequately displays the interplay of Nevin's incarnational and sacramental theology with his sociopolitical analyses and reflections. Borneman has performed a great service by showing the sociopolitical implications of Nevin's overall philosophy and theology even where Nevin himself may not have offered extended treatments. As such, *Church, Sacrament, and American Democracy* is must reading for Christian scholars, pastors, and laypeople alike who have an interest either in the Mercersburg theology specifically or in Christian political theology more generally."

—Jonathan G. Bonomo
author of *Incarnation and Sacrament*

"Borneman's work provides a valuable contribution to the growing constellation of studies on that most fascinating of nineteenth-century American theologians, John Williamson Nevin. By focusing his attention on the ways in which Nevin's thought engages the political—which, because of his deep ecclesiological commitment, remains always suprapolitical—Borneman renders scholars (and laymen) a twofold service. First, by attending to the socio-political context of Nevin's life and work, he provides us with a new lens for reading and understanding Nevin's writings, thus deepening our historical understanding of an important thinker about whom we still understand all too little. Second, Borneman contributes to the important and exciting task of bringing Nevin into conversation (as he himself surely would have wished) with a range of creative theologians from across the ecumenical spectrum. Due to the idiosyncratic, wide-ranging, and catholic nature of Nevin's thought, such comparisons nearly always bear much fruit, and Borneman's essay is no exception. Borneman is to be particularly commended for engaging with a broad swath of Nevin's writings, rather than merely majoring on a few key texts, and for his familiarity with a wide range of relevant secondary literature."

—W. Bradford Littlejohn
author of *The Mercersburg Theology and The Quest for Reformed Catholicity*

Church, Sacrament, and American Democracy

The Social and Political Dimensions of John Williamson Nevin's Theology of Incarnation

Adam S. Borneman

WIPF & STOCK · Eugene, Oregon

CHURCH, SACRAMENT, AND AMERICAN DEMOCRACY
The Social and Political Dimensions of John Williamson Nevin's Theology of Incarnation

Copyright © 2011 Adam S. Borneman. All rights reserved. Except for brief quotations in critical publications or reviews, no part of this book may be reproduced in any manner without prior written permission from the publisher. Write: Permissions, Wipf and Stock Publishers, 199 W. 8th Ave., Suite 3, Eugene, OR 97401.

Wipf & Stock
An Imprint of Wipf and Stock Publishers
199 W. 8th Ave., Suite 3
Eugene, OR 97401

www.wipfandstock.com

ISBN 13: 978-1-60899-887-6

Manufactured in the U.S.A.

For my wife, Jessica

Contents

Foreword by Rich Lusk / xiii

Preface / xvii

Introduction / 1

1 From Puritan to Partisan: Nevin's Antebellum Context / 15

2 The Irony of Sectarian Liberty: Nevin's Interpretation and Critique of the Antebellum World / 41

3 Of Humanity and History / 59

4 The Church: Salvation, Sacrament, and the Historical Extension of the Incarnate Christ / 89

5 Nevin in Conversation, Part One—Nevin and the West: Liturgy, Natural Law, and the Two Kingdoms / 111

6 Nevin in Conversation, Part Two—What Has Mercersburg to Do with Moscow and Cambridge? / 129

7 The World's Ascension into a Higher Order of Existence: The Implications of a Sacramental Hermeneutic / 149

Conclusion: The Legacy of John Williamson Nevin and the Mercersburg Theology / 161

Bibliography / 165

Index / 177

Foreword

THE CHURCH IN THE West, especially America, is undergoing a serious identity crisis in our day. The problem with our ecclesiology is ... well, we don't really have an ecclesiology. American Christians aren't quite sure what to do with the church. We don't know what the church should be *doing* because we don't know what the church *is*. Should the church try to be fit and fashionable, accommodating herself to the trends of the present age? Or should the church try to repristinate a supposed "golden age" from the past?

The nineteenth-century Mercersburg movement can help us find a third way, one that recovers the church's true identity by embracing the future without jettisoning the past. Led by luminaries Philip Schaff and John Williamson Nevin, this theological movement sought to combine the best of the church's heritage (the patristic and Reformation eras in particular) with cutting edge scholarship that addressed the concerns and questions of the day. Mercersburg was a deeply ecclesiocentric movement, focused with a laser-like intensity on what came to be known as "the church question." The Mercersburg men became known as "Reformed catholics" for their robust combination of classic Reformed theology with a high doctrine of the church, especially emphasizing the importance of Christian unity. The Mercersburg theologians argued that a high view of the institutional church was a corollary of biblical Christology, and more specifically, the Incarnation. If the church is truly the body and bride of Christ, how could it be otherwise?

The recent resurgence of interest in Mercersburg has helped spearhead a reemergence of ecclesiology in American evangelicalism. The Mercersburg men were considered theological misfits by many in their own day and were largely forgotten for several generations. But now many scholars are finally starting to notice the depths and riches that Mercersburg has to offer us. On the nature of the church, the sacraments, liturgy, pastoral office, catholicity, and a range of other topics, contemporary scholars are beginning to dig up and refine gold from the Mercersburg mine. A number of biographies and specialized theological and historical studies on the Mercersburg leaders have been popping up in recent years, most of them to our benefit.

But this Mercersburg renaissance is far from complete. In particular, the wider sociopolitical dimensions of Mercersburg have been left untouched. Adam Borneman has stepped in to provide this missing piece and fill a crucial void at a very appropriate time. One of the reasons the theology of Mercersburg struggled to get a warm reception in the past was its rejection of certain very American presuppositions. American Protestants have tended to view the pluriformity of the denominational system as a blessing rather than a curse and have focused on the private religious experience of individuals, while rejecting the need for external, ordinary means like a pastor and sacraments. American Protestantism is a religion of private judgment and liberty of conscience. The result is that the church has been given over to sectarian revivalism, democratic individualism, and uncritical nationalism. The church in America has been increasingly marginalized because a divided church with a privatized theology cannot provide an integration point for society. A diluted ecclesiology cannot sustain prophetic critique. Hence, Americans have looked to the state (that is, the American nation), rather than the church, to bear God's purposes in history and serve as humanity's last, best hope. "One nation under God" has trumped "one holy, catholic, and apostolic church."

Nevin clearly saw the problems of Americanized Christianity and gave a stout, albeit unpopular, diagnosis: the church in America had become more American than Christian. Nevin knew that the maturation and perfection of humanity would not be found in the spread of American democracy but in the proliferation of Reformed catholic churches. The goal of humanity would not be recognized in America's "manifest destiny," but in the life of the incarnate Christ, extended through his body, the church. Nevin, to be frank, saw the church as the goal and aim not only of Christ's redeeming work, but of all of human history. Creation reaches its *telos* in the new creation, the perfected people of God.

Not all students of Mercersburg will agree with each and every interpretation and application of Nevin's work set forth in this monograph. Nevertheless, Borneman's work is an important contribution to the ongoing recovery and reappropriation of Nevin's insights. Borneman examines Nevin's thought within his historical context, a time of rising revivalism and swelling nationalism, and shows him to be a compelling political theologian with a vital message to deliver to the church today. Further, Borneman shows that Nevin's ecclesiocentric politics is simply part of his total theological project; his political and cultural views are not tacked on, but flow organically out of his view of the church as the body of the incarnate Christ. Borneman demonstrates that if we listen closely to Nevin, and carefully tease out the implications of his work, we will find a message that enriches our understanding and coheres well with the best political theology being done in contemporary scholarship. Borneman helps us understand Nevin's own understanding of the church's role in history and society, especially in the context of the still-in-progress American democratic experiment.

I warmly commend Borneman's work, not simply because it is yet another study of Mercersburg, but because it serves as a unique and valuable entry point to an aspect of Nevin's work that has been hitherto inadequately explored.

Rich Lusk
Pastor, Trinity Presbyterian Church
Birmingham, AL

Preface

It was during a seminary course, American Christianity, taught by Dr. Garth Rosell at Gordon-Conwell Theological Seminary, that I first discovered the theology of John Williamson Nevin. Reading through E. Brooks Holifield's magisterial *Theology in America*, I suddenly found myself absorbed in a chapter entitled "The Mercersburg Theology: Communal Reason." I felt as Jonathan Edwards did upon discovering Locke's *Essay Concerning Human Understanding*, reading with more pleasure than "the most greedy miser [finds] in gathering up hands full of silver and gold from some new discovered treasure."[1] Holifield had unwittingly introduced me to a theological movement that seemed to resolve so many of my longings as a discontented student of Reformed Theology. To be sure, the Mercersburg theology has its shortcomings and inconsistencies, but the way in which Nevin and Schaff integrated history, ecclesiology, and a sacramental sensibility into American Calvinism appealed—and still appeals—to me in a profound way. After reading Holifield, I proceeded to immerse myself in Nevin's masterpiece, *The Mystical Presence*. I was hooked.

In retrospect, there was a confluence of factors stemming from Dr. Rosell's course that have proven to have significant implications for this current project. In addition to being introduced to the Mercersburg theology, I was also assigned to read Richard Carwardine's *Evangelicals and Politics in Antebellum America*. Carwardine offers a perspective on nineteenth-century American religion and politics that, to my knowledge, is unparalleled. As I read through Carwardine (in conjunction

---

1. According to Hopkins (Edwards's personal friend and early biographer), Edwards, toward the end of his life, held up a copy of Locke's essay and openly declared to some of his friends that when he read Locke at the age of fourteen, he did so with more pleasure than "the most greedy Miser [finds] in gathering up handsful of Silver and Gold from some new discover'd Treasure." Cited in Wallace E. Anderson, ed., *The Works of Jonathan Edwards: Scientific and Philosophical Writings* (New Haven: Yale University Press, 1980) 17. Hopkins's work was *The Life and Character of the Late Mr. Jonathan Edwards*, which was published in Boston in 1765.

with Nathan Hatch's *The Democratization of Christianity*), I had a nagging suspicion that the Mercersburg theology had something more to say to the trends of American democratization and fragmentation than students and scholars had indicated. My hope is that the present study vindicates that suspicion. Furthermore, it was in Dr. Rosell's course that I found a kindred Mercersburg spirit in Jonathan Bonomo. Aside from Jonathan's recent insightful work on the Eucharistic controversy between John Nevin and Charles Hodge, he has continued to be an encouragement to me in my efforts to contribute to the growing community of Mercersburg scholarship.

One of the reasons I decided to pursue a Master of Theology degree was so that I might have the opportunity to study the Mercersburg theology in more depth. Under the direction and supervision of Dr. Gordon Isaac and Dr. Richard Lints, I was afforded such an opportunity in the way of writing a thesis, the title of which would eventually be *Nature, Mankind, and the Incarnation: A Framework for Interpreting the Sociopolitical Dimensions of John Williamson Nevin's Ecclesiocentric Theology*. Due to the flexibility, insight, and constructive criticism offered by Dr. Lints and Dr. Isaac, the project quickly became one of the most gratifying experiences of my young academic career. I am grateful that it lives on in the form of the present study, and am certain that the project would not have been granted this second life without their attentive and supportive direction.

While working tirelessly the early drafts of my ThM thesis, I enlisted several trustworthy and erudite colleagues to proofread and provide editorial comments. Mark Catlin, Mark Knudsen, and Jason Wood gave of their time to this task, drastically decreasing the time I would have had to spend proofreading and editing. Mark Catlin has remained on board for the current full-length project by preparing an index. His efforts, indispensable for this type of publication, deserve a great deal of gratitude from me and from readers who find themselves thumbing through the index of this book. Others have provided insight on various topics throughout the monograph, and they will be cited accordingly.

As for the project in its final form, there are two individuals who deserve my utmost appreciation. Nicole Conrad, editor extraordinaire, has, in addition to her full-time teaching schedule, poured over this project for hours upon hours with her keen proofreading ability and a razor-sharp eye for detail. She has demonstrated remarkable insight at every stage of the editing, proofreading, and formatting process, providing reassurance along the way that we would indeed see a finished product! Her efforts are deserving of the highest commendation from me and from anyone who should pick up this book and benefit from it. Lukata Mjumbe, my friend, brother in Christ, and partner in the ministry, has demonstrated profound generosity with his financial contribution to this project. His enduring support and encouragement, while hardly surprising, serves as a powerful testimony not only to God's grace, but also to the way in which God blesses us in order that we might be a blessing to others. I offer to him my sincere gratitude, with hopes that I might be an extension of his graciousness by blessing someone else in turn.

I would be remiss not to thank Rick Lints, Jonathan Bonomo, Brad Littlejohn, and Rich Lusk for reading early drafts of this monograph and offering endorsements for the project. Rev. Lusk has also been kind enough to compose a foreword, a few brief pages that not only introduce the study with great insight, but also indicate his enduring support as a fellow pastor-theologian.

Finally, I want to thank those closest to me. My parents, Bob and Mary Dell Borneman have, from my earliest stages, instilled within me an unwavering confidence in all that I pursue. This publication is only the most recent evidence of that fact. Most importantly, I want to express my love and thanks to my wife Jessica, who, like me, never anticipated that a ThM thesis would turn into what has become a nearly three-year long project. In addition to abiding my late nights and Saturday afternoons hovering over the computer, stacks of books lying around the house, and my endless musing on all things Nevin, she has remained a constant source of love and encouragement. Simply put, I am well aware that this book might not have happened had it not been for her being at my side.

Adam S. Borneman
Birmingham, AL
November 15, 2010

Introduction

THIS IS A BOOK about the historical and sociopolitical dimensions of sacramental theology. It explores these dimensions by looking at a unique historical circumstance in which sociopolitical factors were quite extraordinary and the theological proposals were no less exceptional. John Williamson Nevin's theological polemics of the antebellum period in America afford such a case, as he articulated a theology that was (and is) foreign to the mainstream of American theology and popular American religious consciousness. Nevertheless, this great architect of the Mercersburg theological tradition offered a theology that is sophisticated in its own right, a fact to which his fellow intellects often testified.[1]

While the majority of recent works that deal with Nevin's theology have focused on his hermeneutics and sacramentology, a few have attempted to examine the social and political dimensions of Nevin's theology. Unfortunately, such attempts have fallen short in two respects. First, they have failed to adequately situate Nevin within the context of nineteenth-century democratization and revivalism, neglecting moreover to take into account various expressions of political theology in the antebellum era. Second, and perhaps most significantly, these attempts have been unable to demonstrate the coherence of Nevin's sociopolitical thought with his broader theological project.[2]

---

1. Hodge regarded Nevin as his "most brilliant" pupil. Toulouse and Duke, *Makers*, 228.

2. Such shortcomings, I believe, are not rooted in dishonest scholarship as much as a failure to take into account the Nevin corpus as whole, and thus the incapability of reading Nevin on his own terms. This is exhibited by scholars' seeming inability to rightly situate Nevin's sociopolitical thought within his decisively theological framework. As such, while James Bratt has examined Nevin's theology through a culture-war lens, and Richard Wentz has attempted to paint a "postmodern portrait" of Nevin as a distinctly American, public, even reactionary theologian, neither has been able to demonstrate how Nevin's social and political musings cohere with his broader hermeneutics and the

In light of such shortcomings, the aim of the present study is to advance studies in the Mercersburg theology in a number of ways. First, by exploring the extraordinary religious and political factors of the antebellum era, including the complicated alignments and affiliations among Scotch-Irish Presbyterians and the German Reformed, this study provides crucial insights into Nevin's historical context that have been largely overlooked by his modern interpreters. Second, complementing the effort to contextualize Nevin in greater detail, this study compares Nevin's views with the political reflections of other theologians and intellectuals of his day, including those of his colleague, Philip Schaff, as well as various interlocutors including Charles Hodge, Horace Bushnell, and Orestes Brownson, and the Transcendentalist movement. Third, Nevin's rhetorical engagement with culture and politics is shown in this study to be part and parcel of his broader theological project. Essays such as "Party Spirit" and "The Sect System," for example, are appropriately framed within Nevin's ecclesiological and sacramental concerns. Fourth, moving a bit outside of Nevin's immediate context, this study will also investigate the theologian's broader intellectual context by placing Nevin in conversation with various streams of political theology, including various streams of Reformation theology, nineteenth-century orthodox theologian Vladamir Solovyov, and the more recent Radical Orthodoxy movement. Lastly, this study will consider the implications of Nevin's theology for today. What are the implications of Nevin's idealist, sacramental hermeneutic? What is to be gleaned from Nevin's view of the church in relation to society?

In many ways, the impetus for such an undertaking may well be the words of Nevin's closest biographer, Theodore Appel, who wrote that, for Nevin, "philosophy and theology had no interest or value, apart from their actual bearings on the welfare of man and the progress of society."[3] Such words will remain cryptic as long as we are negligent in our efforts to dig deeper into Nevin's writings. To be sure—and in fairness to previous scholarship—the cultural relevance of Nevin's theology, particularly in terms of the church-state relationship, is not easily surmised from his extant writings. As Richard E. Wentz explains,

---

most fundamental principles of his theology. See Bratt, "Antebellum Culture Wars" and Wentz, *American Theologian*, 8.

3. Appel, *Life and Work*, ix.

> Nevin does not spell out the relationship of Christian faith to the dynamics of republican political and social order. However, there is enough available of the structure of his thought for us to make confident inference . . . (His theology) offers no blueprint for social and political change. Instead, his theology offers both the insight and the faith and imagination necessary for appropriate and continuing response to the movement of history.[4]

Following Wentz to the degree that the broader structures of Nevin's thought do in fact afford enough information to make such inferences, the present study investigates these structures in hopes of making more concrete observations about the sociopolitical dimensions of his theology, demonstrating moreover the coherence of Nevin's thought.

At the outset, it is important to take note of the fact that for Nevin all political theories and critiques are fundamentally theological or, more specifically, ecclesiological in nature. As such, his view insists that true sociopolitical analysis is ultimately a theological exercise and that societal problems are to be solved by taking seriously the historical church, the efficacy of the church's sacraments, and indeed the one to which these institutions point, God incarnate in Jesus Christ. It is the presence of the incarnate Christ in the church and its sacraments which reveals the unity and wholeness for which the cosmos is designed. In the political realm, this wholeness stands firmly against partisanship and sectarianism. On the level of humankind, it serves as a reminder that one's personal identity is in fact governed by his relation to others and to the essential, organic constitution of the human race. In sum, Nevin's sociopolitical analyses can be shown to cohere with his broader theology of incarnation when interpreted in terms of his threefold ontological hierarchy, in which mankind, insofar as he is united to the incarnate Christ, serves as the end and perfection of the natural world. As such, this study serves as the first book-length effort to bring Nevin's sociopolitical analyses into harmony with the method and fundamental tenets of his theology.

---

4. Wentz, *American Theologian*, 102.

SIGNIFICANT THEMES OF THIS STUDY

Nevin's Ontological Hierarchy

Nevin's hierarchical framework may appropriately be understood in terms of an *analogia entis*. The "analogy of being," traditionally understood, constitutes an ontological continuum in which lower and higher orders of existence have an innate attraction for one another. In Nevin's hierarchy, as DiPuccio explains, "The lower orders adumbrate and anticipate the higher, while at the same time the higher orders take up and assimilate the lower just as an organism incorporates material from its environment . . . The lower is thus made to transcend itself through the action of a higher power, thus fulfilling the created purpose or design of each class."[5] While generally more implicit throughout his corpus of work, Nevin's hierarchical view is developed rather explicitly in a handful of his writings, not least in a Baccalaureate speech delivered in August 1853. Speaking on the theme of "Man's True Destiny," Nevin explained,

> The organization of the world, as a system of nature, comes to its completion in his person . . . Man is himself . . . the end of nature, the point where its whole process reaches its ultimate destination . . . What is in this way continually proclaimed by the general constitution of the world, finds its full echo in the moral nature of man himself. Whatever relation his intelligence and will may bear to the present world as such, they carry in their very constitution, at the same time, no less distinctly, a necessary reference also to something beyond this world, to a higher economy . . . It is not enough that we have been created for such end, nor yet that we may see and feel the necessity of it, as, on our part, something beyond this world. The case calls for purpose and will, in an object which is known to be real. This comes before us here in the form of a supernatural revelation, brought to its full accomplishment in Christ.[6]

The culmination of this "full accomplishment" may be said to reside in the resurrection of Jesus Christ and the dawn of the new creation. As Nevin writes,

> The body of Christ Himself was glorified in this way when He rose from the dead; the bodies of His people, we are told, shall hereafter be made glorious in like manner; and there is to be at

---

5. DiPuccio, *Interior Sense*, 36.
6. Nevin, "Man's True Destiny," 612.

the last, in some way which we cannot now understand, a glorification also of the whole natural creation—new heavens and a new earth (2 Pet. iii 13).[7]

Nevin, then, offers a modified Hegelian view of reality in which higher forms of existence incorporate lower spheres through a dialectical process. In Nevin's words, "Life here is in this way a scale of degrees, a succession of ascending planes, each of which prefigures and prepares the way for that by which it is followed."[8] Specifically, his model incorporates a threefold, hierarchical relationship between the natural "lower organic sphere,"[9] moral mankind, and the Incarnation of Jesus Christ.

This is arguably the central feature of Nevin's theology, in terms of both content and methodology. In Nevin's system, the Incarnation of Jesus Christ serves as the crucial event of history. Although *in* history, the Incarnation also reconciles all of history to God, thus raising history into the higher order of existence for which it was originally designed. Mankind, as the image of God, serves uniquely as the creature that possesses both an organic relation to the lower, natural, created order and possesses qualities that manifest God's character. As such, mankind serves as the end and perfection of nature insofar as he becomes truly human in his union to the divine. By virtue of this process, the lower organic sphere of social and political existence is reconciled unto God sacramentally, and the fragmented elements of society are incorporated into the divine, objective whole. The visible locus of this whole is the church, who, by way of the ministry of word and sacrament, reigns in the disparate remnants of the fallen, splintered creation.

Sacraments and Politics

A fundamental assumption throughout this study is that, for Nevin, the presence of the incarnate Christ in the Eucharist reveals the unity and wholeness for which the cosmos is designed. In the political realm, this wholeness stands firmly against partisanship and sectarianism. On the level of humankind, it serves as a reminder that personal identity is in fact governed by its relation to others and to the whole of humanity. In

---

7. Nevin, "Undying Life," 612.
8. Nevin, "Philosophy of History" in DiPuccio, *Interior Sense*, 36.
9. Borrowing from DiPuccio, *Interior Sense*, 47. The natural, lower organic sphere is understood in the current study as that which constitutes *actual* (as opposed to ideal) socio-political existence.

short, principles which promoted individualism and sheer subjectivity were, in Nevin's eyes, antithetical to the fundamental principles of the Incarnation and sacrament. He lamented, ". . . the sect system tends to destroy all faith in the holy sacraments. . . . Our view of the sacraments is always conditioned by our sense of the mystery comprehended in the idea of the Church, and forms thus, of course, at the same time, a simple, but sure, touchstone of our faith in the Church itself."[10]

For Nevin, the sacraments of the church are more than a bare symbol that pictures for the world what unity and wholeness look like. They are more than a mechanism or apparatus for the world's reconciliation to God. While the sacraments both depict and serve as the means for the union of creature and creator, creation itself is shot through with the organic, historical, sacramental character of God's presence in his son, the incarnate Christ. This is captured remarkably well by Scott Collins-Jones:

> Nevin's thinking on the sacraments reflects his understanding of the unity of the orders of creation and redemption. For him the sacraments are not mere symbols of supernatural grace, but real means of it. He believed that this was true for creation as well, which was in a real sense *sacramental* through and through. The world does not just point to or symbolize the spiritual, but was filled with it. The two divinely ordained sacraments, which reveal the mystery of the new creation through an organic union of the spiritual and the material, point to the same organic union in all creation, revealed most clearly in the Incarnation. The world has not reached its divinely appointed *telos*, the new heaven and the new earth, but the organic principle of the Incarnation and the new creation is really at work in it.[11]

Nevin's theology of incarnation and Eucharist renders the dualisms, divisions, and dichotomies created by the cultural shifts of the nineteenth century as false and unnecessary. These shifts or trends were marked most fundamentally by the dual separation of the believer from the "body politic of the Church" and the individual's faith from his or her physical body.[12] This fragmentation emerged "under the auspices of

---

10. Nevin, "The Sect System," in Yrigoyen, *Catholic and Reformed*, 148.
11. Collins-Jones, "First-Fruits," 4.
12. Clapp, *Border Crossings*, 99. Harvey, "Re-Membering," 106, explains, "Sequestering religion in the private sphere reserved the public realm exclusively for the coercive rule of both state and market, and helped to provide an effective mode of social discipline

a social arrangement that sanctioned a moral identity of the church with the state and its commercial republic."[13] Nevin believed that the fragmentation of society and disintegration of its authority structures had gone well beyond notions of human freedom and subjectivity, which, in theory, he supported. In dismantling the oppressions of the modern state, the Enlightenment had thrown the baby out with the bathwater by rejecting the objectivity of the church and its sacramental power.

Political Dimensions of the Worshiping Church in Modern Theology

While it would be inappropriate to implicate Nevin as a political theologian in the modern sense, it would nevertheless prove instructive to consider how Nevin's theology speaks to current predominant political theologies. Exercising caution not to impose contemporary theological paradigms onto Nevin's theology, current efforts to demonstrate the relationship between liturgy and politics would benefit a great deal from Nevin's insights.

Theologian and ethicist Bernd Wannenwetsch has provided helpful categories in which one might situate various political-theological traditions.[14] While his rather broad categories will not be entirely adequate for any one theologian or theological tradition (he does not presume to have provided such), they are nevertheless instructive for thinking paradigmatically about the nature of political theology and the general tendencies of various approaches to the subject.

First, Wannenwetsch notes those who stress the church as a "political antitype" or counter-society. Theologians who fit into this model (Wannenwetsch suggests Augustine and Milbank as examples, though this is debatable) affirm the right to insist on the truth of politics rather than the functionality of politics. Rather than distinguishing between "spheres," as in later traditions, these theologians distinguish only between true and false political action.[15]

Second is the model in which the church, unlike the previous model, is seen to "rub off" on the state. This model has the church pursuing

---

to those in control of these political entities to claim absolute sovereignty over the bodies of their subjects. With Christian identity safely confined to the realm of individual values, the work of the church was increasingly devoted to nurturing the 'soul.'"

13. Harvey, "Re-Membering," 107.
14. Wannenwetsch, "Liturgy," 87.
15. Ibid., 87.

the "ideal type" of politics and in turn providing the state with social principles (William Temple is implicated here). This model is important because, as will become increasingly evident in the present study, it resonates with Nevin's view at a number of points. That being said, Wannenwetsch notes an important characteristic of this approach that marks a clear divergence from Nevin. He rightly notes the tendency of theologians in this model to disregard the concreteness of the church's practices in favor of a "universalizing strategy offering principles that are derived from abstracts such as 'sacramentality' rather than drawing out the conceptual implications of the sacramental practices themselves."[16] In Nevin's judgment, this tendency would be quite unacceptable.

Finally, citing Barth and Hauerwas as examples, Wannenwetsch notes those who see the worshiping church as the "paradigm" which represents the "unique politics of God." The worshiping church, in this model, does not seek to provide secular authorities with religious rationale, but rather pictures for the world another way of acquiring and enacting power.[17]

While Wannenwetsch's categories are far from exhaustive, they nonetheless accurately reflect the ways in which a number of influential theologians of the modern era have drawn upon and attempted to develop various political-theological traditions. To be sure, Nevin does not fit squarely within any of these categories, but it is nevertheless important to understand how and why that is the case. The question of Nevin's theological rapport with William Temple, for example, raises a number of interesting questions about the nature of sacramentality in relation to politics. Therefore, although it would be inappropriate to commandeer Nevin's theology and label it the "ideal type" or "political antitype," it would undoubtedly be instructive to take into account what Nevin might have to say to the modern and postmodern approaches to worship, sacraments, and politics.

WARRANT FOR THIS STUDY

James D. Bratt and Richard E. Wentz are notable among interpreters of Nevin who have attempted to situate Nevin in his sociopolitical con-

---

16. Ibid.
17. Ibid., 87.

text, and several of their insights will prove helpful in the current study.[18] Bratt captures well the broader political approach employed by Nevin, describing it as a "Churchly, sacramental theology," which was essentially a way of doing "politics by transcendent means, the only means adequate to the difficulties at hand." He summarizes Nevin as follows:

> (Nevin) saw the church question as paramount, absorbing all other problems of the age. All naturally conceived and secularly wrought solutions, he insisted, shared humanity's fateful limitations. Life required a supernatural redemption, which had begun only in the incarnation of Jesus Christ. Here was the objective fact of a new life, a divine and supernatural force present in history, offering power for real change. But that power was available only in the Church, Christ's living body in the world, and there preeminently through the sacrament.[19]

Yet, despite his accurate summation of Nevin's thought, Bratt falls short in his study of Nevin, compromising his interpretation at several points. To be sure, Bratt asks the right questions, and his intuitions regarding Nevin's view of the political sphere appear to be moving along the right trajectory, but the support material he employs for certain aspects of his argument seems insufficient, and his overall interpretation results in an intemperate emphasis upon the alleged dualisms of Nevin's thought. Additionally, Bratt's invoking of Niebuhr's famous Christ and Culture typology is somewhat puzzling and rather anachronistic. He writes, "Nevin sometimes intimates Christ against culture, then the Christ of culture, more often Christ and culture in paradox or Christ above culture, without substantiating the option he surely desired, Christ transforming culture."[20] Such an analysis, which portrays Nevin as a somewhat confused and seemingly incoherent systematician, is perhaps more so indicative of an inappropriate methodology on the part of the

---

18. James D. Bratt's essay, "Nevin and the Antebellum Culture Wars," aims to take seriously the "lively political connections" of Nevin's extended family as well as the volatile political circumstances in which Nevin lived and worked during his most formative years as a theologian. Bratt draws upon several of Nevin's writings in order to demonstrate the political tone employed by the Mercersburg theologian, suggesting that "the culture war lens discloses in (Nevin's) theology a deeper range of meanings than those usually explored, one that both warrants and raises questions about his claims to practicality and that provides a fair measure of his work's merits and difficulties." Bratt, "Antebellum Culture Wars," 2.

19. Bratt, "Antebellum Culture Wars," 11.

20. Ibid., 14.

interpreter than of blatant inconsistency in Nevin's theology. For Nevin, such a typology would violate the organic continuum of church and the "outward" existence of the world. It misunderstands the church's nature and function as an ark and medium of salvation.

Richard Wentz, in his recent work, *John Nevin: American Theologian*, is careful not to evaluate Nevin's theology and cultural critiques in terms of their cultural utility and pragmatic value, instead recognizing that Nevin's approach is transcendental and sacramental; it is a theology from above. Wentz's work, in this respect, is right on target. Nevertheless, it likewise falls short in several respects. Most notably, despite his recognition of Nevin's "sacramental approach," Wentz seems to have flipped the roles of Nevin's incarnational paradigm and his critique of antebellum religious culture so that the latter serves as the basis for the former. The sacramental approach, in other words, is reactionary to cultural circumstances. William DiPuccio agrees. He criticizes Wentz for seeing "Nevin's critique of nineteenth-century American religion (revivalism and individualistic/sectarian forms of religious expression) as preparatory to his reinterpretation of catholicity, which, in the end, must reach beyond the pale of Christendom to embrace other faiths as well."[21] As such, Wentz likewise fails to place proper emphasis on Nevin's high ecclesiology and the way in which the Incarnation of Christ plays a normative role in his worldview. His account of Nevin, moreover, leaves the reader wondering whether Nevin's church has historical or confessional boundaries. Thus, while Wentz's depiction of Nevin as "public theologian" is helpful at points, it generally fails to capture the ecclesial character of Nevin's life and theology.

Interpreters of Nevin will have difficulty in surpassing DiPuccio's treatment of Nevin's hermeneutical lens and intellectual context in his outstanding effort, *The Interior Sense of Scripture: The Sacred Hermeneutics of John W. Nevin*. The present study is certainly indebted to DiPuccio on a number of points, particularly in the analysis of Nevin's philosophical views and hermeneutics. Nevertheless, DiPuccio's work is not designed to address the concrete historical realities of Nevin's antebellum context. Certainly his treatment of Nevin's philosophical critiques moves in this direction, but beyond discussing Nevin's "incarnational paradigm" and its engagement with the prevalent philosophical methods of his day, DiPuccio has little to say regarding Nevin's direct engagement with the

---

21. DiPuccio, Review of *American Theologian*, 152.

concrete or actual events of antebellum society. The value of DiPuccio's work is not debased in this respect; rather, it is simply the case that he has not taken his work in this direction.

More recently, the works of DeBie, Littlejohn, and Bonomo have likewise proven to be valuable contributions to Mercersburg studies.[22] DeBie's work serves as a fine complement to DiPuccio's, if not surpassing it in a number of respects. His treatment of Nevin's hermeneutical trajectory in relation to its American philosophical context is as accessible as it is informative. Chapter four of the present study draws from Littlejohn and Bonomo on ecclesiology and sacramentology, respectively. I would be remiss not to commend both their erudition and clarity on these topics.

Thus, there remains a gap in Nevin studies. On the one hand, attempts to situate Nevin in his sociopolitical context have not fully dealt with Nevin's extraordinarily high view of the church, its history, its exclusivity, and its sole foundation, the Incarnation of Jesus Christ. On the other hand, in-depth treatments of Nevin's hermeneutics, sacramentology, and ecclesiology, have not as yet engaged Nevin's more politically charged writings or his interpretation of America's role in the antebellum world. One of the goals of this study is to unite these divergent approaches to Nevin's thought.

OUTLINE OF CHAPTERS

The present study considers Nevin's project both in terms of content and structure, as the first four chapters in succession loosely follow Nevin's hierarchical framework, proceeding from the "lower organic" sphere of history and politics to mankind, to the incarnate Christ in the life of the church. It is, as such, a study in methodology as much as it is a study in theology.

The first chapter takes into account Nevin's social and political context. Emphasis is placed on disestablishment, democratization, and revivalism. In addition, I will take into account the reflections of a number of Nevin's contemporaries (Hodge, the Transcendentalists, Bushnell, Brownson, and Schaff) on matters of politics, culture, slavery, and other themes of the antebellum era. The overarching aim of this chapter is to

---

22. DeBie, *Speculative Theology*; Littlejohn, *Quest for Reformed Catholicity*; Bonomo, *Incarnation and Sacrament*.

present the fragmentation of American politics and religion as a significant theme of Nevin's theological writings.

Chapter two will open with a discussion of Nevin's family history, their ties to politics, and Nevin's approach to one of the crucial issues of his day—slavery. Perhaps most significantly, chapter two offers a viable entryway into the sociopolitical dimensions of Nevin's theology by focusing on his articles "Early Christianity," "Party Spirit," and "The Sect System." A review and analysis of these articles is introduced by taking into consideration Nevin's broader understanding of the United States' role in world history. This chapter establishes that Nevin's engagement with social and political issues is decisively theological.

Chapter three investigates Nevin's philosophical and theological presuppositions as well as his corresponding theology of history and theological anthropology. First, it will be necessary to provide an account of the philosophical trends that dominated the antebellum era. In addition to establishing Nevin's departure from such trends, this chapter reflects both on Nevin's insistence that the Incarnation serves as the culmination of history and his view of mankind as the end and perfection of nature.

Moving into the primary *loci* of Nevin's theology, the fourth chapter deals with Nevin's view of the church as the historical extension of the Incarnation, and thus necessarily the accommodating features of his sacramentology and soteriology. Throughout the chapter, the Incarnation is again presented as the "cardinal principle" of Nevin's theology,[23] but here, attention is also given to how the Incarnation relates to mankind via the sacraments. Accordingly, elements of Nevin's theological anthropology are recalled by addressing his view of sin and imputation in comparison to Bushnell and Hodge, respectively.

Constituting part one of "Nevin in Conversation," Chapter five puts Nevin into conversation with his western theological tradition, with a focus on those theologians within the reformation tradition. While Littlejohn has done a great service by exploring the various ways in which Nevin speaks to a number of traditions, the present study more specifically examines points of engagement with the political theological tradition, including natural law, two kingdoms theory, and sphere sovereignty, among others.[24] Principally to be demonstrated is the way

---

23. Nevin, "Letter to Harbaugh," 408.
24. See Littlejohn, *Quest for Reformed Catholicity*.

in which Nevin both draws upon and departs from his theological predecessors.

Chapter six serves as part two of "Nevin in Conversation" by comparing Nevin's approach both to Vladimir Solovyov's political philosophy as well as Radical Orthodoxy's participatory ontology and sacramental approach to politics. This chapter is the most speculative of the study, as Nevin does not appear to have read Solovyov and can only be seen as anticipating Radical Orthodoxy on various points. On the whole, the goal of this chapter is to introduce possibilities for further studies in Nevin's theology.

Chapter seven is the last full chapter of the study. It summarizes the approach of Nevin and the Mercersburg theology to antebellum culture and the church/state paradigm of the early American republic. The chapter also recasts the implications of Nevin's project in terms of mission and the relationship of worship to politics. Nevin, as will be demonstrated, believed that the primary role of the church was to *be* the church, not in a passive or separatist manner, but in such a way that it would retain its liturgical, sacramental identity.

In closing, I offer some brief remarks on the legacy and lessons of Nevin and the Mercersburg theology. Many of the challenges Nevin posed to the church and society of the nineteenth century are no less relevant to his students of today. Sadly, the church, along with society, has only become more sectarian, more fragmented, and more compartmentalized. This is in many ways due to the inability of individuals to recognize the formative "liturgies" of society that so deeply influence one's worldview. Nevin offers helpful correctives to this problem, not least in the way of reforming the church's liturgical life. My hope is that the study as a whole will capture Nevin's sentiment in this respect, and that his passion for Christ and his church will only become more evident.

1

From Puritan to Partisan

Nevin's Antebellum Context

NEVIN'S "ACTUAL" POLITICAL CONTEXT[1]

THE MOST INCISIVE WRITINGS in the Nevin corpus were composed during a time when political and religious cultures in America were both scrambling for stability and anxiously seeking to understand their complicated relationship to one another. Indeed, it is becoming increasingly difficult for scholars to avoid the profound role that religion played in the culture wars of the early republic and the years leading to the Civil War. The ongoing effort to offer a fresh interpretation of this crucial era of American history renders the life and work of someone like Nevin all the more fascinating, for scholars have increasingly recognized that the theological battles of the period profoundly reflect and even inform the political battles.[2]

Establishing the rather complicated antebellum context of Nevin's life and work is not simply an exercise in conventional historical methodology. Because the idea of historical development figures so prominently in Nevin's theology, it is crucial for any interpreter to acquire a sense of how Nevin saw history unfolding.[3] For Nevin, history is indeed

---

1. As opposed to the "ideal" and universal, the "actual," in Nevin's theology, referred to the finite. See DiPuccio, "Dynamic Realism."

2. This has been most astutely shown by Richard Carwardine's masterpiece, *Evangelicals and Politics in Antebellum America*, as well as more recent works such as Mark A. Noll's recent publication, *The Civil War as a Theological Crisis*.

3. As will be discussed in chapter 3, for Nevin, history is not merely an event which refers to abstract truth about God, but, as revealed in the Incarnation, it is the organic expression and medium of God's truth. History in Nevin's idealist, dialectical scheme is revelatory and meaningful insofar as it reveals God's "providential history" in the life

God's history, and thus national and world events must be interpreted accordingly. Such is clear in Nevin's reflections on how the history of the United States had eventuated in Civil War:

> All that may have been new or great, or full of interest, in the previous history of the country: its discovery more than three centuries ago; its colonies and colonial times; its war of independence; the foundation and adoption of its constitution; and whatever has been of account in the enlargement of its resources or in the development of its powers since; all is found at last, I say, gathering itself up into the grandeur of this last crisis, and showing itself to have been significant only as it has served to prepare the way for its advent.[4]

We turn, then, to consider carefully the historical trends that affected Nevin the most—trends which he saw as playing a decisive role in the unfolding of America's history, the history of the natural world, and the eschatological union of natural and supernatural in the Incarnation of Jesus Christ.

Democratization and the Second Party System

The democratization of politics and religion in the post-revolutionary, antebellum era raises important questions about political-religious alignment.[5] While political allegiances among American Christians in the modern era are somewhat predictable, the antebellum religious and political situation was immensely complex and constantly shifting. This is due not only to the fact that America was still creating for herself a new identity as a republic, but also to the wide variety of immigrant com-

---

of Christ. For Nevin, this "history" is found in Christ's church, the historic extension of his incarnation.

4. Nevin, "Lancaster Commencement Address," in Appel, *Life and Work*, 638.

5. In his aptly titled *The Democratization of Christianity*, historian Nathan Hatch has suggested that the antebellum era, particularly in light of the new Jacksonianism, demonstrates the recurring dialectic in Christian history between atomization and authority. It was during this era, particularly in the first half of the nineteenth century, that the pendulum swung violently from ecclesiastical objectivity and authority towards populist religion and the revivalist cause. The dialectic is of course enormously complex. Above all, what needs to be emphasized is the way in which "democratic dissent" and the accompanying doctrines of republicanism during the early antebellum era produced within mainline Protestantism an increasingly anti-authoritarian sentiment as well as the seeming inevitability of denominational fragmentation. See Hatch, *Democratization of American Christianity*, 15–16.

munities that were pouring into American communities along the east coast. Evangelicals scrambled to engage the culture of a rapidly changing nation, leading to strife and discord within the Protestant church. As Carwardine notes,

> The evidence from the mouths and pens of evangelicals themselves, and of those who observed them, suggests a multiplicity of divisions and antagonisms amongst evangelicals which, far from being superficial exceptions to an underlying Protestant unity, had significant implications for their political outlook. These religious conflicts were not based on economic differences, although issues of status and economic outlook certainly impinged, but revolved around profound cultural antagonisms. For this reason during the second party system no "evangelical Protestant vote" was cast consistently for one party or the other.[6]

The American evangelical trend towards fragmentation was quite unique. Similar trends were not to be found among European evangelical counterparts, who operated contently within their respective establishmentarian contexts. This was the case for reputed Anglicans William Wilberforce and Charles Simeon, as well as Scottish Presbyterian Thomas Chalmers and Irish Presbyterian Henry Cooke. By contrast, the new democratic republic of a post-revolutionary America seemed to provide avenues for people to participate in society apart from establishmentarian institution. This was evidenced by unprecedented Protestant dissent from churches with high sacramentology who claimed to be vested with the means of salvation, denunciation of institutions of higher learning promoted by the elitist establishment, and, of course, rejection of the British monarchy. Such violent cultural shifts within American religion would ultimately lay the foundation for the birth of voluntary societies and para-church ministry efforts.[7]

---

6. As Carwardine, *Evangelicals and Politics*, 99, notes, "Patterns of evangelical voting do suggest some congruence between church membership and theological perspective on one side, and party choice on the other; but these varied considerably according to demographic, denominational, and other contexts, were not wholly consistent even within local churches, and suggest that many evangelicals felt only a loose attachment to party . . . Loyalties shifted during the course of the second party system, but those changes did not extend to achieving what some at least desired, the creation of a Christian party in politics."

7. See Noll, *America's God*, 174–75.

The very notion of "party" took on an entirely new range of meaning with the inception of the "second party system."[8] The origin of this system can arguably be traced to the early years of the antebellum era, when revivalist factions of Yankee New England began to coalesce, setting the stage for the Whig Party's arrival in the 1820s. This substantially evangelical contingent viewed themselves as the more progressive party of American politics, and their efforts allowed the "benevolent empire" of social activism and voluntarism to persist during the first half of the century.[9] Whiggery shared with Federalism a high view of the state's enforcement of moral and social order, but also forced a realignment of the party's supporters by infusing politics with a new evangelicalism that reached well beyond the borders of what many perceived as a strain of Yankee-elitism in the Federalist Party.[10] The brooding nativism of New

---

8. This system, lasting until 1854, included the Democratic Party, the Whig Party, and several other less influential parties such as the Anti-Masonic Party (1827–1834), Liberty Party (1840), and eventually the Free Soil Party (1848–1852). It was, arguably, the defining characteristic of the Jacksonian era, its most defining feature being the Whig Party's formation in opposition to President Andrew Jackson's supposed executive tyranny (beginning in 1834). Unlike other systems of two-party rivalry in the nineteenth century, Whigs and Democrats competed with each other in every state of the nation except South Carolina. Although each party was stronger in some states than in others, nationally they were closely balanced. Between 1836 and 1852 Democrats won the presidency in 1836, 1844, and 1852, while Whigs prevailed in 1840 and 1848. Although Jackson himself was the primary focus of partisan combat so long as he remained president, between 1837 and 1852 the two parties adopted coherent and sharply contrasting stances in platforms, in roll-call votes in Congress and state legislatures, and on the hustings on governmental economic policy, governmental sponsorship of social and moral reforms, and territorial expansion. Starting in the mid-1840s, however, each of these parties began to split along sectional lines over slavery extension, and that sectional rupture would ultimately help cause the system's demise in the mid-1850s. See McCormick, *Second American Party System*.

9. "Benevolent Empire" refers to the revivalist-prompted missionary societies and nationwide reform efforts during the nineteenth century.

10. This is not to say that Federalism was a tyrannical or over-centralizing force. On the contrary, it has been compellingly argued that antebellum federalism was in fact decentralized, reflecting the theory of "dual sovereignty" or "dual federalism." See Scheiber, "American Federalism." It is equally important to note that "Yankee" carried different connotations in different contexts; sometimes elitist, sometimes commoner. Following Conforti, *Imagining New England*, 154, "On the one hand, as Yankee-Doodles, they represented the Republican virtue and attachment to liberty of New England common folk. On the other hand, the Yankee label persisted, especially in Federalist circles, as an epithet now encumbered with new, troublesome Revolutionary associations: the New England commoners' increasingly bold assertion of their rights, native ability, and distrust of deference and hierarchy."

England would soon come to fruition in this context, demonstrating this "elitist" strain.[11]

The Democrats, likewise, believed in social order, but they remained highly suspicious of the establishment—particularly the New England establishment—a sentiment which ultimately united immigrants and Catholics in the middle states with slave holders in the South. This alignment would hold strong until Catholic immigration and industrialization precipitated the birth of the Republican Party shortly before the dawn of the War Between the States. Religiously, the Democratic contingent was more ritualistic and traditional than the evangelicals of New England. The ritualist disposition was, in contrast to the revivalist movement, less interested in cultural engagement and more focused on the church's sanctity and its "in the world but not of the world" role.

Political affiliations were likewise affected as alignments between certain social statuses and political positions solidified. Although the divisions between Democrats and Whigs were not strictly class based, the Whig Party was nevertheless perceived as more respectable and upwardly mobile. Thus, a great number of poorer evangelicals who gained wealth and higher social standing during the era tended toward the evangelical "establishment" and the Whig Party. By 1840, Gienapp argues, the revolution was complete: "With the full establishment of the second party system, campaigns were characterized by appeals to the common man, mass meetings, parades, celebrations, and intense enthusiasm, while elections generated high voter participation. In structure and ideology, American politics had been democratized."[12] This "revolution" of sorts reflected, informed, and was woven throughout American religion, especially in its Protestant manifestations.

The relevance of the second party system to Nevin's life and career is unmistakable, not only because it serves as a dominant feature of his immediate political context, but also because it reflected and encouraged the type of religious revivalism that Nevin so abhorred. Since the arrival of the first colonists, the consensus had been in favor of societal and ecclesiastical mediation. Even the Puritans, who were indeed "separatist" in one sense, still regarded institutions like the family, church, and society as necessary covenant mediators for God's grace. Reflecting broader

---

11. Nativism gained support especially in Boston, New York, Philadelphia, and Baltimore.

12. Gienapp, "Politics Seem," 15.

political trends, evangelicals countered this movement by jumpstarting their own communities apart from the established order; first ecclesiastical, then voluntary.[13] Thus, the ramifications of revivalist, democratic ferment could be seen most clearly in the rejection of a salvation mediated by institutions. Simply put, "From the perspective of American experience, a natural affinity seemed to exist between key evangelical convictions and a polity of disestablishment."[14]

Disestablishmentarianism and Other Revivalist Causes

A failure to take into account the trends of revivalist religion, particularly in their relation to American democratization, would result in a rather distorted interpretation of Nevin. The significance of his tract *The Anxious Bench*, for instance, would be greatly underestimated without knowledge of the type of evangelical fervor that was being promulgated by the likes of Charles Finney throughout the ranks of American Protestantism. Finney, one of Nevin's most significant theological opponents, took advantage of democratic ideology and showed just how powerful revivalist preaching could be, particularly by emphasizing individual conversion and a doctrine of the individual's agency in Christian moral action. The "bench" represented for Nevin not only the perverse theology of Finney's "new measures" revivalism, but also the increasingly sectarian nature of American culture. He wrote, "New measures, in the technical modern sense, form a particular system, involving a certain theory of religious action, and are characterized by a distinctive life, which is by no means difficult to understand. Of this system the Anxious Bench is a proper representative. It opens the way naturally to other forms of aberration in the same direction, and may be regarded in this view as the threshold

---

13. Noll, *America's God*, 173–75. See also, Hatch, *Democratization of American Christianity*, 65, who explains that the "no creed but the Bible" way of American Christianity was sweeping the nation. "By appealing to abstract principles such as the Bible alone and the ancient order of things, Christian churches were constructing roofs over their heads. But they lacked the ecclesiastical walls of liturgy, governance, theology, and instruction that are normative in a given church tradition."

14. Noll, *America's God*, 174. Initially, federalist sympathizers, including the majority of conservative clergy bemoaned the loss of institutional objectivity. The Federalists' failure to preserve the Standing Order in Connecticut, for example, was viewed by Congregationalist Lyman Beecher as bringing "irreparable injury" to the church. See Schmidt, *Souls*, 4, citing Beecher, *Autobiography*, 1:252. Beecher later viewed these events as the "best thing that ever happened to the state of Connecticut."

of all that is found to follow, quite out to the extreme of fanaticism and rant."[15] Ultimately, the result, as Schmidt notes, was that "evangelicalism based on voluntarism, a theology compounded of Taylorism, Finneyism, Methodism, and the institutionalization of revivalism had made a clean sweep in nearly all denominations by 1850."[16]

The new democratic sentiment being disseminated throughout the country prompted countless numbers of groups and individuals to pursue social and political reform on their own initiative. The great hope of the evangelical revivalist cause in the antebellum United States was that converting individuals to the Christian faith would be the most effective and most efficient way to transform society as a whole. It was believed that the pious lives of the converted would necessarily result in public displays of benevolence, beginning with relations between individuals and ultimately extending to the very foundational structures of society. Notably, such movements were just as effective in encouraging similar efforts among secularists. As such, the term "revivalism," while originating among evangelical Christians, can by no means be limited to the sphere of the church. It is, rather, a term which can be more broadly applied to the entire social, political, economic, and religious life of the antebellum era.[17]

This sweep gained its greatest momentum during the second Great Awakening toward the end of the eighteenth century. The awakening promoted a new American Arminianism, the democratic nature of which imposed an enormous amount of pressure on more traditional Calvinist communities. These "new measures" and "new divinity" trends had strong appeal among the lower classes by promoting a higher view of the individual and his role in the church and the world. As such, the pressure was not merely doctrinal or theological, as the traditional five points of Calvinism—total depravity of humanity, unconditional election of God's people, limited atonement, irresistibility of grace, perseverance of God's elect—carried meaning that pervaded all of human existence and as

15. Nevin, *Anxious Bench*, 12.
16. Hewitt, *Regeneration and Morality*, 36. See also Schmidt, *Souls*, 25.
17. Timothy L. Smith's pivotal work, *Revivalism and Social Reform*, reveals the powerful impact that such trends had during the antebellum era. His main thesis is that "far from disdaining earthly affairs, the evangelists played a key role in the widespread attack upon slavery, poverty, and greed. They thus helped prepare the way both in theory and in practice for what later became known as the social gospel." Smith, *Revivalism and Social Reform*, 8.

such, a substantial element of the antebellum worldview. A compromise on such doctrinal tenets thus was part and parcel of the democratization of Protestantism. Sociologist George Thomas concludes that "revivalism was primarily an acceptance of the new order that both legitimated and was legitimated by the individuated market and the new myth of rational individualism. It comprehensively worked individualism into a unified cosmic order of things, from family relations to individual action to national growth."[18] It almost goes without saying that Nevin was diametrically opposed to all that promoted this "new order."

THEOLOGICAL REFLECTION AMONG NEVIN'S CONTEMPORARIES

Whether one is mounting a comprehensive analysis or working within a narrow stream of Nevin's thought, vital for the task is an adequate account of the theologian's contemporary intellectual context. An account of several nineteenth-century intellects and their views is therefore appropriate. For the sake of clarity and focus, it will suffice to relate that which pertains especially to politics, history, and insofar as the social element is concerned, slavery. Moreover, those great minds discussed here are those which provide the greatest insight into Nevin's own thought; most of them either worked with Nevin or engaged with him in debate. We begin with one who falls into the latter category.

Charles Hodge

Charles Hodge declared quite openly his political leanings when he wrote, "Every drop of blood in our veins is of the federal stock."[19] This federalism would take Hodge on a journey from Federalism to Whiggery to the Republican Party, but the basic federalist principles he had inherited from his family remained consistent. Such was summarized rather concisely by his son, Alexander:

> He was always an attentive and interested witness of political events, and entertained and expressed the most decided opinions. He was trained by his family in the opinions of the old Federalist party of Washington, Hamilton and Madison, and he held them tenaciously as principles to the end of his life. He had a poor

---

18. Thomas, *Revivalism and Cultural Change*, 7. Cited by Noll, *America's God*, 189.
19. Hodge, "Church and the Country," 333.

opinion of President Jackson, and of the Locofoco party, and was a warm advocate of the protective tariff, and of the United States Bank. He always adhered to the old Whig party until its death; then in 1857 voted for Fremont, the first Republican candidate for the Presidency, and continued to be a decided Republican as long as he lived.[20]

From Hodge's perspective, the shifts were in the politics of the nation, not in his principles. Federalism served as a necessary means for balancing the unbridled individualism of the post-revolutionary era. As a political philosophy, it provided a sense of governing restraint in the midst of an otherwise populist ideology. Hodge's federalism was indeed a theologically-informed, morally-principled federalism, and the gradual movement of Hodge to Whiggery and to the Republican Party reflected his political consistency. His shift to the Whig Party is perhaps most clearly displayed in his distaste for Andrew Jackson's political advances, writing, "Although I feel as deeply as ever the great advantages which our ecclesiastical liberty confers upon us, and think that we have reason to rejoice in the general prevalence of truth and piety in most sections of our country, I am now aware to a greater degree, than formerly, of the evils which attend even the best system."[21]

Hodge believed in strong federal union, balanced and regulated democracy, and gradual social progress. He saw the major players in this political system to be government, churches, and benevolent voluntary societies, all of which he believed should be driven by a populace that was educated and devoutly Christian. His federalism, however, not only indicated a certain brand of politics, but also signified his understanding of how churches and benevolent societies should function. As Torbett explains, "Hodge, in keeping with the values of these three institutions, balanced a qualified social egalitarianism with a similarly qualified elitism. He balanced a qualified love of personal liberty with a similarly qualified regard for formal authority."[22]

Hodge's political principles were remarkably consistent with, and profoundly informed by, his comprehensive theological system. His emphasis upon the essential unity of humankind can be gleaned not

---

20. A.A. Hodge, *Life of Charles Hodge*, 230.

21. Ibid., 210–11. See also Carwardine, "Politics of Charles Hodge," 258–59.

22. Torbett, *Theology and Slavery*, 68. See also Carwardine "Politics of Charles Hodge," 249–58.

only from his caution towards Jacksonian populism, but more fundamentally in his advancement of "federal" (from latin, *foedus*) theology. Herein lies Hodge's insistence that all of humankind descended from the same couple, Adam and Eve, and that as such, all are culpable of the same original sin.[23] This universal guilt was not, as it were, due to some historical, ontological oneness (as in the case of Nevin), but rather to the simple biblical fact. The common sense hermeneutic with which Hodge approached the Bible eventuated in this understanding of mankind's unity, namely a unity of knowledge and nature, since "all people perceive the same truth and, at least on a natural level, are affected by it in the same way."[24]

Because he viewed humankind's unity through the lenses of Common Sense Realism and "biblical fact" rather than through an organic, idealist ontology (in which lines of separation are more fluid because the human being is understood to exist always in relationship), Hodge did not object to the American enlightenment's version of church-state separation or to the fundamental distinction of "spheres" in society. He maintained that all spheres of society, including individuals, the church, and the civil government, should be built upon and governed by Christian principles.[25] His *jus divinum* understanding of God's administration in the world allowed Hodge to maintain that these spheres could remain fundamentally separate while still being obligated to abide by such principles. As such, the state is duty-bound to retain a sense of Christian principle even though it is not required to do so in relationship to the church. To be sure, church and state are designed to interpenetrate, particularly since the church has the obligation to encourage and even insist upon a code of ethics, values, and morality, but the lines of separation are always retained. As Torbett notes, Hodge maintained that "each entity must work within its respective sphere . . . during the long period of time in which he wrote on slavery Hodge was concerned with protecting the distinct rights and duties of each entity from unjust interference from the others."[26] Nevertheless, he likewise repudiated any theory of government whereby those in power were to somehow remain

---

23. This will be discussed in further detail in chapter 4.
24. Torbett, *Theology and Slavery*, 81.
25. Ibid., 81, citing Hodge, "Relation of Church," 691–93.
26. Ibid., 87.

"neutral" in matters of religion.[27] Hodge insisted that the moral voice of the church was too important to sacrifice for the sake of an absolute separation, a view which the great majority of his fellow theological intellects would likewise affirm. Ultimately, for Hodge, all spheres are to work together with their respective powers and responsibilities to create a balanced, just society.[28]

The moral voice of the church, however, was not to be merely a principle unaffected by the shifting political circumstances. For Hodge, there was a time for balancing the principle of separation with a morally informed pragmatism. "There are periods in the history of every nation when its destiny for ages may be determined by the events of an hour," Hodge once wrote. "There are occasions when political questions rise into the sphere of morals and religion; when the rule for political action is to be sought, not in considerations of state policy, but in the Word of God."[29] For Hodge, the war and the critical issue of slavery had given way to extraordinary circumstances in which the Bible, morality, and theology came to the fore and necessarily informed the full scope of political discourse.

Hodge was not a pro-slavery man. He recognized the institution as a great evil, one which he believed should eventually come to an end. Nevertheless, he could not condemn it as a sin and thus felt that one could not expel a slaveholder from the church.[30] No less the logician than in his approach to systematic theology, Hodge was in search of precise definitions and sound argumentation on the matter of slavery.[31] At the

27. Hodge, "Sunday Laws," 734–42.
28. Torbett, *Theology and Slavery*, 96.
29. A. A. Hodge, *Life of Charles Hodge*, 461.
30. Ibid., 356.

31. In an 1844 letter, responding with great agitation to a recent publication in the *Witness*, he wrote, "If the Abolitionists of Great Britain wish to do us any good, let them first define what slavery is, making due discrimination between slave-holding and the varying laws by which, in different countries, slave-holding is regulated. And then let them prove that slave-holding, not the slave laws of this or that State, but slave-holding, is contrary to the Word of God. It cannot do us any good to tell us that it is wrong to be cruel, to be unjust, to separate husbands and wives, parents and children, or to keep servants in ignorance. Our churches do not sanction any of these things, though our laws often do. Instead of really arguing the question, and affecting the conscience through the understanding, such men as the writers in the *Witness* take up reports of this or that case of cruelty, and hold it up as an indication of the character of whole classes of men in this country." Ibid., 359.

end of the war, Hodge addressed the matter by situating emancipation within the scope of God's redemptive history:

> It is enough to humble the whole Christian world to hear our Presbyterian brethren in the South declaring that the great mission of the Southern church was to conserve the system of African slavery. Since the death of Christ no such dogma stains the record of an ecclesiastical body ... The first and most obvious consequence of the dreadful civil war just ended, has been the final and universal overthrow of slavery within the limits of the United States. This is one of the most momentous events in the history of the world. That it was the design of God to bring about this event cannot be doubted ... Almost all foreigners, and a large class of our own people predicted the success of the South, and the chances were, so to speak, in favour at least of a compromise, which would leave slavery untouched within the limits of the States. But God has ordered it otherwise ... The inevitable difficulties and sufferings consequent on such an abrupt change in the institutions and social organization of a great people, must be submitted to, as comprehended in the design of God in these events.[32]

Hodge was one of the more vocal theologians of his day. His articles, essays, and letters indicate that he was highly—and indeed thoughtfully—engaged with the numerous pressing political issues of his day, issues which proved to be deeply formative in the history of the country. Nevertheless, Hodge never betrayed his commitment to being a theologian, and as such, held fast to his Bible and its principles even on matters that seemed to be beyond the pale of the church and theology. It is difficult to fault Hodge in this respect, even if in retrospect one would prefer for him to drink a bit more sparingly from the well of Common Sense Realism and aspects of the accompanying enlightenment political theory. Even where one does want to critique Hodge in theory, one cannot but help admire his pragmatism when it was warranted. His remarks on the war and slavery, for instance, demonstrate great honesty, caution, and logic. It is for this reason that Hodge cannot be fit so easily into most categories we might assign to the era and that the theologian must be taken seriously as one who provides indispensable insight into the world of the nineteenth century.

---

32. Hodge, "President Lincoln," 439–40.

The Transcendentalists

Transcendentalism is an often overlooked aspect of Nevin's context and intellectual backdrop. This is perhaps due to the fact that the movement makes only scant appearances in Nevin's writings (where it is condemned).[33] Nevertheless, it is an unfortunate oversight since the movement's significance and impact during Nevin's lifetime, particularly in the Northeast, can hardly be overestimated. What is more, aside from Transcendentalism's vast impact as an intellectual, literary, and philosophical tradition, the movement shares with Nevin an appreciation for themes that originated in German romanticism and idealism.[34] Indeed, the philosophical categories and trajectories of Transcendentalism were in many ways much closer to Nevin than were the themes of Common Sense Realism, which Nevin regarded as empty, atomistic, and arbitrary.[35] Thus, while it is beyond the scope of the present study to consider in detail the social and political views of the Transcendentalist movement, it will suffice to give a brief account of the Transcendentalist understanding of the individual in relation to society.

Only recently has serious work been done in the area of Transcendentalist social and political theory, partially due to the fact that the likes of Emerson simply did not undertake much of any political writing.[36] Most pertinent to Nevin's thought—and indeed to the thought of most American theologians at the time—is the insistence among Transcendentalists, especially Emerson and Thoreau, that the individual was the fundamental source of societal transformation. This approach, at one level, makes Transcendentalism and revivalism strange bedfellows, but it is precisely for this reason that a cursory account of Transcendentalism is warranted.[37] As Frost explains, Emerson and Thoreau "kept to the sidelines politically and argued that genuine political regeneration could only come about through individual spiritual

---

33. Nevin, "Lancaster Commencement Address," 648. Nevin, "Rauch's Psychology," 106.

34. See Frost, "Religion," 356, citing Atkinson, *Essential Writings*, 81, 86.

35. In this way, Nevin shares with Emerson a distaste for materialists such as Locke. See Frost, "Religion," 356. Nevin's philosophical views are discussed in further detail in chapter 3.

36. Ibid., 373.

37. See Hutchison, *Transcendentalist Ministers*; Also Hankins, *Second Great Awakening*.

renewal."[38] As such, the movement serves as yet another testimony to how powerful and profound the revivalist impulse was, an impulse which Nevin spent an enormous amount of time and energy trying to correct.

Both Thoreau and Emerson had a deeply romanticized view of the natural world, believing, furthermore, that a divine spirit animated all creation. The individual, from their perspective, was a part of this greater whole, but the individual was also the sole source of moral authority and meaning within creation. The Transcendentalists, therefore, placed great value upon and encouraged creativity, spontaneity, and a contemplative, existential way of life. As Emerson once wrote, "Mind is the only reality, of which men and all other natures are better or worse reflectors. Nature, literature, history, are only subjective phenomena . . . His thought—that is the Universe." Granted, there was room in Emerson's system for "outer" influences, but such were regarded as no more than inspiration or ecstasy.[39]

With respect to the individual's participation in society, Emerson, for one, was consistent in his scathing criticisms of what he considered to be a market that inherently resulted in fragmentation, alienation, and ultimately in a dehumanization of the American worker. "Man is metamorphosed into a thing, into many things," he wrote. "The planter . . . is seldom cheered by any idea of the true dignity of his ministry . . . The Tradesman scarcely ever gives an ideal worth to his work . . . The priest becomes a form; the attorney, a statute-book; the mechanic a machine; the sailor, a rope of ship."[40] He believed, like Nevin, that humanity was designed for a unified and harmonious existence, teaching that "man is one" and therefore politically and socially equal.

The Transcendentalist critique of materialistic philosophy as well as the movement's constructive efforts towards an idealist philosophy of the individual and society certainly fall in line with Nevin's broader project. That the individual is in essence part of a whole which is greater than the sum of its parts is likewise a belief that Nevin shared. Nevertheless, the common ground ends there. Nevin unflinchingly rejected the way in which Transcendentalism had appropriated idealistic philosophical and theological categories into a sheer humanism, characterizing

---

38. Frost, "Religion," 355.
39. Atkinson, *Essential Writings*, 82–83. See Frost, "Religion," 356.
40. Gougeon, "Politics and Economics," 40.

Transcendentalism's adherents as leaving the world behind "to expatiate among the clouds."[41]

Horace Bushnell

In an 1837 address to Yale College, theologian Horace Bushnell related his political views by employing the famous words of John Milton:

> "Alas, sir!" exclaimed Milton, suddenly grasping this whole subject as with divine force, "a commonwealth ought to be but as one huge Christian personage, one mighty growth and stature of an honest man, as big and compact in virtue as in body; for look, what the grounds and causes are of single happiness to one man, the same ye shall find them to a whole state." Here, in a single sentence, he declares the true idea of a state, and of all just administration.[42]

Here, the romantic allusions to organic growth as well as the unity of the one and the many reveal the basic tenets of Bushnell's hermeneutic. His approach to politics and social structures further discloses this view as one which stresses the organic unity of society and the role of the family. Such is part and parcel of Bushnell's family life and theological career as it developed in New England. Emerging from his distinctly New England congregational context, Bushnell placed a heavy emphasis on the educational, democratic, and religious efforts that contributed to the enculturation of individual freedom in society.[43] In this respect, Bushnell fell in line with the more conservative tradition of New England politics, which affirmed God's sovereignty over institutions or "spheres" within society. As such, he can be aligned—at least early in his theological career—with the federalist tradition in New Haven, along with Timothy Dwight and conservative Unitarians.[44] Eventually, however, Bushnell would be writing like a Whig, calling himself a Democrat, and joining Lincoln's Republican Party. This irony seems to have grown "out of a basic tension between two important values of his social orientation: unity and stability on the one hand and individual spontaneity

---

41. Nevin, "Rauch's Psychology," 106.

42. Bushnell, "Native Quality," 93. See Milton, John, *Complete Prose Works of John Milton*. Vol 1, edited by Don Wolfe. New Haven: Yale University Press, 1953.

43. Haddorff, *Dependence and Freedom*, 122–23.

44. Ibid., 123.

and creativity on the other . . . he combined a love of order with a love of freedom."[45]

The New England influence upon Bushnell is not so much due to a convenient political affinity between Bushnell and his contemporaries as it is to Bushnell's valuing of early Puritan politics, which he believed could be best preserved by way of New England society. Aligning himself with the likes of Thomas Hooker and the Connecticut Congregationalists of colonial Hartford, Bushnell would eventually make the compelling case that the faithful Puritan founders, long before the revolution and drafting of the American constitution, advocated forms of government and liberty that were far more influential than the "elaborate political theories of Locke or Rousseau."[46] The Puritans, he believed, rightly understood that the various institutions of society are ordained and designed by God, not by man. Thus, to develop a political theory which begins with "social contracts" and "natural" rights is to fundamentally misunderstand the genesis, flow, and nature of society and its institutions.[47]

The educational, moral, and civic values within society, Bushnell believed, could be appropriately modeled by the interlocking institutions of the family, the church, and the state. Order in society was pursued and maintained as these institutions worked together to define social obligations.[48] This model of society was anything but arbitrary; rather it was a model that reflected the way in which the individual was to be instilled with the values of a virtuous, just republic. "Individualism," as it was understood by Bushnell's contemporaries, violated this model as well as the organic nature of God's creation and design for society. Instead, the individual's very constitution was the result of institutions in society. The individual could not, as the new materialistic empiricism had begun to insinuate, be separated from the structures, institutions, and dynamism of society.

That being said, it is not the case for Bushnell that each institution is equally important or influential. One may rightly surmise both from Bushnell's close knit family and his work on the theme of *Christian Nurture* that the theologian gives unique priority to the family.[49] It is the

45. Torbett, *Theology and Slavery*, 128. See also Barnes, *Virtuous Republic*, 47–48.
46. See Haddorff's analysis, *Dependence and Freedom*, 123–24.
47. Ibid., 124. See Conrad Cherry, "Structure of Organic Thinking," 3–20.
48. Bushnell, *Christian Nurture*, 96.
49. Ibid., 90–122. On Bushnell's immediate family, see Barnes, *Virtuous Republic*, 11–12. See also Torbett, *Theology and Slavery*, 124.

family's responsibility, as having the most direct and unmediated influence upon the individual, to instill within the individual the Christian faith, along with its moral values and sense of civic responsibility. This is an important distinction that sets Bushnell apart from other theologians. To be sure, others—not least Hodge and Nevin—emphasized greatly the role of the family to catechize, instruct, and introduce children to the life of the church and society, but Bushnell attributed primacy to the family and, more specifically, to mothers. The nation's success in the arenas of politics, science, and economics was ultimately dependent on moral character—character which began at home.[50] Bushnell was so bold as to employ the family as a model for the state, writing, "Each state should have the interest in itself of a family, a sense of character to sustain, a love of its ancestors and its children, a just ambition to raise its quota of distinguished men, to be honored for its literature, its good manners and the philosophic beauty of its disciplinary institutions."[51]

Bushnell joined the majority of his contemporary intellectuals in his aim to balance freedom and order in society, principles which were deeply and necessarily woven into the fabric of American political philosophy. More specifically, like Hodge and a number of other theologians, he recognized the various institutions that work together for a just society. Nevertheless, departing from Hodge and aligning more closely with Nevin, Bushnell also insisted on a historically informed approach to politics. This is most evident in his battle over Puritan origins and colonial history.[52] Consider, for instance, his words concerning the founders:

> But then we need to add that law is law, binding upon souls, not as human will, or the will of just one more than half the full grown men over a certain age, but a power of God entering into souls and reigning in them as a divine instinct of civil order, creating thus a state—perpetual, beneficent, the safeguard of the homes and of industry, the condition of a public feeling and a consciously organic life. This it is that makes all government sacred and powerful, that it somehow stands in the will of God; nay, it is the special dignity and glory and freedom of our government, that it rests, so little, on the mere will or force of man, so entirely

50. Barnes, *Virtuous Republic*, 127.
51. Bushnell, "Native Quality," 95.
52. On this point, see Haddorff, *Dependence and Freedom*, 126, drawing upon Bushnell, "Unconscious Influence," 186–205.

on those principles of justice and common beneficence which we know are sacred to God. And it is the glory also of our founders and first fathers that they prepared us to such a state. Had they managed to weave nothing into our character more adequate than we sometimes discover in our political dogmas, we should even have wanted the institutions about which we speculate so feebly, and should have been as hopeless of any settled terms of order, as we now are confident of our baseless and undigested principles.[53]

Within this historical framework, Bushnell maintained that society was essentially organic in such a way that its institutions were permeable and porous. Insofar as this reflected Bushnell's ontology, this marked a divergence from the traditional *jus divinum* hermeneutic of Hodge. It also marked an additional shift towards the Mercersburg hermeneutic, even if Bushnell's view remained too anthropocentric and naturalistic for Nevin's taste. Insofar as Bushnell viewed history and politics through the romanticized lens of organic unity, his most poignant words are to be found in his Yale commencement address of 1865:

> So the unity now to be developed, after this war-deluge is over, ... will be no more thought of as a mere human compact, or composition, always to be debated by the letter, but it will be that bond of common life which God has touched with blood; a sacredly heroic, Providentially tragic unity, where God's cherubim stand guard over grudges and hates and remembered jealousies, and the sense of nationality becomes even a kind of religion ... I can only say that [these fallen alumni] having taken the sword to be God's ministers, and to vindicate the law as his ordinance, they have done it even the more effectively in that they have died for it ... Bitter has been the cost of our pitifully weak philosophy [that imagined government to be a trifle]. In these rivers of blood we have now bathed our institutions, and they are henceforth to be hallowed in our sight. Government is now become Providential,—no more a mere creature of our human will, but a grandly moral affair ... We have not fought this dreadful war to a close, just to put our government upon a par with these oppressive dynasties [of old Europe]! We scorn the parallel they give us; and we owe it even to them to say, that a government which is friendly, and free, and right, protecting all alike, and doing the most for all, is one of God's sacred finalities, which no hand may touch, or conspiracy assail, without com-

---

53. Bushnell, "Founders, Great," 93.

mitting the most damning crime, such as can be matched by no possible severities of justice.[54]

Horace Bushnell not only served as a formidable interlocutor for Nevin on matters of theology proper, but also as an interpreter of American society whose basic premises were shared by Nevin. Most significant in this respect is Bushnell's view of society as an organic, historical, interconnected web of institutions. This fundamental assumption was shared by Nevin (though, as we will see, with a different set of emphases), indicating from the outset that Bushnell is likely more suggestive than Hodge regarding Nevin's own theological vision of society. To be sure, there is a hermeneutical divergence between Nevin and Bushnell, but in terms of historical progression, the value of enlightenment political theory, institutional interconnectivity, and anthropology, the two theologians complement each other quite well.[55] We have in Bushnell, then, a theologian who can tell us a great deal about Nevin's thought, even in instances of disagreement.

Orestes A. Brownson

Among Nevin's contemporaries who articulated a theologically informed view of politics and culture, perhaps none provides more clues to Nevin's thought than the Catholic theologian Orestes A. Brownson. Beginning with their theological correspondence in the early 1850's in the form of book reviews and essays, the two theologians demonstrated rather quickly that while they differed hermeneutically and methodologically, they pursued similar ends, namely a churchly, sacramental theology and the reconciliation of the subjective and objective notions of faith, free-

---

54. Bushnell, "Our Obligations," 328–29, 341, 352. See also Noll's analysis in Noll, "Both . . . Pray," para. 17. Noll insightfully notes, "What seems clearer now, more than a generation after Clebsch and Cross published their fine work, however, is that Bushnell's romantic nationalism of the redeemed *Volk* was as liable to be corrupted as it was to promote the millennium Bushnell anticipated. However powerful as theology, it was extraordinarily dangerous theology of the type reversing celestial and terrestrial categories and paving a way for the divine-right nationalism that gave us World War I, the Red Scare, the internment of Japanese Americans during World War II, and the recent dismemberment of Yugoslavia."

55. As will be discussed in chapter 4, Nevin is critical of Bushnell's naturalism, preferring a hermeneutic and an ontology which can be rooted in the transcendent and supernatural. It is a matter of debate as to what degree Nevin's criticism of Bushnell was warranted, as Bushnell certainly implicates notions of the transcendent. It is, perhaps, more so a matter of emphasis than it is radical divergence from one another.

dom, and authority.[56] Brownson provides insight into Nevin's political thought not because their correspondence ever dealt with politics *per se*, but because Brownson's theological trajectory lines up well with Nevin's, particularly on those aspects which informed each theologian's understanding of freedom, authority, human relationship, and the primacy of the church. Not only do Brownson's theological commonalities with Nevin conspicuously emerge, but they are highly suggestive of Nevin's thought where he is seemingly silent.

Brownson wrote far more on the subject of politics and government than Nevin. It is ironic, in retrospect, that his theology as a whole was largely unhistorical and overtly supernatural, a critique that Nevin rightly leveled at Brownson on several occasions. Brownson, explains one biographer, attempted to formulate a view of government that both eschewed notions of theocracy while also remaining consistent with Christian principles. His hope was to unite religion and politics in principle, not institutionally.[57] To this end, Brownson insisted that all political thought must be rooted in and driven by theology. He writes, "There is no state without God, any more than there is a church without Christ or the Incarnation. An atheist may be a politician, but if there were no God there could be no politics. Theological principles are the basis of political principles."[58] Brownson thus refuses to isolate questions of the state from theology. Insofar as our theory of the state raises metaphysical questions, and it does, this theory necessarily begs a line of theological questioning and formulation. In turn, he explains, "our theology determines our metaphysics, our ethics, and our politics. It is idle to attempt to separate the political question from the ethical, the metaphysical or the theological."[59]

Like Nevin and Bushnell, Brownson was suspicious of the seemingly conventional "social contract theory." He viewed this formulation as one which violated God's sovereign authority over human wills and relationships, particularly as they existed in the context of communion with God and the surrounding world. Communion was understood by Brownson to be fundamental to human existence since humanity exists in relationship. As such, relationships are rightly formed under the

56. See Carey, *Orestes A. Brownson*, 209–15.
57. Ibid., 123.
58. Brownson, *American Republic*, 409.
59. Brownson, "Origin and Ground," 258.

authority of God's divine providence and sanction rather than by capricious contract. Limits in society are to be understood primarily in terms of God's law and will; "contracts" remain as a flawed necessity for the concrete world of politics. True human relationships find their genesis in and by communion with God, humankind, and nature: "We, as members of the church, are said to live a divine life by communion with the church, and by that communion only... The church here symbolizes humanity in its relations to God, and life by communion with her means, when translated from the symbolical language of faith into the language of science, life by communion with God in man, or the communion of man with his race."[60]

To be sure, "communion" for Brownson stemmed most fundamentally from his theology of the Eucharist, which he had largely adapted from Pierre Leroux's philosophical doctrine of communion. In words that may just as well be applied to Nevin, Carey explains that Leroux "saw in the Incarnation and the Eucharist a philosophical doctrine of communion that had universal significance for understanding the progress of humanity... Leroux defined the human in relational terms. The self existed or rather lived only and always in relation: to God, to nature, and to other human beings. The self, therefore, was always a social or relational self—living only in so far as it was in interaction with god, nature, and humanity."[61]

Thus for Brownson, that the state cannot be isolated from God is rooted in the fact that no human relation can be understood apart from "life by communion," and ultimately, from communion with God in the church and its sacraments. Religion, according to Brownson, is inseparable from every living act of man, whether it be an individual or social act. As such, "men must conform either their politics to their religion or their religion to their politics." He adds, "Christianity is constantly at work, moulding political society in its own image and likeness, and every political system struggles to harmonize Christianity with itself. If, then, the United States have a political destiny, they have a religious destiny inseparable from it."[62] Far from relegating society or the political order into distinct spheres or realms, Brownson saw the constitution of mankind to be far more fluid and dynamic, constantly overlapping and

60. Brownson, "Channing on Social Reform," 149.
61. Carey, *Orestes A. Brownson*, 105, 107.
62. Brownson, *American Republic*, 411.

interpenetrating. He understood that the premodern western world had confused the relationship of church and state, but was just as sure that the modern American insistence upon removing religion from other "secular" areas of life was to deny the fallen condition of humanity and the state's desperate need for redemption by God.[63]

Philip Schaff

Philip Schaff, Nevin's colleague at Mercersburg, took a certain pleasure in affirming, "I am Swiss by birth, a German by education, and an American by choice."[64] His "choice" to be an American is perhaps no more clearly expressed than in his love of the American constitution and his optimism for the future of the country which he had come to call home.

More expressly, Schaff's work, *America: A Sketch of the Political, Social, and Religious Character*, exhibits the historical theologian's fascination with the ways in which America had departed from European norms of politics and culture. This departure, he believed, constituted a unique unfolding of world history. Such could be attributed to the success of Protestantism, the influx of Anglo-Germanic immigrants during the early years of the republic, and, most importantly, the Constitution. This great document "protects us against the despotism of a state church," writes Schaff, "and guarantees to us the free exercise and enjoyment of religion, as an inherent, inviolable, and inalienable right of every man."[65] As such, the Constitution "forms an entirely new phenomenon in the history of the world."[66]

Both church and state, in Schaff's view, were instituted by God but have their own "sphere of jurisdiction." These "spheres" are not isolated or completely autonomous; they are distinct but inseparable, analogous to the relationship between body and soul. While the former is concerned with eternal matters and the other with the temporal, they are equally necessary. Schaff is worth quoting at length concerning their respective roles:

> The one looks to heaven as the final home of immortal spirits, the other upon our mother earth. The church is the reign of love; the

---

63. Carey, *Orestes A. Brownson*, 182.
64. D. Schaff, *Life of Philip Schaff*, 1.
65. Schaff, *Church and State*, 5.
66. Schaff, *America*, 37.

state is the reign of justice. The former is governed by the gospel, the latter by the law. The church exhorts, and uses moral suasion; the state commands, and enforces obedience. The church punishes by rebuke, suspension, and excommunication; the state by fines, imprisonment, and death. Both meet on questions of public morals, and both together constitute civilized human society and ensure its prosperity.[67]

Schaff accepts the separation of church and state as it exists in America precisely because he does not see this separation as absolute, noting several *loci* of society where there is inherent, necessary overlap. Here he includes marriage, the role of Sabbath in the workweek, and public schooling.[68] Thus, fundamentally, the spheres of church and state necessarily overlap, not only because they were both instituted by God, but also because they flow from God's most essential institution, the family. Here, one cannot help but notice the striking similarity with Bushnell's view of society's institutions.

For Schaff, those who espoused and promoted absolute separation of church and state were mistaken. The state needed the religious morals exhibited and promoted by the church. In fact, "The state is more in need of the moral support of the church than the church is in need of the protection of the state."[69] Not only was such an ideology futile in theory, but the history of the country had, to this point, demonstrated that such an absolute separation was neither possible nor desirable. This pragmatism is at first betrayed by Schaff in his own words: "Whatever may be the merits of the theory of the American system, it has worked well in practice. It has stood the test of experience. It has the advantages of the union of church and state without its disadvantages. It secures all the rights of the church without the sacrifice of liberty and independence, which are worth more than endowments."[70]

Given that Schaff shared with Nevin disgust for over-privatization and sectarianism within the church, it is perhaps odd that he should view voluntarism as a positive result of church and state separation. The value of such, he believes, lies in the fact that voluntarism has returned Christianity to dependence on its own resources. It is, more specifically,

---

67. Schaff, *Church and State*, 10.
68. Bowden, "Civil Authority," 156.
69. Schaff, *Church and State*, 44.
70. Ibid., 78.

"the voluntary principle . . . of self government." This principle encourages and necessitates that the church rely upon its own resources and demonstrate before the world its ability to thrive without the aid of the secular arm of the government.[71] This type of voluntarism in the context of church and state separation provides for the church's "declaration of independence towards the state," and indeed, "an emancipation of the state from bondage to a particular confession."[72] Schaff further explains the profit of the church in such circumstances:

> A Christian government can be made an infinite blessing to a people; and to have such a government must be a matter of joy. But in the first place, the freedom and independence of the church is, after all, a precious boon. In the second place, it is very hazardous for the church to expect too much of that union, and to put her trust in the temporal arm, especially in our days, when truly Christian princes and statesmen have become much more rare than in the times of the Reformation. And in the last place, the Church will do well to hold herself in readiness for the possible event of a violent rupture of that venerable bond, if not for a formal persecution by the temporal powers, if they should fall again, by some unexpected turn, into Red Republican hands.[73]

Such a system, Schaff believes, allows there to be a respectful separation in terms of outward operation while simultaneously protecting the Christian substance of the nation from the potential abuse of temporal authority. That is, the nation remains Christian by refusing to have its heart and mind under the authority of the state. When Christianity is allowed to be expressed freely out of personal conviction, Schaff explains, it has far greater power over the mind than when enjoined by civil law.[74]

Another reason for Schaff's rejection of an absolute separation of church and state lies in his preservation of the view that Christianity is designed to "leaven and sanctify all spheres of human life." Particularly where the temporal and eternal spheres converge, the Christian faith ought to be advanced for the sake of justice, morality, and even religious instruction. The natural, organic growth of the nation calls for the church at times to provide nurture and guardianship over the children of

---

71. Ibid.
72. Schaff, *America*, 91.
73. Ibid., xiii–xiv.
74. Ibid., 91.

God in all spheres.[75] Simply put, Schaff "was too committed to a theory of development in history not to look for continuing penetration and transformation of the state by Christianity." The theologian is not vague on this point, explaining that "Christianity aims to leaven and sanctify all spheres of human life, as well as all the powers of the soul,"[76] and adding moreover, "We would by no means vindicate this separation of church and state as the perfect and final relation between the two. The kingdom of Christ is to penetrate and transform like leaven, all the relations of individual and national life."[77]

On the matter of slavery, Schaff offered a condemnation that was relatively common amidst the many other voices of the middle states. With other formidable theologians and churchmen of his time, he denounced the institution while also remaining cautious about how to end it:

> [Slavery] is certainly in most palpable contradiction to the first principle of that government, that all men are born free and equal; or, as it should be more properly expressed, are born or destined for freedom. What an anomaly, that the freest country in the world should maintain and defend a relic of barbarism and heathenism, which humanity and Christianity, reason and revelation, and all the civilized nations of Europe condemn with one voice! But when and how this social evil, not introduced by the national American government itself, but inherited from the colonial period, rooted in the heart of the land, and interwoven with all the material interests of the South, is to be done away, is one of the most difficult questions, which statesmanship has ever had to solve.[78]

No less than in other political matters, Schaff once again displays his great admiration of the American Constitution and the principles of government therein. In fact, if there is distinction to be made between Schaff and his theological contemporaries, it is precisely in this admiration. This not to say that Schaff detracted from his Christian principles on political matters or that others did not express belief that the country is Christian in substance, only that his appreciation for American prin-

---

75. Ibid., xiii.
76. Bowden, "Civil Authority," 151.
77. Schaff, *America*, 90.
78. Ibid., 49.

ciples was more clearly displayed than other theologians who encountered the same circumstances. Hodge, for one, seems to have opted not so much for argumentation along the lines of the American constitution as he did the Bible. Perhaps most striking is the way in which Schaff and Nevin differed on this point, given their broad hermeneutical and theological similarities, similarities which were arguably not to be found among another pair of theologians of their time. Nevertheless, Schaff's appreciation for the Constitution, combined with his romanticized version of an organic history, suggests that the historian was in fact more akin to Bushnell than Nevin when it came to American social and political issues.

Even in his later reflections in the midst of a war-torn nation would Schaff muster his poignant optimism for the country's days ahead. His belief that history was unfolding organically and dialectically prompted Schaff to deduce that, despite the "streams of noble blood" and the many "sacrifices" of the government and the people, God would continue to guide events to an ultimate resolution. "The country," he romanticized, "has passed through the fiery trial and has now entered into the maturity of manly strength and self-sufficiency."[79]

Schaff was not alone in his idealist (and even optimistic) interpretation of America's recent history. His colleague at Mercersburg likewise proclaimed that the war had "been to the nation like the baptism of the Red Sea." Quoting Paul's second letter to the Corinthians, he declared, "Old things have been made to pass away by it; and now, lo, all things are becoming new."[80] And yet the two architects of the Mercersburg theology, Schaff and Nevin, had arrived at these similar interpretations despite having vastly different backgrounds. Accordingly, we turn now to examine Nevin's life and work as it pertains to antebellum politics and culture.

---

79. Schaff, *The Civil War*, 16–17. See Noll, "Both . . . Pray."
80. Nevin, "Lancaster Commencement Address," 638.

2

The Irony of Sectarian Liberty

Nevin's Interpretation and Critique of the Antebellum World

THE UNIQUE CULTURAL AND religious milieu of Nevin's life and career raises important questions about the theologian's more immediate circumstances and how he engaged the myriad issues therein. Here, we will consider the Scotch-Irish and German Reformed Pennsylvanian communities in which Nevin spent the majority of his lifetime. Nevin's writings suggest that his concern for these communities was not necessarily over their political orientation or involvement (which was remarkably complex), but rather their inability to prevent ecclesial fragmentation and disunity, thus rendering impotent their public role.[1] To this end, the chapter will first briefly take into account Nevin's family history and the implications of Nevin's upbringing.

NEVIN: A BIOGRAPHICAL SKETCH

The Nevin family, likely deriving their name from the popular Scotch-Irish name MacNevin, had settled in the Cumberland Valley of Pennsylvania (after a brief stint in New York) in the mid-late eighteenth century. The location and timing of the family's residence here is of no small import, as the Cumberland Valley, close in proximity to the Mason-Dixon Line, would prove to be a juncture for feisty political battles and dynamic religious forces.

Nevin revered his parents as "conscientious and exemplary professors of religion," affirming that he had been "carefully brought up in the

---

1. It is likely not a coincidence, moreover, that Nevin's Scotch-Irish and Anglo-German contexts parallel the clash of German idealism and Scottish Common Sense that was so prevalent in his own theological polemics.

nurture and admonition of the Lord, according to the Presbyterian faith as it then stood."[2] The Presbyterian faith that Nevin knew as a child was a faith that placed great emphasis upon the notion of a covenant family, the catechesis of children, and the preparation of children for the Lord's Supper. "In one word," he wrote, "all proceeded on the theory of sacramental, educational religion."[3]

Hugh Williamson, Nevin's paternal great-uncle and a staunch Federalist, served as a delegate from North Carolina to the Continental Congress and the Constitutional Convention before representing Philadelphia for two terms in Congress. Similarly, Nevin's father, John Sr., was sent by his fellow citizens of Kasey's Run to represent them in Congress—a duty which was deterred by his death in 1829.[4] Finally, Robert Jenkins, Nevin's father-in-law, was an ironmaster of Lancaster County who served as a member of Congress from 1807–1811.[5]

The Nevin-Jenkins relationship is worth noting due to Robert's friendship with future president, James Buchanan of Lancaster. Nevin would also befriend Buchanan, and the two men, serving as chairman of the trustees and past-president of Franklin and Marshall college, respectively, would eventually work together to keep the school from falling prey to Nevin's opponents in the early 1850s. And later, upon return from his presidency to Lancaster, Buchanan lived in a home adjacent to the Nevin farm. It was a relationship characterized by long conversations that lasted well into the night—conversations driven by politics, philosophy, theology, and certainly the War Between the States that had called upon three of Nevin's sons.[6]

2. Nevin, "My Own Life," 2.

3. Ibid., 2.

4. Bratt notes that John Sr. "declined to run for Congress out of his diffidence at public speaking." Bratt, "Antebellum Culture Wars," 2. See also Appel, *Life and Work*, 25, 27.

5. Ibid., 2.

6. Ibid., 3. Buchanan's life overlapped with Nevin's in several respects. He was born in Mercersburg and, like Nevin's father, attended Dickenson College. Before joining the Jacksonian Democratic movement, Buchanan, like Nevin's uncle, Hugh, was a Federalist member of Congress. Furthermore, Nevin's father-in-law, Robert Jenkins, was a successful business man and a close political ally of Buchanan's, also serving as a Federalist member of Congress (1807–1811). Buchanan had purchased his Wheatland estate in Lancaster in 1848 and returned there in 1861 after his presidency. Buchanan had grown up in a Presbyterian home, but took a newfound interest in spiritual matters upon his return to Lancaster. He began attending chapel services at Franklin and Marshall College, where Nevin regularly preached. Nevin, taking note of Buchanan's participa-

Clash of Cultures

As part of a Presbyterian community of Scotch-Irish descent, Nevin was instilled with many of the values and mores of a group that had demonstrated a great deal of resentment towards the English. It was, after all, largely the unjust treatment that Ulster had suffered at the hands of the British that led to Scotch-Irish migration to America during the eighteenth century. This had resulted in strong support of the American Revolution and Jeffersonian Republicanism by the Scotch-Irish communities, who constituted over forty percent of the population in the Carolinas, Virginia, and the middle states. Conversely, New England boasted of an enormous population where eighty percent of whites were of English origin.[7]

The dividing line one might expect between Scotch-Irish and English-Yankee religion, however, is quite complex. In fact, the antagonism between these groups rarely corresponded with denominational lines.[8] In many cases, internal division within denominations played just as much of a role, if not greater, in demarcating party allegiance. In particular, the Presbyterian Church exhibited significant division between several groups: On the one hand was the Scotch and Scotch-Irish majority; on the other, the English, Welsh, and other minorities of New England. The former, with their tight grip on the doctrines of Westminster and Reformed Orthodoxy, generally fell into line with Jacksonian Democracy and held greater sway in cities such as Philadelphia, spreading also throughout the southern and western states. The latter of these groups, known as the New School Presbyterians, had been reared in New England revivalism, fitting quite nicely into the socially and politically

---

tion, took the former president as a student of Christianity's basic tenets. Eventually, Buchanan resolved to join a church and, after weighing the possibility of joining the Presbyterians, Episcopalians, or German Reformed, joined the Presbyterians with the stipulation that he would not have to accept the doctrine of predestination. See Hart, *High Church Calvinist*, 174–75.

7. There were many exceptions to the rule of Scotch-Irish Republicanism, notably in Tory regions of North Carolina. Carwardine, *Evangelicals and Politics*, 118. See Thompson, *Presbyterians in the South*, 1:20–21; Kelley, *Cultural Pattern*, 70–75; McDonald and McDonald, "Ethnic Origins," 182–83, 195, 198–99.

8. Carwardine, *Evangelicals and Politics*, 118, notes the exception of Quakers, whose English ethnicity connected them almost entirely with Federalism and, later, with Whiggery.

"progressive" Whig Party.[9] The Presbyterian Schism of 1837–1838 was deeply rooted in these theological-political divisions within the denomination, an occasion which ultimately convinced Nevin to leave the denomination for the German Reformed in the late 1830s.[10] He believed that the German Reformed denomination would serve quite well as a locus for liturgical reform, and he admired the traditional, confessional nature of the denomination—a quality that certainly spoke to its liturgical as well as its political disposition.

Oddly, one aspect of Nevin's political context that has not been taken seriously is the political involvement and stance of the German Reformed denomination. While it would be sheer speculation to suggest that Nevin fell in line with the political positions of his own denomination, it is not unreasonable to propose that his writings took the political temperament of his denomination seriously.

During the early years of the republic, German and Dutch communities remained highly suspicious of the Anglo-Yankee and Federalist establishment, with the result that most of these communities were staunchly Republican under the first party system. This trend continued under the second party system as the German and Dutch joined the

---

9. Carwardine, *Evangelicals and Politics*, 118, cites personal letters and articles from the era, and is worth quoting at length on this point. He explains, "Many, probably most (Presbyterians), had put their faith in the Republicans in the 1790s and 1800s. A lack of partisan coherence continued to mark the church, taken as a whole, during the early years of the second party system. But the Presbyterian attachments were not wholly random, as alignments after the denominational schism of 1837–1838 demonstrate. New School men appear to have pulled heartily for Whiggery . . . (and many) were active in the moral reform societies of the 'benevolent empire.' . . . Though the elite of Old School ministers, north and south, appear to have been disproportionately Whig (to do in part with their social conservatism and concern for social order), in general Whig Old Schoolers like Charles Hodge, Stephen Colwell, John Hall, Robert J. Breckenridge, and John L. Nevius were no more typical of the denomination than those of the stripe of Ashbel Green, Nathan L. Rice, C H. McCormick, Robert L. Dabney, or William A. Scott. The latter were often of Scotch-Irish stock, found their strength in the middle and southern states, regarded the New School and the institutions of the benevolent empire with some suspicion, and sought in the Democratic party refuge from 'church and state' Whiggery." See also Kelley, *Cultural Pattern*, 128; Shade, "Political Pluralism"; Shade, "Pennsylvania Politics."

10. Nevin, though not explicitly referencing the schism, later wrote, "I cannot help seeing and feeling that a very material change has come upon [the Presbyterian Church] . . . and this in a way not without serious interest for my own religious life." Nevin, "My Own Life," 2.

ranks of the Jacksonians. The German electorate was likewise strongly Democrat, with the exception of the Brethren and Moravians.[11] In addition to popularity in the Deep South and the younger western states, Democratic presence was particularly strong in the middle states, not least in Pennsylvania. Democrats had generally been much more hospitable to immigrant communities than their rival political factions. This affiliation would hold true at least until the presidential election of Abraham Lincoln, who surprisingly garnered much support from the German communities of Pennsylvania.[12]

As he would relate later in life, from Nevin's point of view, this immigrant community had strived successfully to free itself from its incipient isolation and meager social position in the state, having entered into a "free, active communication with the general life of the State."[13] It was therefore imperative that the institutions of the state stay in conversation with the Anglo-German population, "the literature and science, philosophy and religion of Germany itself, serving to promote, at the same time, an intelligent regard for the German life at home . . ." Such was to coincide, of course, with the "perpetual patronage and support of the German Reformed Church."[14] This aspect of Nevin's life is far from trivial, as his sentiment would eventually develop into a profound love for this unique community.

Slavery

In 1829, having taken a job teaching at Western Seminary, Nevin moved to Pittsburgh and dove headlong into a number of responsibilities: teaching full-time at the seminary, preaching most Sundays in local churches, serving on various humanitarian and religious organizations' boards, and editing *The Friend*, a publication of the Young Men's Society of Pittsburgh and Vicinity (a precursor to the YMCA). During this time, Nevin participated more directly in debates over slavery (as well as

---

11. Carwardine, *Evangelicals and Politics*, 117–18. See Kelley, *Cultural Pattern*, 64–65; Tully, "Ethnicity, Religion and Politics," 494, 530–36; Shade, "Political Pluralism," 102.

12. Carwardine, *Evangelicals and Politics*, 306. By 1855, the German Reformed denomination counted 75,000 members. This was certainly due to an influx of immigration during the latter part of the antebellum era, but the presence of the German Reformed had been felt in the region for several decades. Carwardine, *Evangelicals and Politics*, 6.

13. Appel, *Life and Work*, 448.

14. Ibid., 448.

temperance and whether to have theatres in the city).[15] That Nevin held an anti-slavery position (as demonstrated especially in earlier writings) ought not to be surprising. His family had been decidedly anti-slavery for generations. When Nevin's father graduated from Dickenson College, he gave a speech entitled "The Sin of Slavery." Of his father, Nevin would later write, "In two things he was quite ahead of his present generation—total abstinence from ardent spirits, and a moral hatred of all slavery." For the Nevin family, anti-slavery was but one component of their broader values of stability, order, and social progress.[16]

The Friend, on occasion, addressed the issue of slavery from various angles, not least in the case of the controversial affair at Lane Seminary in the spring of 1834 and Judge Birney's advocacy for the slaves' immediate emancipation in the form of a letter to the Kentucky Colonization Society.[17] These examples sufficed during this time for Nevin as "specimens simply of my way of preaching abolitionism."[18]

In March of 1835, Nevin's responsibilities as editor of *The Friend* came to an end. Humbly, if not regretfully, he wrote, "Here, then, our relations to the subscribers of the *Friend* must be brought to an end. We trust that, notwithstanding the occasion of offence we may have given to some, we may still have the respect and good will of all; and with sentiments of corresponding regard, and the wishes for their prosperity on both sides of the grave, we bid them all an affectionate farewell."[19]

This "occasion of offense" was the publication's condemnation of the sin of slavery, which certainly did not bode well with what was a substantial pro-slavery contingent in Pittsburgh. Nevin included in his "farewell address" a bold expression of his position on slavery: "Slavery is a sin, *as it exists in this country*, and as such it ought to be abolished. There is no excuse for its being continued a single day. The whole nation is involved in the guilt of it, so long as public sentiment acquiesces in it as

---

15. Hart, *High Church Calvinist*, 54–55.

16. See Appel, *Life and Work*, 27, 61; Bratt, "Antebellum Culture Wars," 3.

17. "Controversial affair" refers to the series of debates organized by Theodore Weld, a student at Lane Seminary. Weld and twenty-four other students had recently transferred to the new school from the Oneida Institute in New York. The debates revolved around two main questions: first, whether or not slavery should be immediately abolished; and second, whether Christians should support colonization of American blacks in Africa. See Harrison, "Lane Seminary Debates," 403–4.

18. Appel, *Life and Work*, 72–73.

19. Ibid., 70, citing Nevin's essay in *The Friend*.

a necessary evil."[20] Addressing the hotly contested positions of colonization and emancipation, he adds, "We are no longer at a loss either on the subject of Colonization. We believe fully that as the case *now* stands, the one interest is contrary to the other; just as moderate drinking societies are at war with the temperance reformation . . . the cause of emancipation, in order to succeed, must be divorced altogether from the whole plan of colonizing the blacks, as heretofore and at present pursued for that purpose."[21]

In many ways, one might regard Nevin's parting words as archetypal for a writing career that would be driven largely by polemics. In a part of the country that was so sharply divided—both politically and theologically—over the issue of slavery, it was certainly expected that such public discourse would garner a variety of responses. Whatever the response may have been, it is notable that for Nevin, his years writing for *The Friend* were not easily forgotten.

As late as 1870, reflecting more broadly upon his position on slavery, he reminisced, "I have been fanatically taken to task in later life for not cursing slavery hard enough at the altar and from the pulpit. In my Pittsburgh days, as already intimated, it was the other way; my wrong stood, it was fanatically said, in allowing myself to talk or write of slavery at all as a bad thing."[22] Such is suggestive of the type of response he received during his tenure with *The Friend*. Indeed, Nevin's relative silence on the matter of slavery later in life is indicative of his frustration, recalling that he was "looked upon and spoken of, in certain quarters, as actually a disturber of the public peace," despite the fact that the publication "never took any party stand in regard to slavery one way or another; it went in favor of Colonization . . ."[23]

The Partisan Nevin?

The work of James Bratt is remarkably helpful in situating Nevin politically.[24] As he explains, Nevin's organic view of history and society and his vehement rejection of American individualism resonated with the Whig

---

20. Ibid., 73.
21. Ibid., 74.
22. Ibid., 70.
23. Ibid., 71.
24. In what follows I am indebted to Bratt, "Antebellum Culture Wars," 7–9.

party more than it did the Democrats. His critique of "party spirit" and his hope for the kingdom of God on this side of eternity were likewise in line with Whiggery. However, his traditional liturgical bent and his affiliation with the Scotch-Irish and German immigrant communities are indicative of a Democratic stance. In addition, his praise of the Mexican War as that which, by virtue of establishing new U.S. territory, would afford more opportunities for communal autonomy and freedom also revealed Democratic leanings. He wrote, moreover, that the day for "nativism" was "fast drawing to an end," thus demonstrating a pro-immigration, Democratic stance. Ultimately, however, the issue for Nevin was not Whig versus Democrat; it was, rather, whether a democratized America could balance human freedom with submission to God's authority.

NEVIN'S POLITICAL-THEOLOGICAL POLEMICS

For Nevin, political solutions are rooted not in politics *per se*, but in the reform of the church. His critiques do not emerge from his concerns over nationalism and American democracy as much as his theological concerns regarding the church, mankind, and their roles in relation to the incarnate Christ. His analyses, as such, are not based on a secularized postmillennial worldview or the optimism of modernist anthropology (both of which were prevalent during his lifetime); rather, his view insists that true sociopolitical analysis is ultimately a theological exercise. In this way, Nevin rejects what he believes to be the dualisms and false dichotomies precipitated by enlightenment political theory.

America's Role in World History

Nevin's theology was highly speculative and idealistic, and his cultural musings reflected the same tendency. With few exceptions, Nevin's political commentary was broad and sweeping, rarely taking an explicit stance on a political issue or publicly endorsing a party or candidate. In assessing his sociopolitical critiques, then, one would do well to follow Nevin's model and start with a wide lens before focusing on the particulars. Nevin's critiques are laden with his idealistic theology, as will be seen in his analysis of the Civil War era, including the ante- and post- bellum years. It is here that students of Nevin will find his theology of church and state, or perhaps more appropriately his theology of Christ for the world, most clearly disclosed. Certainly more trenchant are Nevin's critiques of Puritanism along with its endemic sectarian nature, which in his view has done irreparable harm to the church as well as the social and political fabric of the nation.

Nevin believed that, periodically, there are representative nations that rise up in the midst of history in order to draw other nations into a higher order of existence and, ultimately, into an existence on the other side of history—the new creation. The turbulent political climate of the antebellum United States marked a time in which America was seeking a new synthesis that, in Nevin's mind, would give rise to her distinctive role in world history. He writes,

> These spiritual and moral forces, now deeply at work everywhere in our modern civilization, no less, I say, than the more outward powers before spoken of, are tending with accumulating strength toward the introduction of a new order of life for the world at large, a new era altogether in the world's social and political history; and in doing so, it is plain that they are throwing themselves more and more, with united volume, into the onward, moving destiny of our vast American Republic.[25]

Nevin's "worldview" did not drastically shift during or after the war. Much of the nation's optimism and idealism—especially among the evangelical population—had been rocked by immigration, industrialization, and war, resulting in a large scale abandonment of "benevolent empire" postmillennialism and the "city on the hill" identity. Nevin's dialectical interpretation of history's development, however, allowed him to accept the "accidents" of history without abandoning hope in God's plan for the nation and the world. The Civil War demonstrated the United States' previous "embryonic existence." Despite the new order of being ushered in by the "pains and throes of the late war," Nevin said, "in a most profound sense, it may be said that a nation has been born in a day."[26]

Wentz duly notes, "as a theatre for the world, the American nation gave voice not merely to its own internal strife but also to forces at work in determining 'the course and destiny of the world's life in a universal or whole view.'"[27] The depiction of America as a "theatre for the world" was Nevin's way of describing the young nation's instrumentality in universal history. The crucial characteristic of this instrumentality is the "new

25. Nevin, "Lancaster Commencement Address," in Appel, *Life and Work*, 641.
26. Ibid., 638.
27. Wentz, *American Theologian*, 110, citing Nevin, "Nation's Second Birth."

order of life" that prevails in America. This new order, he believed, was the dawn of a new historic era in which America was to be a beacon of freedom unto which all the world could aspire.[28] The American project ought not to be an opportunity for setting oneself apart in a nationalist, sectarian sense—a city upon a hill—but rather an effort to raise all of human existence into a higher order. "It has been plain for a long time past," he explains, "that the character and state of the world at large were likely to be powerfully affected in the end, by the progress of society in America."[29] As a theatre for the world, the young nation ought to serve as means for nations to reinterpret their aspirations in terms of the American story, a story which, ideally, expresses the freedom that humanity can find in Christ. America, in this sense, is viewed as the latest synthesis of world history. As such, she must seek to incorporate the life of the world into herself, raising the pitfalls and accidents of history into a more holy existence. The goal, in other words, is not to merely discount the failures of other nations; the goal is rather to recognize and integrate both the successes and failures of human history into the greater whole of God's providential plan.

Nevin's view coincided with the popular "manifest destiny" ideology at certain points, but there were significant differences. For one, popular notions of manifest destiny tended to be too nationalistic for Nevin. America should be careful not to naively and arrogantly boast in her own destiny without consideration for God's work beyond her borders. She should always remain open to her internal and external development, not closed and "set apart." Focusing too much on internal human history at the expense of external "catholic" history would constitute a grave error. As Nevin further comments, using the Mexican War as an example, "With the political morality of the Mexican war, we have here nothing to do whatever ... In this case ... we must distinguish between

---

28. "When we read in the present state of the world, the approach of a new historical period, whose character and course are to be determined prevailingly by the new order of life which reigns in America, we are not so foolish as to conceive of this under the form of a simple triumph of our national spirit, as it now stands, over the political institutions of the old world ... The revolutionary spirit of the age[(has its significance] in the yet undeveloped life toward which transitionally it points and leads. This lies in the direction which the course of history has already begun to take in America ... by means of the theatre here opened." Nevin, "The Year 1848," 28–30 in Wentz, *American Theologian*, 98.

29. Nevin, "The Year 1848," 20.

what is human in history, and what is properly universal and divine. The first may be worthy of all reprobation, where we are still bound to adore the presence of the second. It is with the second only, the interior objective life of history, its true and proper world sense, that we are concerned at all in our present contemplation."[30] As such, America's unique destiny ought to be one that takes seriously unity in diversity and the organic nature of God's outworking of history. Nevin could applaud the sense of mission found in America, as the antebellum era included countless efforts—some more laudable than others—to expand freedom to people in uncharted territory.

Accompanying the notions of manifest destiny and mission, however, was also an underlying sense of pride in America's newfound independence, which Wentz describes as "an adolescent perception of boundless power and energy."[31] This pride is precisely what fed the type of nationalism and sectarianism that Nevin determinedly fought during the latter years of the antebellum era. "It was but a 'sophomorical style of self-gratification' and tended to think of America 'as a settled and given fact' rather than as a theater for a new order of world history."[32] The dangerous tendency in America was to emulate the very characteristics of those who had long held her captive, namely Europeans. Nationalism was rampant among European states, and it bred a triumphalistic, and ultimately an imperialistic, worldview that failed to appreciate the "wholeness" character of world-historical development.[33] Such an ahistorical, insular view of one's existence in the world denotes a fundamental misunderstanding of the dialectical process of God's divine plan and would certainly serve as a sinful hindrance to its development. Nevin was convinced that "Our faith in God

---

30. Ibid., 23.

31. Wentz, *American Theologian*, 99.

32. Ibid., 98, citing Nevin, "The Year 1848."

33. "In various ways, the unsettled state of Europe, involving as it does the failure of so much that has been trusted as permanently secure, is rapidly turning the scale of comparative promise and hope against itself, and in favor of our youthful republic. The rate of exchange, to speak in commercial phrase, has been suddenly reversed, by the terrible shock now given to all moral and political institutions in the trans-Atlantic world; and both our credit and capital are made to rise, with the depreciation of so much spiritual property abroad." Nevin, "The Year 1848," 21.

rather, and in history, as God's work, requires us to be fully persuaded that (the world's life) has only begun."[34]

Puritans and Partisans

Drawing upon the work of William R. Taylor and Robert L. Kelley, James Bratt has noted that commentators of the era would "casually tie Yankee traits to their Puritan provenance."[35] Consequently, "Substitute the Constitution for the Lord's Supper, or Founding Fathers for the Reformers, and the conservative case against immediate abolition emerges."[36] Cited are instances in Nevin's *The Mystical Presence* where Nevin rebukes "the modern Puritan view" for having fallen away from the "old Reformed view, and for "eviscerating the institution of all objective force."[37]

Bratt's point is well taken, but the argument would in fact be more adequately supported with excerpts from Nevin's second article on "Early Christianity," in which Nevin imagines a New England Puritanism, "her associations and consociations, with their system of parity and rank democracy, passing over in so short a time to a well ordered hierarchy, revolving round a single centre."[38] His ensuing critique of Puritan ecclesiology is laden with political rhetoric. He writes, "The idea of the church (for the Puritans) is stripped of all mystery; it falls to the level of any other social or political institution; to believe in it is just as easy, as to believe in the Copernican system or the Parliament of Great Britain . . ."[39]

For Nevin, this brand of Puritanism has mistakenly viewed the church as a man-made institution where God's involvement is much like the oversight offered by the government. Puritanism, it seems, practices under the latent republican—and indeed enlightenment—axiom that "The voice of the people is the voice of God."[40] In contrast, Nevin promotes the Apostolic and Patristic notion of an episcopate church, a system of church government which "is the very reverse of all such in-

---

34. Ibid., 19. See also Wentz, *American Theologian*, 105, 107.

35. Bratt, "Antebellum Culture Wars," 11. See Kelley, *Cultural Pattern*, 222–23; Taylor, *Cavalier and Yankee*.

36. Ibid., 11.

37. Ibid., 10–11, citing Nevin, *Mystical Presence*, 117.

38. Nevin, "Early Christianity," in Yrigoyen, *Catholic and Reformed*, 222.

39. Ibid., 222.

40. Ibid., 232–33.

dependency and popularity as are made to be the basis of ecclesiastical order in New England."⁴¹

In 1840, Nevin was called upon to give a lecture at Mercersburg on the theme of "Party Spirit." The year was marked by what would come to be known as the "Log Cabin" campaign, a notoriously divisive campaign that embodied the very theme on which Nevin was to speak.⁴² In addition, as noted by Nevin's earliest biographer Theodore Appel, for Nevin, "Party Spirit" would have likewise characterized the denomination where he had spent the majority of his lifetime up to that point, the Presbyterian Church, where a nasty schism between "Old School" and "New School" had taken place in 1837–1838. "Party Spirit," Nevin said, "is not simply zeal for the views, opinions, or measures of a certain party or class of men, with whom we may feel it to be our duty to co-operate in the promotion of just and honorable ends ... Party Spirit is an abuse, a misdirection of the social principle ... It employs it but only for its own selfish purposes and ends ... The partisan cares most for himself; for his own emolument or the gratification of his own base passions."⁴³

The tendency of party spirit was neither unique to America nor to the nineteenth century. In fact, Nevin insisted that it had been present since the very inception of the Apostle Paul's ministry: "Parties in the Church Catholic [the Apostle Paul] regarded with abhorrence as the pest of religion, and as the bane of that heaven-born charity, in which essentially he supposed the power of the Gospel to consist ... 'In a word, the genius of the Gospel is irreconcilably at war with the Spirit of Party.'"⁴⁴

41. Ibid., 237.

42. This was a name given to the 1840 Presidential campaign of William Henry Harrison. During the campaign, Democrats incessantly mocked Harrison's age and referred to him as "Granny," hinting that he was senile. Said one Democratic newspaper: "Give him a barrel of hard cider, and ... a pension of two thousand [dollars] a year ... and ... he will sit the remainder of his days in his log cabin." Whigs cleverly responded by declaring that Harrison was indeed "the log cabin and hard cider candidate," a man of the common people. In addition, they depicted Harrison's opponent, President Martin Van Buren, as snobbish and out of touch. Ironically, Harrison had come from a wealthy, prominent family and Van Buren a poor, blue-collar family.

43. Nevin, *Party Spirit* in Appel, *Life and Work*, 118. The "Social Principle" to which Nevin refers will be discussed more thoroughly in chapter 3. With regard to its use here, Nevin comments, "There is a common mind belonging to each age and to every country, to every province and class of society, which surrounds men as an atmosphere and in the end forms the character of the individual and the community." Appel, *Life and Work*, 118.

44. Ibid., 124.

Its manifestation in America signified a cruel irony, however, according to Nevin, America's given role in providential history was to raise the world into a higher order and ultimately render selfishness, materialism, sect, and schism obsolete.

Party spirit is not merely a phenomenon that occurs at the political level. Rather, it is endemic in the social fabric of the nation, "having entered vitally into the constitution of human nature."[45] This was acutely revealed by the rampant individualism and sectarianism in American politics and religion. Nevin understood that external influences had played a role in the development of party spirit, particularly at the national level. This trend, however, was not his greatest concern; rather, it was that such influences would be woven into the fundamental worldviews of ordinary citizens, robbing them of their dignity as individuals and creating an "ungovernable frenzy" and ultimately a "dark and malignant fanaticism."[46] To fall prey to party spirit was to live in opposition to America's divinely ordained role as a self-sacrificing theatre for the world. "At what an expense of virtue, with what wreck of principle, are not our party struggles ordinarily conducted through the entire nation?" he pleaded.[47]

For all the political rhetoric, the religious dimension of "party spirit" was clearly Nevin's greatest concern, directing his most damnable language at the church's relationship to "the Spirit of Party." "Religion suffers in full measure to this present hour," he bemoaned,

> Need it be said that the Spirit of Party is directly opposed to the Spirit of the Gospel? The one destroys what the other would build up. It drinks up the life blood of the Church; cuts the sinews of faith and prayer; and blunts the edge of all spiritual motives. The still small voice of the Spirit cannot be heard where it reigns. Truth also finds no mercy under its hands. Shorn of her vital spirit, she is retained and honored at the best only as an embalmed corpse; a bandaged mummy, stiff and still; with a creed for its sarcophagus.[48]

Thus, while the sinful, fallen tendencies of the war-bound nation stood in contrast with his hopes of a righteous, providential role, Nevin's

---

45. Ibid., 118.
46. Ibid., 118.
47. Ibid., 120.
48. Ibid., 122.

greatest concern was certainly how these tendencies had infected the church. The church, after all, is the very locus of God's work to elevate the nation into the life of the divine. In the church, Nevin believed, the plague of party spirit had infected not merely the fundamental principles of the gospel, but along with it the church's exegesis, biblical interpretation, and indeed each Christian, who "sees the forms of his previous thoughts reflected back upon him as oracles from God."[49]

Nevin further addresses the matter of party spirit and sectarianism in its relationship to the church and the antebellum cultural landscape in his two articles on "The Sect System," appearing in the 1849 *Mercersburg Review*.[50] The work is strikingly similar to Nevin's earlier "Party Spirit," but demonstrates more clearly how his political rhetoric is ultimately wrapped up in ecclesiology. Like "Party Spirit," "The Sect System," speaks to both the political and religious spheres of American life. Nevin often used language to describe one that he would without hesitation apply to the other: "All sects, in proposition as they deserve the name, are narrow, bigoted and intolerant. They know not what liberty means. They put out men's eyes, gag their mouths, and manacle their hands and feet. They are intrinsically, constitutionally, incurably popish, enslaved by tradition and prone to persecution."[51] As such, the "Sect System" is primarily a treatise directed at church sectarianism that carries political overtones. These overtones reveal Nevin's tendency to employ political language in a pejorative manner as a means of exhorting the church to operate above the sinfulness of American politics. He writes, for example, that in the

---

49. Ibid., 122.

50. Bratt, "Antebellum Culture Wars," 10, notes a section in which he sees "direct political parallels" with the "sect spirit." In order to demonstrate the parallels, he inserts political language (indicated by brackets) into Nevin's critique of the sects. For Nevin, he suggests that both politics and sectarian religion "run into low cunning, disingenuous trickery and jesuitic policy. Religion [like politics] degenerates with it into a trade, in which men come to terms with God [the nation] on the subject of their own salvation [citizenship and office], and lay away their spiritual acquisitions as a sort of outward property for convenient use." Nevin might well have agreed with this rendering; it was not uncommon for him to criticize both the political institution and the sectarian "institution" in a similar manner. However, the approach here is somewhat eisegetical, having forced language and ideas into a text where they simply do not fit. This is particularly odd since there are several other sections of Nevin's "The Sect System" that would have been much more conducive to this sort of approach, sections which directly attack socio-political realities in their relation to the sect system.

51. Nevin, "The Sect System," in Yrigoyen, *Catholic and Reformed*, 144.

sect system, "It is felt to be as easy to start a new Church, as it is to get up a new moral or political association under any other name."[52]

A careful look at the "The Sect System" helps to reiterate the fact that for Nevin, political ideology and partisanship is not the source of the sectarian tendency; it is a reflection of this tendency, which is ultimately rooted in the church's misunderstanding of her role in the world. In other words, for Nevin, to address the political institution in itself is merely to address the symptoms, not the disease. Politics provides but a glimpse into a deeper reality behind "concrete" history; it is not the reality itself. He writes:

> There is a vast chasm also, in the political or outward toleration itself, as it may be called, to which the sect system affects in general to be so favorable. It is full of zeal, apparently for human freedom in every shape, the rights of man, liberty of conscience, and the privilege of every man to worship God in his own way ... Roger Williams is taken by his sect to be the father emphatically of our American Independence ... And it is of the first Baptists in particular, we are told, that these words of Hume in favor of the Puritans stand good: "By these alone the precious spark of liberty was kindled, and to these America owes the whole freedom of her constitution." ... The truth is, as any one may see who has any familiarity at all with the character and history of sects, that no more unpropitious atmosphere for liberty and independence can well be conceived, than that which they everywhere tend to create. Those precisely which make the greatest boast of their liberty, are as a general thing, the least prepared either to exercise it themselves or to allow its exercise in others. The sect habit, as such, is constitutionally unfree.[53]

"The Sect System," was ultimately an indictment against the American church, particularly in its latent Puritan manifestations, for having abandoned the "Catholicity" which, according to Nevin, had been retained by the early Protestant reformers. For Nevin, the political "parts" of American sectarianism were never as fundamental to society as ecclesiologic "wholeness." This is why sectarianism is such a perilous trend in the church. The problem is not merely that the church has bought into American political ideology, but that in doing so, it has betrayed her fundamental role as the objective, unified locus of God's cosmic recon-

52. Ibid., 146.
53. Ibid., 141–43.

ciliation.[54] His hope was that the church, recognizing its distinct role as a medium of salvation for the world, and in contrast to the fragmenting nature of American politics, would retain its catholicity; that is, its wholeness. It must insist on its identity as an objective, concrete reality, not subject to the turbulent currents of divisive politics.[55]

"The Greatest Question of the Age"

Nevin, in a brief commentary on his home state of Pennsylvania in 1853, afforded his audience a glimpse into his understanding of God's redemptive scheme as it related to the sociopolitical landscape of antebellum America.[56] Notable is the way in which the aged theologian peers through the social and political life of Pennsylvania in order to address its moral and spiritual health, the qualities of which he believed would lead the state and indeed the nation into its divinely appointed role. The address, moreover, is reflective of a mature Nevin who is adept at clearly outlining the relationship between the concrete realities of political life and the moral and spiritual role of mankind. Nevin recognized that Pennsylvania retained a wealth of resources, not merely in her industry but more importantly in her intellectual culture and patriotic zeal. He wanted to make sure, however, that such resources were not prized without regard for the "constitutional character of the mind itself, the quality of the moral soil . . ."[57] Nevin's emphasis upon the spiritual and moral health of the state and nation is based on his view that mankind, in his unique moral and spiritual nature, holds out for all of the creation the possibility of being united with God in Christ. The hope of the natural world, in all of its various political (and in this particular address, educational) manifestations, resides in moral and spiritual man, insofar as man is raised into the life of Christ.[58]

---

54. For Nevin, that the church has forfeited some of her identity to party spirit and sectarianism is acutely evident in her dilapidated view of sacraments.

55. Ibid., 146–47.

56. The occasion, June 7th, 1853, was the formal reopening of Franklin and Marshall College in its new location in Lancaster. Nevin referred to Pennsylvania as the "sleeping Giant," which, ". . . possesses a greatness and importance which must at once be acknowledged by the whole world. Politically, it forms the keystone of the arch, on which rests the structure of our glorious Republic." Appel, *Life and Work*, 445.

57. Ibid., 446.

58. This theme will be examined in further detail in chapter 3.

That Nevin's sociopolitical concerns are ultimately theological—and more specifically, ecclesiological—was perhaps most poignantly indicated in his 1867 commencement address to the students of Franklin and Marshall College. The address takes seriously the dialectical nature of historical development. The crises of the antebellum era were, in this sense, "wrought out organically from the inmost forces of the national life," yearning for their union with God in the incarnate Christ.[59] "The greatest questions of life, the last problems of history," he said,

> are fast crowding upon us for their solution. Here is to be settled, on a grand scale, how far men are capable of self-government in a truly free way; how far the interests of public authority and personal independence can be made to meet harmoniously in the same political system. Here is to be issued and adjudicated practically the old arch-controversy, between the rights of man, as they are called, and the duties of man. Here are to be met, and answered in some way, the tremendous politico-economical and social problems ... Here are to be shown, in the end, we must believe, the mightiest achievements of science, the greatest wonders of art, the most stupendous victories in the service of commerce and trade. Above all in interest for us, here must be settled the great ecclesiastical issues, with which the whole Christian world is wrestling at the present time, and which are felt by thousands everywhere to involve nothing less than the question of life or death for the universal cause of Christianity itself. Yes, my beloved hearers, there is no room now I think to doubt it. Here on this Western Continent is to be the arena where the Church Question, which all truly earnest men feel and know to be the greatest question of the age, is to be fought out, if I may use the expression, to its last consequences and results.[60]

Elemental to Nevin's Reformed orthodoxy is the "wholeness" of Christ and his church. Party spirit and sectarianism are not threatening merely in their societal effects, but more so because they violate the very *fundamentum* of reality, namely the body of Christ, which is not to be divided and subjected to the dictates of each individual. This deeply rooted and profoundly sinful problem was, in Nevin's judgment, encroaching upon the very constitution, not merely of the antebellum political scene, but of creation and mankind.

---

59. Nevin, "Lancaster Commencement Address," 643.
60. Ibid., 643–44.

3

Of Humanity and History

IN HIS ESSAY "UNDYING Life in Christ," Nevin explains that the relation of Christ to the world, "comes into still clearer view when we ascend from the sphere of mere physical existence into the sphere of *humanity and history*, where nature shows itself joined with the self-conscious mind, and the world stands sublimated to its highest sense in the free personality of man."[1] Humankind serves in Nevin's system as the immediate possibility of nature's redemption. Insofar as he demonstrates faith in Jesus Christ, moral, intelligent mankind raises natural history into harmony with the life of the divine.[2] But how does Nevin arrive at this unconventional metaphysic, one which has unavoidable implications for Christian soteriology? Here, we investigate in further detail Nevin's theology of history as well as his theological anthropology, focusing on humanity's role as the end and perfection of nature. To this end, a brief account of Nevin's philosophical context is in order.

PHILOSOPHICAL ALTERNATIVES

Pervasive Undercurrents of American Philosophy

Underlying the political realignment and social activism of the antebellum era were several important ideological shifts and accompanying philosophical influences. These shifts and influences drastically affected political orientations, worldviews, and theological inquiry. Mark Noll suggests that extensive participation by Protestants in the life of the nation during the antebellum period was part and parcel of such shifts. First, republicanism was hailed as the new vision of a free society. It was characterized most fundamentally by a new way of thinking about the

---

1. Nevin, "Undying Life," 612.
2. The use of the masculine pronoun is in keeping with Nevin's usage.

connectionalism of governments, which was now defined in mixed-constitution and democratic terms. Such structures encouraged Americans to rethink their role in society and the nature of social relationships. Second, albeit more subconsciously, an invasion of Scottish philosophy had introduced a brand of common sense moral reasoning that challenged traditional notions of conscious human perception. Third, social activism and the notions of a "benevolent empire" were informed by a new confidence in moral causes and their relationship to broader social agendas.[3] This reasoning was largely due to Enlightenment rationalism which boasted of being able to explain cause-effect relationships in the real world. Fourth, Noll explains, "in offering their religious wares to the cultural markets of the new American polity, Protestants—especially the evangelicals—not only exploited but also internalized at least some aspects of the new nation's republicanism, commonsense moral reasoning, and Newtonian-providentialist social theory."[4]

As such, the antebellum era was truly an era of radical democratization. Fundamental to the republicanism, moral reasoning, activism, and free-market religion that precipitated American Protestantism was a burgeoning ideology rooted in the power of the people and a newfound emphasis upon the individual. The "turn to the self" philosophical revolution of Kant and company had reached American shores in a variety of forms, but the simple fact was that the individual now perceived that he or she could ascend to a position of significance which, until that point, had been known only to society's elite.

Conventional notions of human identity and social existence were thus under attack on several fronts. The idea that the individual is defined by his or her allegiance to an authority or by compliance with a universal law (particularly one of transcendent origin) was quickly becoming obsolete. However, while the ideologies of democracy, republicanism, and social contract were clearly perceived across the antebellum landscape, they were built upon philosophical foundations that were far more subtle. The basic tenets of these philosophical trends deserve attention if one is to engage Nevin's more pointed cultural critiques.

The prevailing worldviews of the antebellum period tended heavily in the direction of the finite and the particular. This philosophical position, nominalism, descended from a tradition that arrived in its

3. On the "Benevolent Empire," see Timothy L. Smith, *Revivalism and Social Reform*.
4. Noll, *America's God*, 209–10.

American form under the influence of John Locke and the Scottish Realists. It represents a view of reality where the individual entity takes precedence, and all relations are therefore regarded as the result of individual consent in the form of a "social contract" (which Nevin called a "monstrous fallacy").[5] Furthermore, nominalism heavily emphasizes empirical inquiry, even in the quest for religious or spiritual truth, an emphasis which fell into line with the prevailing confidence in Baconianism, which had come to dominate the scientific method.[6]

The Baconian method of inquiry insists that all certainty begins with concreteness and actuality, not the ideal or "universal." The implications for religion are therefore far reaching since both "revelation" and "faith" are to be judged in the first instance as objects of empirical inquiry, not deduced from what is believed to be true *a priori* about God. Following this trajectory, the Baconian approach requires miraculous "evidences" for God and faith.[7] As DiPuccio comments, "Consequently, the spiritual and ideal are all but eliminated from the internal nexus of history and daily life, or relegated to the sphere of private conscience as was the case in subjective pietism."[8]

Baconianism was accompanied and bolstered by Common Sense Realism, a philosophical movement chiefly led by Thomas Reid and Dugald Steward, and promulgated in America by the likes of John Witherspoon.[9] The principles of Common Sense spoke volumes to the new democratic ideology. By insisting on the individual's natural ability to perceive the world as it really is, Common Sense Realism is indeed a protest against totalitarianism and elitism. It is no wonder, perhaps,

---

5. Nevin, "Philosophy of History," as noted by DiPuccio, *Interior Sense*, 170.

6. Ibid., 119–20.

7. "Evidentialism," so it was deemed, was further promoted by eighteenth-century British theology in a (seemingly ironic) attempt to defend orthodoxy against deism and pietism. As such, divine revelation was approached as any other scientific fact, requiring empirical verification. Ibid., 125.

8. "This seems to be the (sic) Hodge's position who, with the Westminster Confession (V.III.), speaks of miracles as being 'without, above, or against' secondary causes." Ibid., 121. See Hodge, *Systematic Theology*, 1:617–29.

9. Reid wrote, "If there are certain principles, as I think there are, which the constitution of our nature leads us to believe, and which we are under a necessity to take for granted in the common concerns of life, without being able to give a reason for them—these are what we call 'the principle of common sense': and what is manifestly contrary to them, is what we call absurd." In Livingston and Schüssler Fiorenza, *Modern Christian Thought*, 303.

that "common sense" became the popular mantra that it did in this early American context. By 1870, Common Sense philosophy could boast of a century of dominance in America, both in the academy and popular culture. During the last half-century of the antebellum period, this philosophical approach was not only lurking beneath the presuppositions of Americans but was being actively taught in most American colleges.[10] Despite various competing philosophies that arrived with antebellum immigration and industrialization, not least German Idealism, "Common Sense Realism remained unquestionably *the* American philosophy."[11]

In addition to providing a firm foundation for Baconian science, Common Sense Realism laid the groundwork for a new moral order. A universal but *natural* law principle came to the forefront of American consciousness in an unprecedented way. Common Sense philosopher Francis Wayland reflected on this approach to morality, writing, "He has made light without, and the eye within; moral qualities in actions, and conscience to judge of them; and so in every other case ... An order of sequence once discovered in morals is just as invariable as an order of sequence in physics."[12] This is not to say that the Bible did not retain its moral authority; indeed it did. The individual's common sense access to moral principles, however, was a novel concept that was challenging how the Bible functioned as a standard of universal morality.[13] In particular, the traditional Calvinist view of man as totally depraved, morally as well as noetically, was blatantly challenged by the substantially higher view of mankind espoused by Common Sense philosophy. Free moral agency,

10. It remains a matter of debate as to what degree Old Princeton succumbed to Baconian and Common Sense methods inquiry. McConnel, "Old Princeton Apologetics," 650, suggests that "The acceptance, in some sense, of Scottish Common Sense Realism by the Old Princetonians would have been in general agreement with the American culture of the day, although Princeton lingered in its adherence late in the nineteenth century when American intellectual currents were moving in different directions." Notably, Common Sense Realism was in fact much more pervasive in Unitarianism and the New Haven Theology, as well as in the "new measures" of Charles Finney.

11. Marsden, *Fundamentalism*, 14. The Presbyterian Samuel Tyler is perhaps most notable as one who sought to infuse the new Baconian, evidentialist approach into Reformed orthodoxy. In addition, Princeton's esteemed Archibald Alexander followed suit when he argued, "Unless the Christian religion is attended with sufficient evidence, we cannot believe in it, even if we would." Alexander, *Evidences of the Authenticity*, 89. Also cited by DiPuccio, *Interior Sense*, 125.

12. Ibid., 15.

13. I am indebted to Marsden, *Fundamentalism*, for this summary and the quotations from Wayland.

for instance, was a new concept that garnered much adherence during this time. In Marsden's words, "These premises—which were essential to the economic, political, and religious individualism so widespread in America—were at odds with traditional views of determinism and depravity."[14]

Nevin's Organic Idealism

Nevin adhered to an idealist ontology which insists that reality fundamentally begins with the ideal and the universal, not the finite and actual. He was influenced in this respect by the German philosophy of Hegel and more directly by Johann Fichte, F. W. J. Schelling, and Frederick Rauch. Hegel had argued in his *Science of Logic* (1812–1814) that the basis of reality cannot begin with the finite since the finite is determined by, and is thus dependent upon, other finite qualities. Alternatively, "spiritual" things, such as God and morality, require no further qualification and are not dependent upon finite qualities of concrete existence.[15] Nevin would not have boasted of Hegelianism, but the broader conceptual structures of the German philosopher's work are certainly foundational for his insistence that the universal and the ideal serve as the *fundamentum* of reality. For Nevin, then, the universal always preceded the particular, a principle which was clearly expressed throughout the full scope of his theology. As Holifield explains, "It was this philosophical vision that enabled Nevin to view the Incarnation as an event that occurred in one divine-human person, recast the principle of human nature in which all people shared, and began to actualize the new ideal possibilities by drawing individuals into the working of its law."[16]

The mediating German philosophy that Nevin came to appreciate was perhaps most forcefully impressed upon him by his friend and colleague, Frederick A. Rauch (1806–1841). Unfortunately, their relationship was ended prematurely, as Rauch passed away less than a year after Nevin arrived in Mercersburg (1840). Nevertheless, Nevin took it upon himself to complete the revision of Rauch's *Psychology; or, a View of the Human Soul*. The project proved to have an enormous impact on Nevin's own thought by providing the necessary structures for him to work out

---

14. Marsden, *Fundamentalism*, 16.
15. For a more detailed explanation, see Robert Wallace, *Hegel's Philosophy*.
16. Holifield, *Theology in America*, 477.

his idealistic philosophy, particularly in the relationship between thought and language.[17] An astonishing effort, Rauch had attempted to unite German idealism with the British Empiricism and Scottish Common Sense Realism that pervaded the American academy and popular culture. Nevin was, therefore, a well-suited candidate for its appropriation and then dissemination into American theology and "common sense" religion. He was particularly indebted to Rauch for his language of "organic unity" between the ideal and actual. Nevin was, as a result, able to construct a viable ontology that took seriously the real—as opposed to the sheer phenomenal—in its organic relation with the experiential, perceived, and empirical.[18]

HISTORY AT MERCERSBURG

In Nevin's theological system, the threefold, hierarchical relationship of sociopolitical existence (the lower organic sphere), mankind, and the Incarnation of Christ constitutes a movement whereby the divine "whole" gathers all "parts" of existence unto itself. History is at once the structure upon and the means by which this threefold movement of God's redemption takes place. But what is history?

History Through the Lens of the Incarnation

The Mercersburg notion of organic development allows that the church will experience a process of division and reunification along with the rest of world history. The crucial distinction, however, is that the church in this scheme serves as the primary locus of true history and true humanity. Such a notion, to the degree that it still remained in the American evangelical consciousness, was largely eschewed as unacceptable. As Larson notes, "the immediate problem with American primitivism was its failure to see itself belonging to this catholic body, while the problem with Romanism was their failure to see the higher stage of development within Reformation theology."[19] The Mercersburg critique of antebellum society was therefore necessarily and thoroughly historical, as both Nevin and Schaff believed the endemic sectarian impulse of American

---

17. See Nevin, *The German Language*, 5. On Nevin's appropriation of Rauch's idealism, see DiPuccio, "Nevin's Idealistic Philosophy," 43–67.

18. See Nevin, Review of *Rauch's Psychology*.

19. Larson, "Philip Schaff's Idea," 6.

Protestantism was largely due to the disregard for history exhibited across the evangelical landscape.[20]

With Nevin, Schaff drew upon the mediating school of theologians within a stream of modified Hegelianism.[21] While Hegel had provided the necessary foundation for a dialectical and progressive view of history, the mediating school supplied for Schaff the romantic themes of organic unity and development.[22] As Lotz suggests, "Schaff's application of historical organicism (or "historicism") to church history is evident at every turn. His basic premise is that the church itself is a living entity, an organism—the body of Christ, whose individual members are united in an organic whole by virtue of their union with Christ, the body's guiding head and animating soul."[23] Thus, Schaff departed from Hegel's inherent pantheism by giving priority to the history of the visible church and the union of Christ with his people.

In 1846, Schaff published a work entitled *What is Church History?*, in which he attempted to outline for his readers the different schools of

20. Nevin's *The Anxious Bench* addressed in particular the nineteenth-century manifestation of revivalist Puritanism, focusing on its "low" ecclesiology and individualism. The work is primarily designed to be a refutation of Charles Finney's "new measures," which had been recently promoted by a visiting preacher in a local German Reformed congregation in Mercersburg. The tract, however, addressed a broader concern of Nevin, who had become increasingly disillusioned with the populist impulse within American popular religion and the German Reformed Church in particular. This sentiment would be woven throughout much of his future work as well, notably in the first issue of the *Mercersburg Review*, published in 1849, in which Nevin wrote his two-part article, "The Sect System." The article was directed towards John Winebrenner's *History of All Religious Denominations in the United States* (1848), a compilation of articles written by authors from fifty-three denominations. Winebrenner, who had already been the object of Nevin's criticism five years earlier in *The Anxious Bench*, represented for Nevin the epitome of the free-market, entrepreneurial Christian, and a major source of the "sect plague." Hatch, *Democratization of American Christianity*, 164.

21. Dorner and Neander are notable among those in this school, which fused Schliermacher's religion of consciousness with Hegel's metaphysical idealism. As Dorrien has noted, some mediating theologians wedded Schleiermacher to the transcendental idealism of F.W.J. Schelling. Dorrien, *American Liberal Theology*, 44. See also Holifield, *Theology in America*, 470.

22. Schaff was deeply indebted to Schelling, who had emerged as a philosophically conservative alternative to Hegel. Following Schelling, Schaff rejected Hegel's conclusion that the idea remained paramount, insisting rather on an inseparable relationship between the idea and history. For more on the philosophical foundations of Schaff's view of history, see DeBie, *Speculative Theology*, 51–56.

23. Lotz, "Philip Schaff and Church," 13. Cited by Larson, "Philip Schaff's Idea." I am indebted to Larson for his synthesis of various aspects of Schaff's thought.

thought and approaches to church history.[24] This effort demonstrated the Hegelian tendencies of Schaff, who believed that the church's eschatological "idea," although completely fulfilled in Christ in one sense, must be made manifest in temporal existence. "Church and History altogether, since the introduction of Christianity, are so closely united, that respect and love towards the first, may be said to be essentially the same with a proper sense of what is comprised in the other," Schaff wrote.[25] As such, history was not to be viewed as history *qua* history, but that which is seen through the lens of the church, and God's providence therein. All history finds its central movement in the development of the principle of Christ's life, a divine principle which has been introduced into human nature and is destined to reconcile all things. In this view it becomes church history.[26]

Nevin's development of a theology of history is likewise indicative of a Hegelian indebtedness. However, in Nevin's judgment, what Hegel and many of his heirs lacked was a real sense of human sin and the necessity for a free human response to the divine. Simply put, it needed a more satisfactory theological orientation. In this respect, his departure from Hegel is perhaps most clearly evidenced by his encounter with the work of August Neander.[27] Nevin labored to learn German so that he could read the renowned historian's most renowned work, *General History of the Christian Religion and Church*, in its original language. Upon reading it, Nevin regarded it as the most significant impulse for him to abandon the Puritan subjectivist approach to theology that he had learned at Princeton. He would later write,

> Before my acquaintance with Neander, it seems to me, now looking back upon my life, this sense of the historical was something which I could hardly be said to have even begun to possess at all. Since then it has come to condition all my views of life. I do not mean to say that it became all at once of such force for me through Neander's teachings. It was an idea or sentiment which grew, and took upon it full form, only in the course of following years; but to him I owe it first of all that any such idea began to dawn upon my mind. He first gave me the feeling in some mea-

---

24. Ahlstrom, *Religious History*, 618.
25. Schaff, *What is Church History?* 25. See Larson, "Philip Schaff's Idea."
26. Ibid., 40.
27. Wentz, *American Theologian*, 95.

sure, of what history means for the life of man everywhere, and most of all in the ruling central sphere of religion.[28]

For both Nevin and Schaff, the most important contribution of Neander was found in his Christological emphasis and his realization that theology was concerned with how to live as a Christian, not just intellectual pursuit. Schaff commented on Neander's work, praising it as a "noble monument of sanctified learning" that was "without question the most important product of the modern German theology in the sphere of church history and must long maintain a high authority."[29]

Neander's assertion of history's authority and Christ's central role in history can be gleaned throughout Nevin's writings. In his review of Isaac Dorner's *History of Protestant Theology*, Nevin wrote brashly, "They are bad Protestants, everywhere and always, who insist on making Protestantism unhistorical. The life of the world universally is historical, a moving stream of united, continuous existence. It is so especially in Christianity, which is the central current of this stream."[30] Nevin invariably maintained that an historical view of Protestantism is necessary if it is to be regarded as a true, viable expression of the Christian faith. It will not suffice to say that Protestantism's birth is a sixteenth century phenomenon; rather, the history of the Protestant church must be located

---

28. Nevin, "My Own Life," in Binkley, *Mercersburg Theology*, 27.

29. Schaff, *What is Church History?*, 79. See also Binkley, *Mercersburg Theology*, 26.

30. Nevin, "Dorner's History," 262. While expressing overall dissatisfaction in Dorner's work, Nevin praises Dorner for his demonstration of how the material principle of Protestantism conditioned and determined its formal principle. He agrees that justification by faith and the authority of Christian scripture bears the weight of the Reformation, and, furthermore, that these principles must ultimately rest on Jesus Christ himself. Otherwise, Protestantism becomes an abstraction, finding no ground in the early history of the church. It is thus crucial, for example, to root Luther's doctrine of justification in Christology if it is to be seen as in continuity with the universal history of Christianity. Nevertheless, Nevin criticizes Dorner for not doing justice to this very principle by confining reformation Christology to the atonement. In closing, he offers a correction by insisting, "The whole Gospel starts in Christ, the mystery of the Incarnation, the coming together of God and man in his person. This is the beginning and foundation of all that follows; and in taking in this, the faith that gives us an interest in the atonement (the material principle of Protestantism) brings into us in truth the power of his universal life, as related to the purposes of our salvation. All this we have in the Creed. There Christianity begins in Christ, and rolls itself forward in the grand and glorious life-stream of the Church." Ibid., 288–89.

within the general flow of Christian history from its inception with the Apostles and church fathers.[31]

For all his efforts to demonstrate the relationship between the Reformation and the apostolic church, Nevin is nevertheless careful not to jettison the history Roman Catholicism, explaining, "It is by no means certain that Protestantism, in breaking forth from the womb of the Catholic Church, carried away with it *all* the significance of that Church for the final purposes of Christianity."[32] Here, Nevin agreed with Schaff who saw the Reformation as not in actuality (or by necessity) a hard and fast break with medieval Catholicism. He rejected the prevalent American and European interpretation that Protestantism was somehow connected with "some fractionary sect of the Middle Ages," finding its place among the age of the apostles with the aid of "certain desperate historical leaps."[33]

"What is *historical* development?" was the question raised by Nevin in Volume I of the *Mercersburg Review*. An article entitled "Sectarianism," appearing in the April 1849 issue of *True Catholic*,[34] had accused sectarians of equating what is meant by "historical" with notions of "development." Sectarianism, it was alleged, wrongly assumed that "development" could occur apart from the infallible authority of the historic church. Nevin had rendered a similar indictment, namely that the fundamental error of the sect system is "the independence which it affects, in pretending to reduce all Christianity to private judgment and the Bible, (involving) a protest against the authority of all previous history . . ."[35] He therefore agreed that "development" in the sectarian sense is at best an inferior form of historical existence, failing as it does to enter into the true stream of the world's life, the historic, objective church.

He would not go so far as to say, however, that the general notion of development requires an "infallible living authority," as this would tend to downplay the reality of change throughout church history. For Nevin, if historical "development" is more generally understood as change, then it should not be rejected outright. "We gladly embrace the idea of organic development," he writes, "by which, through all changes, we are allowed

---

31. Ibid., 262.
32. Ibid., 263.
33. Schaff, *Principle of Protestantism*, 31.
34. Episcopal Magazine published in Baltimore.
35. Nevin, "The Sect System," in Yrigoyen, *Catholic and Reformed*, 145.

to believe the Church, *one*, holy catholic and apostolical, from the beginning onward to the last day."[36] The church, in all its organic development, is historical, not because it stays the same, "but because it is the power of a divine fact, which is forever growing itself more and more into the consciousness, the interior life of the world, and which can never be complete till the whole thinking and working of humanity shall appear transfused with its glorious reconstructive power."[37] This fine distinction between history and development was crucial for Nevin, who wanted to show that Protestantism could evolve and change without being inherently sectarian. More specifically, he needed to align Protestantism with the history of the church while justifying its break with Rome. In his judgment, only by appropriation of this historical idealism and organicism could one sufficiently differentiate between history and development, and thus escape the difficulty of affirming the continuity of Protestantism with the early church.[38]

The optimism with which Nevin viewed history and the transforming power of the church marks one of the few instances where he is in broad agreement with nineteenth-century American evangelicalism. This optimism is further confirmed by Orestes Brownson's criticism of Nevin, who, Brownson believed, had an excessively optimistic view of history that did not sufficiently account for sin.[39] Unlike the majority of his evangelical contemporaries, however, Nevin's optimistic view of historical development was rooted in the church's historical continuity and in history's ability to point to Christ, not in the voluntarism of the "benevolent empire."

"To believe in God truly," Nevin writes, "one must see him in nature and history; and this implies an earnest apprehension of both, as full of infinite wisdom and love." This necessity is not to be understood merely in terms of proper theological method; it is rather, a matter of sin and divine judgment. For Nevin, such judgment is incurred when one looks

---

36. Nevin, "Historical Development," 513.
37. Ibid., 513.
38. Holifield, *Theology in America*, 480.
39. Brownson accused "developmentalists" such as Nevin of violating the Christian doctrines of creation and redemption by confusing the natural and supernatural orders of existence. He equated developmentalism "with emanationism, pantheism, and Eutychianism because he believed that developmentalists viewed history as God's realization of his own potentialities in space and time. For Brownson God was pure act; there was no potentiality in God." Carey, *Orestes A. Brownson*, 214.

upon history as nothing more than chaos, without form and void. He insists, rather, upon the idea of a "universal plan and process in the course of the world's life," and that God's truth is manifest in the general life of humanity and the historical development therein.[40]

History of the Individual and of Common Nationality

According to Nevin, the movements of the history of mankind are to be understood as quite different from that of nature since nature, he believed, was more cyclical. "The animal never rises above its own order, but in the case of the moral and historical world the progress is always from a lower to a higher stadium."[41] The history of mankind, therefore, is not just a history of the *natural* order; it is a history which takes into account man's role in redemptive salvation history. For Nevin, to espouse a history of mankind that does not take seriously God's movement within mankind by the Holy Spirit is to offer both an insufficient account of history and an inadequate anthropology.

Both the individual and the broader, generic structures of humanity have their place in historical study; history, in other words, must take into account both the one and the many. It is this dynamic relationship of the individual and the race as a whole which constitutes a vital aspect of history's development. In Nevin's view, they must be studied together if either is to be properly understood and if history is to be rightly written.

Nations, not least indicated by Nevin's treatment of America as a "theatre for the world," are for Nevin a requisite object of historical study. The identity of the nation is demonstrated by a body of people bound by common interest and goals—a body of people through which national history "raises and extends itself." Its "wholeness" resides in its union to ideal, objective history. The nation thus interprets its existence in terms of universal history, not in terms of its particular parts. Common na-

---

40. Nevin, "The Year 1848," 44.

41. Nevin, "Lectures on History," in Appel, *Life and Work*, 591. From 1861 to 1866, Nevin served as a lecturer of history at Franklin and Marshall College. Notes from these lectures have been preserved, offering great insight into Nevin's understanding of history's development and meaning. His hierarchical model of the state, humanity, and Christ can be clearly perceived throughout.

tionality, like the whole of humanity, should not be regarded as the sum or collective of individual persons, resulting in a type of "allness."[42]

Nevin addresses the progress of man's historical development in relation to this "common nationality" by drawing upon his broader anthropology, insisting that the development of man is moral, physical, and spiritual. This development is far more vital for a nation's history than all "external" or natural "improvements" that it might receive. To the degree that it participates in its divinely ordained role, the history of mankind is the locus of history's inward, organic development, prompting the union of individual-national history with world-universal history.

Nevertheless, the method employed by Nevin not only takes into account individual and national history, but it also seeks to unite these histories with universal or "world" history. World (or universal) history, however, is likewise not the sum of the individual and the nation; it is, in its objectivity, greater than the sum of these "parts."[43] There is, in Nevin's view, an objective principle in universal history, which gathers all nations and individuals unto itself. The sense of universal history, as a whole, is comprised of distinct nations which have a purpose in history or a share in bringing about the grand result.[44] "The development must, therefore, be subject to some law, which binds all the parts together into a single whole, always tending towards some definite end or result."[45]

As opposed to traditional Hegelian models where human consciousness and the state constitute the ultimate synthesis, for Nevin, it is the Incarnation, the antithesis of abstraction and mere pronouncement, which resolves all tensions and "apparent contradictions" throughout the seemingly dualistic universe. Although it is *rationally* perceived that God could not at once be utterly transcendent and yet profoundly immanent, in Jesus Christ, God acted in precisely this manner. As a result the "grand sense of the world" has been revealed, and the incarnate Christ was shown to be "the key that unlocks the mystery of human existence." Nevin recognizes that the popular tendency is to search for this "key" in the political and scientific life of man. This search, however, had proven fruitless, indicating that the chief end of man lies beyond these spheres

---

42. See Nevin's distinction between "all" and "whole" in Nevin, "Catholic Unity," 40–41.

43. Nevin, "Lectures on History," in Appel, *Life and Work*, 592.

44. Ibid., 596.

45. Ibid., 592.

of life. The Incarnation of Jesus Christ is not only beyond these spheres, but gives them an entirely new meaning in the course of history, casting light on all corners of human existence.[46]

"So all history becomes true at last only in Christ:"[47]
The Incarnation as the Culmination of History

In his essay entitled "Natural and Supernatural," Nevin explains, "All History again must come to its proper unity in Christ, if he be indeed what he is made to be in the Gospel. Here, as in the constitution of Nature, God must have a plan in harmony with itself throughout; and this plan can not possibly go aside from his main thought and purpose in the government of the world. It must centre in the Incarnation."[48] The "cardinal principle" of the Mercersburg theology was the Incarnation of Jesus Christ.[49] It was the epistemological lens through which Nevin studied theology, constituting, as it were, a transcendental hermeneutic, one which insisted on a top-down view of the world (as opposed to the Common Sense Realism and Positivism which started with the finite and particular). For Nevin, the Incarnation was the starting point for all reflection because it was precisely the fount from which all of creation found its meaning. As DiPuccio astutely explains, "It is the archetype of the cosmos . . . Out of it emerges the controlling law or principle of reality itself."[50] Otherwise, "God can be for men only an abstraction, an unreality, a mental figment, and so of course an idolatry."[51]

In the Incarnation of Jesus Christ, divinity and humanity are joined so as to constitute a "mediatorial" person, through which Christ becomes joined with our human existence and incorporated into the life and being of the world. The world is a "*mere system of nature . . . which is thus brought to find in Him its own last end and only perfect sense*"[52] Nevin describes the process as follows: "He became man; the work of the new creation taking up into itself in this way the work of the old creation, so

---

46. Ibid., 596.
47. Nevin, *Mystical Presence*, 195.
48. Nevin, "Natural and Supernatural," 192.
49. "Letter to Harbaugh," in Yrigoyen, *Catholic and Reformed*, 408.
50. DiPuccio, *Interior Sense*, 25.
51. Nevin, "Bread of Life," 21.
52. Nevin, "Undying Life," 607.

as to be only the fulfillment, in a higher sphere, of its original purpose and sense."[53]

The Incarnation, then, is not merely an event *in* history—although it did reign as the most important event in history—but was also the event that seeks to incorporate all of history into a higher order of existence. Accordingly, history is not only the structure upon which various prophecies or annunciations take place, but is itself "one vast prophecy of the Incarnation, for the beginning to the end."[54] From Nevin's perspective, "The ethical world, the movement of humanity, the world of history as it may be called, begins and ends in Him; it is not chaotic, the sport of blind chance or iron fate; Christ is in it, causing all its powers and forces to converge throughout to what shall be found to be at last the world's last sense in the finished work of redemption."[55] As the historical concretion of the Incarnation, the Christian religion provides a *telos* for world history. It is in fact the universal, albeit "unseen," reality that gives meaning to all historical, concrete existence and is in this sense more "real" than the temporal actualities of particular history. It is the "deepest sense of the world's life."[56]

NEVIN'S "IDEAL" HUMANITY

Nevin's organic, idealist ontology likewise played a vital role in his anthropology, both in terms of mankind's essential identity and his role in world history. In his 1848 essay "Human Freedom," Nevin proposes a philosophical basis for his view of human ontology and freedom. He insists upon the "universal force" which lies behind all particular existence and an ideal character whose existence precedes that of individual objects. In what might be described as almost formulaic prose for Nevin, he goes on to reaffirm his position that all of life is at once ideal and actual and that "the ideal can have no reality, except in the form of the actual; and the actual can have no truth, save as it is filled with the presence of the ideal."[57]

---

53. Ibid., 611.
54. Nevin, *Mystical Presence*, 189. See also Ibid., 187.
55. Nevin, "Vindication," 368.
56. DiPuccio, *Interior Sense*, 27.
57. Nevin, "Human Freedom," 3.

This same philosophical assertion concerning the ideal and actual holds true in the case of mankind. The individual, after all, recognizes himself as such, but also as one among many—as one who belongs to the race as a whole. "He is a man; the universal conception of humanity enters into him, as it enters also into all other men; while he is, besides, this or that man, as distinguished from all others by his particular position in the human world."[58] As in his broader ontology, for Nevin, the "ideal" humanity, while taking priority in what it means to be human, has no reality unless it is actualized in the sphere of the natural; to be a "true" human being, however, is to have one's constitution first in the ideal.

By virtue of his German idealism and his prioritizing of the whole and the essential (as opposed to the "rights" and "freedoms" of the individual), Nevin was set on a philosophical trajectory that inherently rejected several basic tenets of Enlightenment political theory. Principles such as nominalism, which viewed terms and concepts as existing in name only and apart from objective reference, and voluntarism, the doctrine that the will is fundamental to one's existence, were, for Nevin, simply unacceptable. He thus stood in contrast to the broad majority of American intellectuals (including theologians) who took for granted several assumptions: the value of republicanism, particularly in its ability to account for the balance of private character and public well-being (the cause-effect relationship between morality and the welfare of society), the fixed nature of virtue and liberty versus vice and tyranny, and the predictability of sociopolitical development governed by reason.[59] His condemnation of these principles is not merely implicit. He denounces those, for instance, who, by virtue of their sectarianism, celebrate Hume's maxim, "By these alone the precious spark of liberty was kindled, and to these America owes the whole freedom of her constitution."[60]

Ultimately, in Nevin's view, the Enlightenment project was doing little more than promoting a radical individualism that was irreparably damaging to the church and society. Institutions based merely on the voluntarism and consent of individuals who were asserting their "natural rights" had, from Nevin's perspective, placed themselves in a perilous position before a God who insisted that the catholic whole be greater

---

58. Ibid.
59. See Noll, *Civil War*, 17–19.
60. Nevin, "The Sect System," in Yrigoyen, *Catholic and Reformed*, 141–43.

than the sum of its voluntary parts and that human identity is found in Christ and his church, not in "*cogito ergo sum.*"

Finally, before proceeding, a note on dualism, of which Nevin was (and is) often accused.[61] It is an issue which is relevant to Nevin's theological system as a whole, but which deserves attention particularly in light of his understanding of mankind's "natural" and "supernatural" identity. "Nevin's language," one scholar has argued, "consistently elevated inward over outward, grace over nature, and by extension Church over world. The German idealism that gave him history cost him in ontology."[62] Such an interpretation overstates matters a bit. While Nevin was more than willing to employ such tensions in his theology, it is equally important to note his departure from the rationalist formulations of most American Reformed, above all in his emphasis on the church as the unifying organism of all such dichotomies.[63] In this way, as Layman has shown, he was able to overcome the objective (Christ) versus subjective (culture/natural man) dualism inherent in the Princeton system.[64] Nevin, in the *Antichrist*, discusses what he believes to be a "most significant and far reaching feature of the antichristian spirit, namely the hopeless, helpless dualism, that characterizes its whole theory of the Christian life." This is contrasted with what Nevin considers to be the correct view, namely that "God and nature, this last completed in man, come to a true union only in Christ ... Apart from this fact, we can have only pantheism or dualism, or an unsteady oscillation rather between both."[65] As such, Nevin's

61. This fact is somewhat ironic as Nevin was also heavily criticized by Hodge for promoting monism. See DeBie, *Speculative Theology*, 82.

62. Bratt, "Antebellum Culture Wars," 13.

63. David Wayne Layman has echoed DiPuccio by demonstrating how Nevin overcame the dualistic tendency of his earlier writings as his ecclesiology matured. Nevin came to view the church as the "central locus of God's activity, (the content of which) discerned in the unfolding process of time and history." Traces of this approach, however, can be found in early writings. In *A Summary of Biblical Antiquities*, written in the late 1820s, Nevin averred, "... although the Church has been substantially the same in all ages, its measures of spiritual advantage, and its outward constitution, have been greatly altered with the progress of time." Layman, "Holistic Supernaturalism," 198. Quote from Nevin, *Summary of Biblical Antiquities*, 240.

64. Layman, "Holistic Supernaturalism," 198. Layman furthermore suggests that Nevin was able to do this by rejecting a theology built solely on supernatural *message*, i.e., that which is limited to the scriptures or the teachings of Jesus, a theology which in the mind of Nevin was limited to natural reason. Nevin believed this flawed hermeneutic to be the fundamental error of the Princeton theology.

65. Nevin, *AntiChrist*, 48.

view of Christ's organic relation to the life of mankind and the world in many ways presents a profound ontology, not one that was forfeited for the sake of idealistic dualism.

Freedom

For Nevin, mankind's distinction from the rest of the natural order is marked by his morality, intelligence, and free agency; these are qualities that grant the possibility of freedom, personality, and sociality. As such, they are qualities which both demonstrate mankind's sanctified status from—yet still pending their organic relationship to—the natural world, allowing him to be the *imago Dei* that he was created to be. While intelligence, morality, and human agency find their concrete existence in the natural world, they find their genesis in the organic relationship between the natural and supernatural. According to Nevin, the universal ideals take logical precedence, but man actually derives these qualities from a repository where the ideal has embedded itself in the actual. This scheme is crucial for Nevin, who wishes to emphasize humanity's universal essence without debasing the value of natural existence. In the case of freedom, for instance, "Man comes not to moral freedom at once, but is required to rise to it by regular development, out of the life of nature in which his existence starts, and in which it continues always to have its root."[66]

"Men are born for truth, as they are born also for freedom," Nevin once wrote. "The first is the inalienable right of their understanding, the second is the inalienable right of their will."[67] Such words surely resonated with the "inalienable rights" theme of the American Revolution, but Nevin would raise the stakes by insisting that it is not just any freedom that mankind should seek, but rather the freedom that is solely found in the life of Christ. All other notions of freedom ultimately fall short since mankind, in his natural state, will sinfully seek after his own freedom rather than the freedom that God offers in Christ. Simply put, the process of acquiring true freedom is "greatly embarrassed and obstructed by a false law of sin."[68] This law is rooted in mankind's natural constitution and remains as the most difficult obstacle for him to overcome.

---

66. Nevin, "Human Freedom," 23.
67. Nevin, "Bible Anthropology," 363–64.
68. Nevin, "Human Freedom," 23.

The difficulty is not only found in the sinful nature of the individual, but is ever complicated by the fact that sin pervades all of social existence. The solution, however, lies in the law of Christ, which likewise "runs through the history of the world's entire social constitution, from the beginning of time to its end."[69] Only through faith in Christ is this law of sin overcome.

The freedom that God offers is not just the "true" freedom of an unbounded will, but it is the truth itself. Thus, only by way of participation in the life of the incarnate Christ does humankind grasp the unity of "freedom" and "truth" that God has intended. To be united to the life of Christ through his church is to attain an original "birth-right" in God's kingdom and to experience true human freedom. Commenting on John 8:31–32, Nevin writes, "He is the truth; he came into the world to bear witness unto the truth; and his voice to all now is: 'If ye continue in my word, then are ye my disciples, indeed; and ye shall know the truth, and the truth shall make you free.'"[70] Freedom is a blessing of one's participation in the truth of Jesus. The individual, if he seeks true freedom, must enter into the objective reality of God's freedom. "Otherwise it is only the diabolical and damnable counterfeit of will, whose freedom is but the bondage of hell."[71]

Particularly with regard to human freedom, Nevin is consistent in his insistence that human qualities do not emerge first and foremost from within the individual but rather have universal resonance and are communicated as such. Even in terms of the "natural" order, to access these fundamental qualities in one's pursuit of human freedom, the individual must resolve himself into certain particular orders or forms of authority. Only in this way can the individual actualize himself and his will in relation to the whole.[72]

Nevin rejects the view that the will is completely free from "all heteronomic extraneous restraints." True subjective freedom demands an object; it demands an authority. The individual who supposes that freedom equals utter independence is therefore misguided. This is not true freedom since it is no more than a subtle, individualized law unto itself. True freedom, rather, requires a universal law of freedom that is only

---

69. Ibid.
70. Nevin, "Bible Anthropology," 364.
71. Ibid.
72. Nevin, "Human Freedom," 13.

found in the life of the divine. It is an objective law, "by which the individual will is of right bound, and without obedience to which it can never be true to its own nature."[73] As Nevin writes in "Human Freedom,"

> no one can be true ethically to his own position, whether as a child or as a man, high or low, rich or poor, in power or out of power, who, in the use of his liberty, whatever it may be, is not ruled at the same time by a sentiment of reverence for the idea of an objective authority extended over him in some form, in the actual social organization to which he belongs. To be without reverence for authority, is to have always to the same extent the spirit of a slave. In no other element is it possible to think what is true, or to act what is right.[74]

Popular notions of freedom and individual liberty were uniquely pervasive during Nevin's lifetime, and Nevin was fully aware that his views on the subject addressed issues far beyond the walls of the church. The complicated relationship between freedom and authority, in particular, could not have been more culturally relevant. The theologian spent much of his time addressing this specific issue, not least in his 1850 baccalaureate address, where Nevin based the necessity of this relationship on the relationship between creator and creature. On this basis, freedom and authority cannot be seen to exclude each other; it is a false dichotomy built on a faulty view of the world which starts with the self and remains suspicious of any "authority" outside of the self. "Why may not the man who disowns private judgment and private will," Nevin asks, "be just as free in the reverent use of established law and tradition, to say the least, as the man who scorns every such limitation?"[75]

Personality

Humanity, in its freedom, shares with God the fundamental attribute of personality. The existence of a will, both in the case of man and God, is rooted in this feature. To be sure, Nevin qualifies the significant difference between creator and creature by insisting that God's will "is not private or particular, but absolute; subjective indeed . . . objective and universal at the same time; these two forms of existence, subjective and objective, be-

---

73. Ibid., 7.
74. Ibid., 24.
75. Nevin, "Faith, Reverence, and Freedom," 114.

ing with Him absolutely commensurate and identical."[76] While mankind does not share with God this seemingly incomprehensible capacity for the will, his ability to act freely out of his own subjectivity is, in Nevin's view, no less crucial in God's work of redemption. The free expression of man's will is demonstrated most fundamentally in his personality.

Mankind's personality is simultaneously rooted in the supernatural order and his natural, material state. Consequently, the reconciliation of the created order depends upon his intimate relation to the earth. His "personality," despite its transcendent qualities, remains "rooted in the earth, conditioned at every point by the material soil which it has sprung."[77] Therefore, personal man, in his created state, bears a unique relationship to both natural and supernatural existence, holding out redemption to the former while yearning for the latter.

As a medium for personality, Nevin explains, the individual must transcend its immediate boundaries and be merged with its essential universal identity.[78] Nevertheless, Nevin insists that the individual "maintains its separate reality" in this event, thus allowing for the possibility of truly social existence.

> The individual life in this form, with a full sense of its own individual nature, and with full power to cleave to this as a separate, independent interest, must yet, with clear consciousness and full choice, receive into itself the general life to which it of right belongs, so as to be filled with it and ruled by it at every point. Then we have a proper human existence.[79]

No human individual, then, can exist in isolation, for this is to violate the very nature of what it means to be human. The individual, rather, must find his humanity—and thus his salvation—in community. To do so is not a concession or a forfeiting of one's freedom; to the contrary, it is to experience freedom for the first time. For Nevin, this is a given since freedom must always have an object; the individual must be free unto something or someone. While the object of this freedom is ultimately God himself, individuals are likewise obligated in their freedom to enter

---

76. Nevin, "Human Freedom," 12.
77. Nevin, "Moral Order of Sex," 551.
78. Appel, *Life and Work*, 407–10.
79. Nevin, "Human Freedom," 7.

into social existence with mankind. It is what Nevin called "the social principle."

The Social Principle and the Objectivity of the Church

Nevin's ontological and anthropological assumptions are further demonstrated in his belief that "the idea of man ... in order that it may become actual, must resolve itself into an innumerable multitude of individual lives" who are to find their perfection in the "whole" constitution of mankind.[80] This abstract formulation was presented more palatably in "Party Spirit," in which he articulates why a misunderstanding of the "general life" of humanity results in fragmentation and sectarianism, qualities which are contrary to the gospel. A passage of the tract elaborates on what Nevin calls "the social principle." It is a principle, he writes,

> which binds men together in large as well as small platoons, enters vitally into the constitution of human nature, without which individual men would be mere atoms, and man would no longer be man or the common unity of races, nations, tribes, and individuals. Without contact and communion with other spirits like himself, he would have no development worthy of his nature, and no history that constantly leads him from one grade of perfection to another. There is a common mind belonging to each age and to every country, to every province and class of society, which surrounds men as an atmosphere and in the end forms the character of the individual and the community.[81]

Nevin was certain that God's redemption of the natural order included the restoration and triumph of the social principle, by which all tribes, tongues, and nations would come to share in the general life of mankind. This cosmic reconciliation was not merely the collection of individuals; the social principle, like all fundamental tenets of Nevin's system, insists on "wholeness" rather than "allness." As such, it is a principle that equally applies to all social, religious, and political realms, insisting moreover that each realm be united to the objective, supernatural whole for which it was designed. Nevin thus rejects the "change the individual, change the world" philosophy of revivalism. While he would agree that both need to be redeemed, he would also insist upon a tight organic relationship between the two which necessitates a structural or societal

---

80. Nevin, "Moral Order of Sex," 551–52.
81. Nevin, "Party Spirit," in Appel, *Life and Work*, 118.

approach. Redemption or "salvation" includes the individual, the family, and the state, a process which occurs through, by, and in the church.

The institutional dimensions of social existence, therefore, ought not to be regarded as merely accidental or tangential to God's redemptive purposes. Nor will it suffice to relegate certain social or political institutions to a second-rate "secular" status. In fact, the social principle, if rightly understood as being truly organic in nature, insists that the very constitution of mankind owes itself in part to these very institutions. As Nevin wrote in "Catholicism," "but to understand fully the inner mission of Christianity . . . we must look beyond the merely individual life as such to the moral organization of society, in which alone it can ever be found real and complete. Pure naked individuality in the case of man is an abstraction, for which there is no place whatever in the concrete human world. The single man is what he is always, only in virtue of the social life in which he is comprehended, and of which he is a part."[82]

While it may seem obvious to an individual that his or her identity has "outside" influences, Nevin's approach suggests that these influences are much broader and far-reaching than one initially perceives. They are societal, structural, and even cosmic in nature. It follows then that basic institutions such as the family and the state are in continuity with the life of man and share with him a desire for the supernatural order.[83] Inversely, as Binkley simply but accurately concludes, for Nevin, "an individual can have no complete salvation unless these agencies are also saved."[84]

For Nevin, personality and social existence finds its true meaning in Christ and his church. And yet, oddly, Nevin has virtually nothing to say in the way of how the doctrine of the Trinity fits into this scheme. His writings on the subject of human freedom and personality render this absence somewhat puzzling, as Nevin locates the origin of freedom and personality in God without taking what seems to be the next logical step, namely, rooting these features in the relationship between Father, Son, and Holy Spirit. This conspicuous absence may reveal what many readers of Nevin may suspect, namely, a Christocentrism that is so emphasized as to downplay other key tenets of Christian theology. The Incarnation of Jesus Christ is so crucial for Nevin's theology that, at times, he tends to bypass the indispensable roles of the Father and Holy Spirit. While the

82. Nevin "Catholicism," in Appel, *Life and Work*, 377.
83. Nevin, "Human Freedom," 23.
84. Binkley, *Mercersburg Theology*, 85–86.

other persons of the Trinity do have a place in Nevin's system, he does not indulge his readers with a thorough treatment of their relation to one another.[85]

Nevertheless, there are traces of Nevin's concern for the sociality of mankind, particularly within the context of the church, that permeate the broader scope of his theology. In terms of soteriology, for instance, Nevin refuses to follow the majority of his contemporaries in the assumption that Christian salvation starts with the individual. This ignores the humanity's "essential" identity and the necessity of social existence. Binkley summarizes well Nevin's understanding: "The complete salvation and conversion of the world would not be accomplished ... by simply adding the names of more and more individuals to the roles of believers. It was also necessary to bring the living economy of the world more and more under the sway of Christian love and peace..."[86]

Nevin articulated his view rather simply but trenchantly, insisting, "No Church, No Christ."[87] A relationship to Christ is determined by one's identity with Christ's church. In opposition to voluntarism, which taught that the individual and not the church was the primary locus of God's saving act, Nevin insisted that Christian identity (and therefore true human identity) begins with word and sacrament, as administered under the authority of the church. His insistence that "the life of the Church is

---

85. This emphasis can be seen in Nevin's series of articles on the Apostle's Creed. "The economical Trinity, as it is sometimes styled, in distinction from its immanent character, the Trinity in its relations to man, as it goes forth from eternity into time, for the accomplishment of our salvation—the only form in which the mystery can be said at all to have for us any *revelation*—comes fully into view only and wholly by Christ ... No man knoweth the Father but the Son, and he to whom the Son shall *reveal* him. God had manifested himself to a certain extent, came forth in some measure from the awful solitude of his own absolute being, in the work of creation, and in the course of history as it stood before Christ came. But all this fell short immeasurably of the self-manifestation which took place in the *act* of the Incarnation, when the everlasting Word became flesh, and linked itself into one life with the life of the world itself, as raised to its highest power in man. God came forth in this act, manifested himself, laid himself open in the form of life to the view of faith, as never in all revelations before. Only so was it possible for the mystery of the Trinity to bring itself out clearly in the apprehension of the world; and in no other form, than as thus apprehended, can the doctrine be of any true value or force." Nevin, "Apostles' Creed," 318–19.

86. Binkley, *Mercersburg Theology*, 85–86.

87. Nevin, *The Church*, 65–66.

the salvation of the world" is fundamental to this understanding of the "individual" Christian.[88]

A theological anthropology that starts with the individual rather than the church is demonstrated at the lay level by the widespread insistence upon what the Mercersburg theologians called "the Bible plus private judgment." Nevin, along with his colleague Philip Schaff, believed that the "private judgment" revolution that had taken place in America was a misguided one at best, based on fundamentally flawed views of human nature and identity. The following indictment of American Protestantism from the pen of Schaff relates well the sentiments of Nevin and the Mercersburg movement. In his *Principle of Protestantism*, Schaff wrote, "the most dangerous foe with which we are called to contend is not the Church of Rome but the sect plague in our own midst; not the single pope of the city of seven hills, but the numberless popes—German, English, and American—who would fain enslave Protestants once more to human authority, not as embodied in the church indeed, but as holding in the form of mere private judgment and private will."[89] Such was the tone of Schaff and Nevin in their diagnosis that the church was being grossly infected with an over-privatization of religion. Christianity, from their perspective, had become little more than another enterprise of the American free market society, which included a market for religious ideas. Such an environment continued to reinforce the trajectory of American populism in all spheres and at all strata of society.

Nevin was not anti-individual. Proper reason and proper religion, however, only took place when the individual submitted their own subjective reason to universal, objective reason. Private judgment, if it remained private, was not sound judgment. In order for it to be rational and accurate in its interpretation of the outside world, it was necessary for such judgment to show "itself to be truly general."[90]

THE MAN OF FAITH AND THE PERFECTION OF NATURE

Nevin's anthropology is ultimately based upon his view of the Incarnation of Jesus Christ. The Incarnation, however, is not a sheer fact of history that occurs, among other facts, by *divine fiat*. It is, rather, the concretion

88. Nevin, "Catholicism," in Appel, *Life and Work*, 386.

89. Schaff, *Principle of Protestantism*, 154.

90. Nevin, "Faith Reverence, and Freedom," 295; Nevin, "Brownson's Quarterly Review," cited in Holifield, *Theology in America*, 470.

of God's whole creative effort, bringing to light what God had intended in his creation of mankind. It is an *event* which subsumes the very history of mankind, who from the beginning was created to participate in the life of the divine, simultaneously raising the natural created order into a higher order of existence. According to Nevin, the opening chapters of Genesis teach that the world is an organic whole which completes itself in man, and "humanity is regarded throughout as a single grand fact, which is brought to pass, not at once, but in the way of history, unfolding always more and more its true interior sense, and reaching onward towards its final consummation."[91] Mankind thus retains his integrity as the climax of God's creative efforts, of which the Incarnation is the supreme expression.

The continuum from the world's natural state to the life of the divine is located in the moral life of man, who is designed to have union with the divine through Christ. Although man in this scheme is the culmination or "end of nature," Nevin acknowledges that man, in his current natural state, is also incomplete because his fulfillment is found in a higher, objective, constitution—the incarnate Christ. The natural world, becoming a moral, intelligent world through mankind, reaches its fulfillment as it is linked with the divine through the second person of the Trinity.[92]

On August 31st, 1853, Nevin stood before the student body and faculty of Franklin and Marshall College to present a baccalaureate address to the first graduating class in Lancaster. The theme was "Man's True Destiny."[93] According to Nevin, humanity is not simply an offshoot, accident, or even a product of the natural world. As the climax of God's creation, man is more than nature, "though organically one with it as the basis of his being."[94] He is "the perfection of nature, the crown of its glory, the very centre of its light," finding his elemental constitution in

91. Nevin, "New Creation in Christ," 7.

92. Nevin, "Christianity and Humanity," 469.

93. Nevin, "Man's True Destiny," 455. See also, Nevin "Undying Life," 613: "In the spirit of man, past and future are brought together in the power of the present—the transitoriness of time surmounted in the apprehension of the Infinite. He was made, we are told, in the image and likeness of God, to be the head of the natural world and to exercise lordship over it in every lower view—to be in it and of it through his bodily organization, and yet to be above it at the same time through his intelligence and reason, disclosing within himself a new and higher order of life altogether."

94. Nevin, "Human Freedom," 5.

the whole and transcendent rather than the particular and the finite. As such, he is to serve as a means for creation's reconciliation with God. "The organization of the world," Nevin said, "as a system of nature, comes to completion in his person."[95]

In his 1859 essay, "The Wonderful Nature of Man," Nevin discussed man's ontology in terms of physicality, intelligence, and moral nature.[96] He begins with man's physical nature, insisting that it too participates in man's supernatural role. The present world, as a physical system, most naturally experiences the first fruits of its redemption in man's physical body, "through which alone it can make room for his presence under any higher form."[97] Man's inimitability in this scheme, then, is found not only in his will and intelligence, qualities that constitute his moral capacity, but also in his created physicality. Nevin, drawing on the words of the psalmist, sums up his view as follows:

Well might the Hebrew Singer cry out, overwhelmed as it were with the contemplation of his own nature:

> "I will praise Thee, O Lord; for I am fearfully and wonderfully made: marvelous are Thy works; and that my soul knoweth right well."... The declaration applies in full force to the entire being of Man. He is to be gazed upon with a sort of trembling admiration, first of all, in his simply physical nature; still more so, afterwards, in his intellectual nature; but most of all finally, in his moral nature—where only, at the last, the full boundless significance of his life, and along with this, the whole terrible sublimity of it also, may be said to burst completely into view.[98]

The physical, intellectual, and moral dimensions of the life of man reveal to him his supernatural destiny. This revelation, however, must be considered in terms of nature's destiny as well. In Nevin's own words, "The notion of real presence of spiritual powers in the Christian Church for supernatural ends, involving as it does, necessarily, the subordination of the whole order of nature to a higher economy that can be apprehended only by faith, is precisely that which it has no power to endure..."[99] The natural world, finding its "echo in the moral nature of man," can only be

95. Nevin, "Man's True Destiny," 455.
96. See also Nevin, "Christianity and Humanity," 471.
97. Nevin, "Wonderful Nature of Man," 323.
98. Ibid., 319–20.
99. Nevin, "Man's True Destiny," 460.

united with God's divine economy when, by virtue of its link with moral, spiritual man, it becomes a moral, spiritual world. Both nature and man, therefore, require a transcendent redemption, one from above, whereby God reaches down and brings all of creation into the life of the divine. "Nature cries aloud for that which is higher, greater, and more enduring than itself. The world that now is, with man in the centre of it, is a riddle whose burden can find no relief except in the world to come."[100]

Man's destiny, the end for which he exists, is therefore not limited to the present world. It lies beyond the world in a supernatural order of existence which even now ought to govern man's present life. It is not enough, however, for man merely to recognize this end for which he has been created. The fulfillment of this end requires that the supernatural takes hold of man and prompts a free act of the will. It must "make itself known, not as a notion or thought merely, but as an actual reality, comprehending in it the very end itself for which man is thus required to live."[101]

In sum, the life of man must be united to the supernatural through the life of Christ. Barring this union, nature seeking to "complete itself" in him, likewise has no hope for supernatural redemption. Nature finds its apex in mankind, but can ascend no further as long as mankind remains strictly in his "natural" state. Such comes in the form of Christ incarnate, in whom man's destiny—that is, what it means to be a true human being—is realized. Communication with this supernatural revelation occurs only by the power of obedient faith, whereby man, following Christ (and indeed *in* Christ), humbly reduces himself in service to God.[102]

"The whole subject," Nevin insists, "reveals to us the nature of necessity, and value of Faith."[103] Herein lies the vital aspect of man's relation to God in Christ. Man's faith, for Nevin, is that mysterious component which, like incarnate Christ, interpenetrates the natural and supernatural realm. Or in DiPuccio's description, "the reality and presence of the supernatural world are inwardly united with the life of humanity through faith in the same way that the two natures of Christ are joined without

---

100. Ibid., 456.
101. Ibid.
102. Nevin, "Christianity and Humanity," 470.
103. Nevin, "Man's True Destiny," 458.

confusion or separation."[104] In Nevin's words, faith is "the very eye . . . that enables us to 'look at things unseen,' and causes their presence to surround us as part of our own life."[105]

Man's faith, in its communication with the divine, is not contingent upon knowledge of the finite present order. Knowledge always follows faith. Faith, rather, is the "power of acknowledging the supernatural, the miraculous, the real presence of possibilities, and powers, actual operations that go beyond the resources of nature and surmount all its laws in a new order of life, which is made to be actually at hand in the mystery of the Church, through the Death, the resurrection and the Glorification of the Son of God."[106]

In another sense, however, man acquires faith quite naturally since, by original right, he belongs to the higher order of existence already. He was, after all, created in the image of God and thus retains self knowledge and free will, qualities which distinguish him from the "world in every lower form."[107] What reconciles this confusing and seemingly dualistic view of man is that man's faith, according to Nevin, is not sheer assent to facts about God. It is, rather, as a substance or "hypostasis" of things hoped for, a means by which man enters into the bosom of "that everlasting order, whose seat is the Divine Mind." By faith, man "dwells in God," and experiences a real participation in the divine life.[108]

In classic theological terminology, Nevin emphasizes the *fides qua* component of belief as the means by which one enters into the life of God. This life—Christ's life—is found in the church, the actual, historical extension of the body of Christ and the locus of God's salvation. The church, the community of the creed, is that which rightfully instills faith in the individual through word, sacrament, and the "system of catechesis." Thus it is a faith which proceeds from the objective life of Christ— the true humanity—through the life of the church, the ark of salvation where individuals may be received into God's new creation. It is a way of thinking about faith that is diametrically opposed to what Nevin called the "system of the Bench," in which the church had no existence apart

---

104. DiPuccio, *Interior Sense*, 151.
105. Nevin, "Apostles' Creed," 208. See also DiPuccio, *Interior Sense*, 152.
106. Nevin, "Man's True Destiny," 458.
107. Nevin, "Faith, Reverence, and Freedom," 98.
108. Ibid., 100.

from the consent of believers. Faith, in this flawed system, begins with the individual, not the objective life of Christ in the church.[109]

For Nevin, mankind bears God's image as one who is moral, intelligent, free, personal, and social. Humanity thus stands in distinction from the rest of the created order as one who is able to truly commune with God. He is that which finds similarity to God within ever greater dissimilarity (*maior dissimilitudo*). Most profoundly, mankind has the ability to exhibit faith in the God-man Jesus Christ. In this way, faith serves as man's most precious quality. It is the instrument not only for the reconciliation between God and man, but also for reconciliation ultimately between God and the natural, lower sphere of existence. Man operates as the crucial link in God's reconciliation of this lower sphere (and indeed all things) because he exists in organic relation with the world around him. His identity, in other words, is not found in himself, but in the generic life of mankind and the various social and political institutions of which he is part. He is lodged in the generic, sinful life of Adam and therefore yearns for the universal life of the divine, which is offered to him eschatologically—but indeed historically and proleptically—in the Incarnation of Jesus Christ.

---

109. Nevin, *Mystical Presence*, 168, 213. See also Holifield, *Theology in America*, 478.

4

The Church

Salvation, Sacrament, and the Historical Extension of the Incarnate Christ

THE INCARNATION OF JESUS Christ, according to Nevin, is the principle event by which all of history, nature, and mankind are reconciled to God. Constituting the organic nature of reality, the event of the Incarnation is at once historical and eschatological, ideal and actual, thrust upon and woven throughout history in the form of the Christian religion, the life of the church.[1] The church, then, as the historical concretion and extension of the Incarnation, acts through word and sacrament as the mediator of God's cosmic reconciling act in Christ.[2] Nevin, therefore, regarded the church as the vehicle for directing the current of the world's life. But how did Nevin understand this event? What is it, from Nevin's perspective, about the life and liturgy of the church that directs the history of the world?

In order to answer these and related questions, the following aspects of Nevin's theology need to be addressed: The visible church as the historical extension of Christ's body, the Incarnation's relationship to history and sacraments, and the corporate and individual dimensions of salvation. In order to think more comprehensively about the inner workings of Nevin's ecclesiology and soteriology, this chapter will also consider the nature of sin, the sacrament of baptism, and the doctrine of

---

1. My thanks to Jason D. Wood for his helpful comments on this chapter. Jason's insight prompted me to clarify and rework several sections, most assuredly for the better.

2. Both the Incarnation and the Church are to be understood historically, lest their supernatural role be relegated to abstraction. It must be remembered that for Nevin, the supernatural must have concrete existence if it is to participate in reality, which is not dualistic but essentially organic.

imputation. Such will afford a more thorough explication of how Nevin's view of personhood and sociality is aligned with his understanding of the church and Christ's salvation therein. The aim here is to more adequately understand how the church functions in Nevin's system as an event *in* history while also, as the concrete expression of Christ in the world, acting to reconcile history to God.

THE CHURCH: THE HISTORICAL EXTENSION OF THE THEANTHROPIC CHRIST

In his *Discussions in Church Polity*, Charles Hodge explains, "The Church, therefore, according to this view, is not essentially a visible society; it is not a corporation which ceases to exist if the external bond of union be dissolved. It may be proper that such union should exist; it may be true that it has always existed; but it is not necessary. The Church, as such, is not a visible society. All visible union, all external organization, may cease, and yet, so long as there are saints who have communion, the Church exists, if the Church is the communion of saints."[3]

Here, another critical point of divergence between Hodge and Mercersburg emerges, as the most significant emphasis of both Schaff and Nevin's ecclesiology is that the church is visible and necessarily historical. The church is not to be regarded as fundamentally invisible or an institution of sheer abstraction.[4] If the church is the visible, historical extension of God incarnate, then it must exist in space and time. Schaff and Nevin articulate an almost identical ecclesiology by emphasizing the historical, mysteriously temporal nature of the church, a kingdom which has a polity, a citizenship, and laws.[5] Christ incarnate gives this kingdom, this new creation, its historical life and progression. As Nevin once instructed his students, "Jesus Christ must be the foundation of our

---

3. Hodge, *Discussions in Church Polity*, 5–6. On comparing Hodge's and Mercersburg's ecclesiology, see Littlejohn, *Quest for Reformed Catholicity*, 72–76.

4. Leithart insightfully comments on the early history of this distinction: "Augustine's formulation of the idea of an *ecclesia invisibilis* is the dogmatic systematization of the identity crisis that followed Constantine's conversion and promotion of Christianity. Among other things, this is politically problematic. An invisible church has no distinctive way of life that can critique, call, challenge or model an alternative to the wider society. Constantinianism is a historical irony: just when the church believes it has reached the pinnacle of influence and power, its political and social witness gets neutered." Leithart, *Defending Constantine*, 311.

5. Schaff, *History of the Apostolic Church*, 164–66.

life, and the main stream of history must be in the Christian Church. Every other belief is of the essence of infidelity. The law of history, therefore, tends towards Christianity, of which Christ is the principle or life, and it is only as we apprehend it in this way that we can prosecute the study of it with any proper degree of comfort or success."[6] Christ incarnate, then, serves as the origin and antecedent of the ideal church and its hypostatic, organic relation with the actual. As such, the ideal church finds its concrete existence in essentially the same way that Christ came in the flesh. In both cases, the objective ideal mysteriously reveals itself in hypostatic union with the material and particular.[7]

So what is the relationship between the church visible and church invisible? The answer, again, lies in the mystery of the Incarnation. The church, as the extension of God incarnate, represents two natures of the same person. Nevin explains, "The Church exhibits itself to us under two aspects, which are in many respects very different, and yet both alike necessary to complete its proper constitution. In one view it is the *ideal church*, in another it is the *actual church*."[8] While this does not fit squarely within traditional reformed terminology, Nevin's language essentially communicates a similar, if not superior, version of the visible/invisible distinction. In fact, for Nevin, the insistence upon a visible church is precisely what lends credence to the existence of the invisible or ideal church. From his perspective, what does the claim to an invisible church to the exclusion of a visible church say about the Incarnation? Was Jesus invisible? Rather, the visible church reminds the Christian that while Christ has ascended, Christ does in fact have a physical body and that the believer participates in the union of Christ's person through his

---

6. Nevin "Lectures on History," in Appel, *Life and Work*, 596–97.

7. This is a crucial point for Nevin and Schaff because, in their view, a failure to recognize both the unity and separateness of Christ's body will result in an ecclesiology that tends towards Gnosticism on the one hand or Roman Catholicism on the other. The Mercersburg theologians were aware of these perilous tendencies. With Gnosticism, one is prone to separate Christ's body to the degree that his church is regarded as either sheer abstraction or gross materialism. Here the fundamental error lies in not grasping the organic and developmental relationship that takes place between the ideal and the actual. On the other hand, both Schaff and Nevin believed that Rome had limited the church to its empirical, institutional manifestation. The error in this view lies in one's willingness to confine the church to history, or in other words, to regard it as a "part" of history, when in fact its essential ontology springs from a whole that is greater than history itself. See DiPuccio, *Interior Sense*, 182.

8. Nevin, *Church*, 58.

or her relationship to Christ in his eschatological ideal, but temporally concrete body, the church.[9]

The church, in its continuum with Christ's body, is the locus both for God's reconciliation with man and for the possibility for mankind to unite with true humanity, namely, the incarnate Christ. As such, it must retain its true "theanthropic" constitution and character. "The union of the divine and human in her constitution, must be inward and real, a continuous revelation of God in the flesh, exalting this last continuously into the sphere of the Spirit."[10] As Nevin further affirms, "Christ's presence in the world is in and by his Mystical Body, the Church. As a real human presence, carrying in itself the power of a new life for the race in general, it is no abstraction or object of thought merely, but a glorious living Reality, continuously at work, in an organic historical way, in the world's constitution."[11]

There is, therefore, no presence of Christ in the world apart from the church, which is the very form that Christ's body has taken. Nevin writes, "The Church is the historical continuation of the life of Jesus Christ in the world. By the Incarnation of the Son of God, a divine supernatural order of existence was introduced into the world . . ."[12] E. Brooks Holifield perceptively comments on this passage, writing, "The church was the extension of the Incarnation through history. If the Incarnation introduced a supernatural life into the world, then the church was the mystical body that actualized that life."[13] As such, the visible church, in its organic (or perhaps "hypostatic") relation with history, is the proper context for Christ's body and blood to be offered to the world. On this point, Nevin explains,

> . . . let the great fact of the Incarnation be apprehended with full faith, as a world fact—the centre of all history—the fountain of a new creation, which is still present and progressive, not fantastically, but in the way of actual human, historical development, in the Church; let it be felt that the Church is, in very deed, the depository and continuation of the Saviour's theanthropic life itself,

---

9. See Littlejohn, *Quest for Reformed Catholicity*, 68–72, for an excellent discussion of these points.
10. Nevin, *Mystical Presence*, 232.
11. Nevin "Wilberforce on the Incarnation," 186.
12. Nevin, *The Church*, 60–61.
13. Holifield, *Theology in America*, 477.

and as such a truly supernatural constitution, in which powers and resources wholly transcending the common order of the world are constantly at hand, involving a real intercommunion and interpenetration of the human and the divine...[14]

Regarding this point, it is imperative to remember that Nevin retains the necessary distinctions between creature and creator, natural and supernatural, human and divine. In fact, it is precisely the unique nature and role of the church that necessitates these boundaries. Mankind, after all, cannot simply be united to God in a way that Transcendentalism or idealist pantheism would suggest. Rather, for Nevin, the church serves as the sole locus of humankind's communion with and participation in the life of Christ. It is the historical stream of Christ's life, giving life to those who enter its doors and become reconciled to God, by faith, through the gracious ministry of word and sacrament.

INCARNATION AND SALVATION

To be inserted into Christ himself, Nevin believes, is to be inserted into the true humanity that is comprehended in his person. It is, mysteriously, to be reunited with the true human race that would fulfill God's purpose for the new creation. The Incarnation of Christ is the archetype and indeed the very constitution of the human race, offered as the way, the truth, and the life, not only for the salvation of individuals, but for the restoration of mankind. Thus, salvation, according to Nevin, is not something to be predicated upon the individual. This is indicated not only by the "social principle" of Nevin's theological anthropology, but also—and more fundamentally—by his understanding of the Incarnation. The Incarnation, for Nevin, is not merely a repository of God's benefits or, as we will see, a mechanism of the atonement. It is the wellspring of the true humanity, the possibility of humanity's union with the divine.

> That the race might be saved, it was necessary that a work should be wrought not beyond it, but in it; and this inward salvation to be effective must lay hold of the race itself in its organic, universal character, before it could extend to individuals, since in no other form was it possible for it to cover fully the breadth and depth of the ruin that lay in its way. Such an inward salvation of the race required that it should be joined in a living way with the divine nature itself, as represented by the everlasting Word or *Logos*, the

14. Nevin, *Mystical Presence*, 233.

> fountain of all created light and life. The Word accordingly became flesh, that is assumed humanity into union with itself.[15]

Such redemption, then, is not based upon sheer contractual agreement or a certain acquisition of God's benefits, but is in fact based upon one's entrance into a new *way* of life. It means laying hold of the divine by being lodged into the true humanity, the Incarnation, and thus living as humanity was created to live, tasting of and proleptically participating in a supernatural order of existence. The church, then, rather than just offering a salvation voucher to individuals, offers an avenue for human beings to enter into the kingdom of God. It is the entrance of history and humanity into a higher order. Christian salvation, writes Nevin, is " . . . a new life introduced into the very centre of humanity itself. In this view, though bound most closely with the organic development of the world's history as it stood before, it is by no means comprehended in it, or carried by it, as its proper product and fruit. Christianity is more than a continuation simply of Judaism. It claims the character of a new creation, by which old things in the end must pass away, and all things become new."[16]

This new creation, according to Nevin, is not necessitated exclusively by Adam's sin and the fall of humankind. Following the Church Fathers and Aquinas more so than his scholastic reformed predecessors, Nevin believes that Jesus' incarnation is not simply a compulsory mechanism of the atonement. It is, rather, the fundamental need and longing of creation itself, namely, to be raised into a higher order of existence, and, to this end, the moral and ontological ascension of humanity into the life of God.[17]

But what of this union between creator and creature? Nevin explains in further detail,

> We say of our union with Christ, that it is a new life. It is deeper than all thought, feeling, or exercise of will. Not a quality only. Not a mere relation. A relation in fact, as that of the iron to the magnet; but one that carries into the centre of the subject a form of being which was not there before. Christ communicates his own life substantially to the soul on which he acts, causing it to grow into his very nature. This is the mystical union; the

15. Ibid., 156.
16. Ibid., 157–58.
17. Nevin, *Antichrist*, 38.

basis of our whole salvation; the only medium by which it is possible for us to have an interest in the grace of Christ under any other view.[18]

At Mercersburg, then, the Incarnation of Christ was not merely an object of study, a doctrine to be taught, or a system to be learned, but a means of participation in the divine. This participation is not static, but dynamic and indeed hypostatic, as one lived in the course of God's providential history. As such, history, theology, and life are essentially meant to be "in Christ." To be *in* Christ, then, is not to assent to God's legal or moral declaration, but to enter into the true humanity found in the "generic," objective life of God.[19] Likewise, the idea of new creation refers not so much to the creation of individual believers, but to the new, supernatural order of existence held out for history and mankind. This supernatural order includes "resources, powers, (and) divine realities" that are not only unique to itself, but which transcend the "common natural constitution of human life . . . under a true historical form." In this way, the supernatural not only takes on a natural form, but becomes natural by "falling into the regular process of the world's history, so as to form to the end of time indeed its true central stream."[20]

Nevin never wavers from his insistence that the church, as the bearer and extension of Christ's body, serves as the requisite context for mankind's redemption. The redemption of mankind is necessary if the lower, natural sphere, in its concrete social and political manifestations, is to be raised into a higher order. The Eucharist, then, functioning as the primary locus of the believer's union with Christ, serves (insofar as it is received by humanity in faith) as the locus of the world's redemption. But how exactly does Nevin understand this union by faith?

---

18. Nevin, *Mystical Presence*, 159.

19. Ibid., 160. Nevin criticizes Calvin for understanding the "generic" life of Christ. He writes, "The third source of embarrassment belonging to the form in which Calvin exhibits his theory, is found in this that he makes no clear distinction between the individual personal life of Christ, and the same life in a generic view. In every sphere of life, the individual and the general are found closely united in the same subject." Later, in his comparison of the first and second Adam, Nevin explains, "Paul in particular is very clear and very strong, in the representation of this federal or generic character on the part of Christ. He makes his relation to the human race parallel in full to that of its natural head." Ibid., 211.

20. Ibid., 157–58.

NEVIN'S HISTORY OF THE EUCHARIST

The church's role as the ark of salvation is essential to Nevin's understanding of humanity's reconciliation with God, as the salvation that is offered by Christ is exclusively available in the historic manifestation of his body. Nevin, however, does not stop there. It is within the context of the church that Christ is more expressively—and even more truly—exhibited in the sacrament of the Lord's Supper. He explains, "let all this (the apprehension of the Incarnation in the Church), I say, be felt, and it is easy to understand how naturally and necessarily, at the same time, we must be led to see the mystery of the Holy Eucharist, epitome as it is of the mystery of the Christian, salvation itself, in a corresponding light."[21] From Nevin's perspective, a high view of sacrament and a high view of Christianity's historical and supernatural character stand and fall together. He explains, moreover, "Low views of the sacrament betray invariably a low view of the mystery of the Incarnation itself, and a low view of the Church also, as that new and higher order of life, in which the power of this mystery continues to reveal itself through all ages."[22] Disregard for the Eucharist eventuates in a deficient ecclesiology and consequently a misunderstanding of the Incarnation.

Thus, the Eucharist must be recognized as the event whereby believers begin to comprehend the Incarnation's power as a world-historical event, not as a simple memorial that points to a past event in the church's history. In this way, Christ's death and resurrection is ever present for the world's life. It is therefore necessary, in Nevin's view, that the events of Christ's life are not regarded simply as "transient facts in the history of the world." "The mystery of Christianity is here concentrated into a single visible transaction, by which it is made as if it were transparent to the senses, and caused to pass before us in immediate living representation."[23] In this sacrament, the church offers the whole life of Christ (both in flesh and spirit) to mankind so that, ultimately, all of creation might be redeemed and raised into supernatural existence.

In keeping with his broader methodology, Nevin seeks to delineate a historical theology of the Eucharist. He believes that it is necessary to root one's understanding of the Eucharist not only in the Reformation,

21. Ibid., 248.
22. Ibid., 233.
23. Ibid., 232.

but more deeply in the Patristic era. His articles on Early Christianity demonstrate this pursuit. He writes, for example, "The doctrine of the Eucharist ... is not a circumstance merely in the general system of faith, but appears as a truly living and divinely efficacious link, between the mystery of the Incarnation on one side and coming resurrection of our bodies on another; showing plainly that these connections as suggested by Ignatius, were not fanciful or casual, but rooted in the reigning belief of the Church."[24]

In his most famous work, *The Mystical Presence*, Nevin goes to great lengths to present a historical defense of the "Calvinistic" Reformed doctrine of the Eucharist and *unio mystica*. He believes that it is of vital importance to demonstrate, over and against the ahistorical or antihistorical tendencies of sectarian Protestantism, how the doctrine of the Eucharist has retained elements of Christianity's true historical character.[25] Nevin follows his initial statement of the doctrine with a thorough historical treatment of the Eucharist, tracing its history from confessional documents of the Reformation to the Puritan views of American Protestantism. He focuses in particular upon Calvin's view, which he regards as singularly important, and attempts to show how it has been betrayed even by the most ardent of Calvin's followers.[26]

Nevin's exposition of the Eucharist in *The Mystical Presence* is thus in many respects a continuation of his critical analysis of American Protestantism. The work exhibits a trenchant criticism against American religious traditions for denying the objectivity and efficacy of the Eucharist. From Nevin's perspective, bearing responsibility for these "low views" of the Eucharist are those within the Puritan and sectarian streams of American religious tradition. Such traditions, Nevin believes, are wrong to view sacraments as mere outward ordinances, exhibiting moreover a fundamental misunderstanding of the Reformed doctrine in its true substance.[27]

---

24. Nevin, "Early Christianity," in Yrigoyen, *Catholic and Reformed*, 240.

25. This problem was one that lay close to home for Nevin, whose German Reformed denomination was on the brink of revising their liturgy in an attempt to retain their theological heritage in the midst of predominantly revivalist religious trends.

26. Nevin, *Mystical Presence*, 59–98. See Bonomo, *Incarnation and Sacrament*, 26–28. Bonomo provides an insightful summary and analysis of Nevin's Eucharistic theology. I am indebted to his analysis on a number of points.

27. Bonomo, *Incarnation and Sacrament*, 26–28.

Nevin's comprehensive analysis of the Eucharist in the history of the post-Reformation church is not simply a convenient way for Nevin to trump his interlocutors with his extensive knowledge of church history. It must be reiterated that for Nevin, historical investigation is not only a matter of intellectual aesthetics. Because the church is the continuous historical extension of Christ for the world, it must be demonstrated historically how Christ has indeed been offered to creation continuously since the time of the Apostles and Church Fathers. Therefore, in Nevin's judgment, "The Question of the Eucharist is one of the most important belonging to the history of religion. It may be regarded as in some sense central to the whole Christian system. For Christianity is grounded in the living union of the believer with the person of Christ; and this great fact is emphatically concentrated in the mystery of the Lord's Supper."[28] This union between Christ and the believer must be an unbroken—or perhaps undivided—event throughout the history of the church. To divide the Eucharist from history and relegate its meaning to timeless spiritual abstraction is to betray Christ's concrete, organic relationship to the ongoing development of God's creation. It is, in Nevin's view, to betray the Incarnation of Christ.

Mankind's Eucharistic Communion with Christ by Faith

In Nevin's theology of Eucharist, Christ communicates the whole of his life to the believer who receives it by faith. The operative word here for Nevin is "whole," and he regretfully criticizes Calvin for not taking this point seriously enough. Calvin's doctrine of the Eucharist, Nevin believes, suffers from a false psychology which equates one's "body" with material volume. Following this line of thought, Calvin places emphasis on the life-giving power of Christ's flesh over his divine-human nature, emphasizing, moreover, Christ's individual life over the generic, spiritual role as the second Adam. For Nevin, Christ's body is in fact an entire "system" of life, an "organic law" unto which the believer is united by faith. "The old body becomes itself, in a mysterious way, the womb of a higher corporeity, the life-law of Christ's own glorious body; which is at last, through the process of death and the resurrection, set free from the first form of existence entirely, and made to supersede it for ever in the

---

28. Nevin, *Mystical Presence*, 47.

immortality of heaven."[29] When Christ is communicated by faith to the believer, he communicates true humanity in a generic, essential, consummate sense. He offers, in other words, what humanness was intended to be in the image of God. Calvin, Nevin believes, has simply not gone far enough, limiting Christ's body to his material, individual, existence.[30]

Bonomo captures well the fact that "Nevin held that the overall biblical presentation of the mystical union between Christ and the Church forms the theological foundation for a proper understanding of what takes place in the Eucharist."[31] As Nevin writes,

> The bread and wine are not Christ's flesh and blood as such; they are only, (but this in a real objective way), the new covenant in his death, made actual by pledge and seal under this outward form; still a participation in the covenant, requires and implies, in the nature of the case, a participation in the very life, by which alone the expiatory value of the covenant can have any reality or force. The paschal lamb must be *eaten*, physically incorporated with the life of the worshipper, to give him part in the covenant of which it was the seal. A fleshly shadow of the true life union, on the ground of which, and by the power of which alone, we can ever have part in the blessings of the new covenant in Christ's blood. Communion with the covenant involves of necessity communion with the sacrifice.[32]

By virtue of its union with the incarnate Christ through the Eucharist, the church becomes the instrument for reconciling "the living economy of the world more and more into the reign of Christ."[33] However, for the world to ascend into the supernatural, it must feed on Christ and become united with his body as it exists visibly in the church. The church's role, therefore, as a medium of salvation and as that which raises the present order into a higher order of existence is essentially one that is governed by the power of sacrament. But to what extent is the Eucharist's power conveyed to the various dimensions of world history and sociopolitical existence? Is it only efficacious insofar as man is

---

29. Ibid., 167.
30. Ibid., 147–49. See also Bonomo, *Incarnation and Sacrament*, 29–30.
31. Bonomo, *Incarnation and Sacrament*, 31.
32. Nevin, *Mystical Presence*, 238.
33. Wentz, *American Theologian*, 109, citing Nevin, "Catholicism," 17.

drawn to God by its administration in the church? What, in other words, is the relationship of the Eucharist to the modern state?

In the Incarnation, transcendence entered into immanence and began to reconcile the natural world and its history back to God. Since the church is the historic extension of the Incarnation, this process of reconciling the world back to God is pictured through the lens of sacrament and as such may be called a "sacramental principle." This principle serves as the locus for reflection on the meaning of history, the political and social life of mankind, and the end for which the world is designed. Thus, insofar as a metaphysical foundation of political principle or social ethic is concerned, sacrament serves as the *sine qua non*. The Anglo-Catholic Eric Mascall puts it this way, "The sacraments have social implications, the Church has social implications, only because the Church itself is a divine and supernatural society . . . The Church has many functions in society, but it can never become a mere function of society, for it is a society—the Society of God, the life of the Holy Trinity communicated to men."[34]

For Nevin, then, the relationship of the Eucharist to the sociopolitical sphere is one which is indirect yet unmistakable. The body of Christ in the Eucharist serves as the structure or conduit through which the redemption of the world takes place, but such does not obviate the crucial necessity of human faith. The faith of mankind is the vital instrument within this process, since the Eucharist is the medium of communication with Christ "only in the case of believers." The power and grace of Christ in sacrament, in other words, can only be apprehended by faith. In fact, Nevin follows Calvin closely in his assertion that "Those who come to the Lord's Table unworthily, as to a common meal, without being in a state to discern the Lord's body, eat and drink only judgment to themselves."[35] This is why faith, as previously discussed, is so fundamental to the reconciliation of the created order. It apprehends in sacrament the means by which nature is perfected and the world is reconciled to God.

Proceeding from the church's administration of word and sacrament, the Eucharist retains its objective force in the world, inviting the lower sphere into the life of Christ. In this way, the Eucharist may be said to engage or transform the sociopolitical sphere, making it possible for

34. Mascall, *Corpus Christi*, 45, cited by Wannenwetsch, *Political Worship*, 101.
35. Nevin, *Mystical Presence*, 172.

the state to be "vanished away in the Church."³⁶ This is not to say that the state or any other "lower" institution will be eradicated, but that such will find its true life in the church and will cease to exist in the lower sphere. In Nevin's words,

> This indicates, however, its relation to the old order. That is not to be annihilated by it, but taken up into it as a higher life. The Incarnation is supernatural; not magical however; not fantastic or visionary; not something to be gazed at as a transient prodigy in the world's history. It is the supernatural linking itself to the onward flow of the world's life, and becoming thenceforward itself the ground and principle of the entire organism, now poised at last on its true centre. In this sense Christianity is indeed a *fact*; even as the first creation was a Fact; a Fact for all time; a world-fact.³⁷

There is, therefore, nothing in the lower organic sphere that is beyond the church's sacramental power.³⁸ It is a power which is necessarily woven throughout creation, so as not to betray its fundamental purpose.

This seemingly cosmic sacramentology, gleaned from the broad scope of Nevin's corpus, is explicitly attested to in an 1851 class lecture: "The whole constitution of the world is sacramental, as being not simply the sign of, but the actual form and presence of invisible things."³⁹ All of life's dimensions, then, to the extent that faith is present, are incorporated into this sacramental whole. They are subsumed into the cosmic, organic whole that is embodied in the Incarnation of Jesus Christ.⁴⁰ It cannot be

---

36. Nevin, "Early Christianity," in Yrigoyen, *Catholic and Reformed*, 299.

37. Nevin, *Mystical Presence*, 157–58.

38. Nevin, "Catholicism," 14. Nevin, "Church Year," 456–61. See also Wentz, *American Theologian*, 59–60. Nevin's emphasis upon Christ's organic, generic, all encompassing relation to mankind and the general stream of world history certainly lends credence to this view.

39. Erb, *Dr. Nevin's Theology*, 373. As noted above, DiPuccio, *Interior Sense*, 25, suggests that for Nevin, the Incarnation is indeed the "archetype of the cosmos."

40. Notably, while this line of thought places Nevin at odds with the vast majority of American Protestant theologians, it is also one that locates him in various Orthodox and Roman Catholic streams of thought. One contemporary Catholic theologian, for example, writes, "All life's dimensions—person and society, world and history—are dynamically interrelated and constitute a single sacramental whole. Endowed with a symbolic power, creation and our humanity can be an epiphany of God. All life is experienced as ultimately 'holy' through the incarnation of the *Logos*. The sacramental universe is steeped in this Christian sacramental principle. It offers not only a holistic meaning to salvation, but also an overarching vision within which one perceives

overstated that for Nevin faith is the lynchpin for this event, since, by faith, humankind extends the power of the Eucharist to all dimensions of society. To be sure, the Eucharist's objective force is not contingent upon this faith, but its transmission to the world depends upon it.

For Nevin, the relationship of sacrament to society is one which finds its meaning in the historic church, where mankind, by faith, participates in Christ and is then exhorted to extend the power and grace exhibited in the Eucharist to all spheres of life. In this way, the Eucharist is indeed cosmic in scope, constituting the church's life and mission to the world. Salvation, as such, is not merely the redemption of individual souls, but a restoration—a recreation—of the cosmos.

SIN, BAPTISM, AND IMPUTATION

Nevin's understanding of the church and salvation, particularly with respect to his broader theological anthropology, can be further uncovered by taking a closer look at his doctrines of sin, baptism, and imputation. This may seem like an odd collection of themes to consider, but in doing so, one gains a more comprehensive understanding of Nevin's view of mankind's relationship to Christ, both individually and collectively.

One way of approaching this task is to focus on Nevin's debates with the most respected theological voices of his day. For one, Nevin's engagement with the views of Horace Bushnell (whom Nevin often praised) demonstrates Nevin's incessant stress upon the ideal and supernatural as well as his high view of the church's role to foster the faith of the believer. Also notable is Charles Hodge, perhaps Nevin's most formidable theological opponent, who swam within a stream of the Reformed tradition that Nevin came to trenchantly criticize. We will proceed with a brief comparison of Nevin and Bushnell on sin and baptism, as well as Nevin and Hodge on the matter of imputation. These comparisons should serve well for understanding Nevin's view of humanity, particularly in relation to Adam's sin and the fall.

Both Nevin and Bushnell followed a scheme which assumed that God's eternal purposes logically preceded and included the fall of man. Nevin, however, departed from Bushnell who saw sin as a *necessary* transitional stage in the process of mankind's development. He criticizes the

---

sacraments as interrelated and meaningful, necessary and integral to real life." Martinez, *Signs of Freedom*, 5.

view of Bushnell, who believed, "The condition of man in Paradise was not, and could not be, a direct onward movement in its own form to confirmed holiness, and so to glory, honor, and eternal life. It was necessary that he should taste evil, in order to become afterwards intelligently and resolutely good. His innocence could be strengthened into its full ripe virtue, only by being required to descend into the rough arena of the world through the fall, for the purpose of needful discipline and probation."[41]

The problem with this view, Nevin believes, is that it violates the essential goodness of God's creation and therefore its divine origin. It renders sin as something wrought in the very constitution of the world, the fruit of man's freedom, ultimately leading to Manichean dualism.[42] For Nevin, Adam and Eve had the ability to choose between what was moral and immoral and chose the latter, resulting in the sin and guilt of the world. Nevin does not postulate or hypothesize about the nature of Eden beyond this point and spends little time or effort in the way of offering a substantial treatment of sin and the fall of man.[43] Nevertheless what can be gleaned from Nevin on this point is a consistent theme of his criticisms of Bushnell, namely, a failure to understand the priority of the supernatural.

To be sure, Bushnell sought to demonstrate that the natural and the supernatural operate together as "one system of God."[44] His most well known work, *Christian Nurture*, is largely built upon this very thesis. Nevin, through his organic and incarnational lens, could applaud this approach to an extent, but ultimately saw it as fatally flawed. He was unnerved by Bushnell's tendency to implicate the supernatural in natural terms. This is perhaps most clearly seen in Bushnell's prioritizing of the nuclear Christian family in the inculcation of faith in a child. Thus, while Bushnell retains a remarkably high view of Christ's incarnation and the supernatural objectivity therein, Nevin believes that he also runs the risk of losing the full force of Christ by relegating the faith to the natural sphere.[45]

41. Nevin, "Natural and Supernatural," in Appel, *Life and Work*, 540.
42. Ibid., 541.
43. See Binkley, *Mercersburg Theology*, 80.
44. Bushnell, *Nature and the Supernatural*. See also Holifield, *Theology in America*, 465.
45. Nevin, "Natural and Supernatural," in Appel, *Life and Work*, 539.

For Nevin, Bushnell's fervent advocacy of the natural not only minimizes the necessary elements of the supernatural order, but it also threatens to diminish the reality and depth of human sin. Nevin feared that Bushnell had not taken seriously enough the supernatural power of sin. "If our nature is radically corrupt," he asked, "how can it be expected to unfold itself by simple religious culture into a truly Christian form? The case would seem to require at least a supernatural change to begin with . . ."[46] Bushnell responded to Nevin only to say that the significant theological differences between the two men were mostly semantic, and that the parents' instillation of the faith into a child is, of course, prompted by divine grace. Nevin's traducian or realist view of sin, however, suggests that the matter was not merely of semantic discrepancy, and his criticisms of "Christian nurture" persisted.

Given Bushnell's consistent affirmation of the organic nature of reality and his accompanying rejection of scholastic and federal theological traditions, one cannot but wonder if he was unfairly targeted by Nevin. A cursory reading would indicate that the two theologians are swimming in the same theological stream. A closer look, however, reveals that while Bushnell is theologically sympathetic to Nevin on a number of points, their priorities remain at odds. Consider, for instance, an additional reflection from Bushnell, who explains, "Nor is any thing more clear, on first principles, than that no man is responsible for any sin but his own. The sin of no person can be transmitted as a sin, or charged to the account of another. But it does not therefore follow that there are no moral connections between individuals, by which one becomes a corrupter of others. If we are units, so also are we a race, and the race is one—one family, one organic whole; such that the fall of the head involves the fall of all the members."[47]

Bushnell, with Nevin, recognizes the organic unity between the individual and the race as a whole. However, a subtle divergence is found in Bushnell's emphasis upon moral connection, the prioritizing of "units," and his recurring use of family as a model for humanity's organic unity. Here we have terminology that Nevin simply would not employ because it does not adequately convey the supernatural element at stake. Nevin's criticism is further warranted by the following passage from Bushnell:

---

46. Nevin, "Educational Religion," 2461, cited by Payne, "Nevin on Baptism," 129.
47. Bushnell, *Views of Christian Nurture*, 196.

Even the old Jewish law, that one Jewish parent made a Jewish child, is brought into the church, and one believing parent "sanctifies" the child. In all of which, it seems to be clearly held that grace shall travel by the same conveyance with sin; that the organic unity, which I have spoken of chiefly as an instrument of corruption, is to be occupied and sanctified by Christ, and become an instrument also of mercy and life. And thence it follows that the seal of faith, applied to households, is to be no absurdity; for it is the privilege and duty of every Christian parent that his children shall come forth into responsible action, as a regenerated stock. The organic unity is to be a power of life. God engages, on his part, that it may be, and calls the Christian parent to promise, on his part, that it shall be. Thus the church has a constitutive element from the family in it still, as it had in the days of Abraham. The church life—that is, the life of Christ—collects families into a common organism, and then, by sanctifying the laws of organic unity in families, extends its quickening power to the generation following, so as to include the future, and make it one with the past.[48]

The significance of the contrast between Nevin and Bushnell on this point can hardly be overstated, not simply because it vindicates Nevin's criticisms, but because it serves to underscore Nevin's view of the individual and the collective. For Nevin, while the church collects families into a common organism, such is not to be discussed apart from the church's supernatural origin, the incarnate Christ.

The above selection from Bushnell brings us to the doctrine of baptism, an issue for which Nevin's engagement with Bushnell's theology of Christian nurture once again proves useful. Nevin and Bushnell agree that children should essentially grow up in such a way that they cannot recall a day that they did not know Christ. This view insists that individual identity is constituted not by the self, but by the community which inculcates and instills the faith into the individual. It follows that the individual's identity is wrapped up in the organic life of the family and in the church's collection of families.

Both theologians reject the atomist view of religion that had given rise to Protestant sectarianism during the antebellum era. As has been discussed, this view starts with the particulars of human existence with the result that the individual is regarded as the primary—if not the

---

48. Ibid., 206.

sole—judge of his or her identity in relation to the world and certainly in relation to Christ's church. The debate surrounding baptism is rather telling in this respect, as many of the incipient revivalist movements rejected the practice of infant baptism on the basis that the infant could not understand, and therefore not profess, his or her identity in relation to Christ.

In addition to his outright rejection of the revivalist's understanding of sacraments, not least in the case of baptism, Nevin also critiques movements within the Reformed tradition that he believes are attempting to mechanize the sacraments or regard them as bare symbols. No less than in the case of the Eucharist, Nevin regards baptism to be objectively efficacious. This efficacy is to be understood not in terms of an *ex opere operato* grace, but rather as denoting the unique role of baptism in carrying and conferring God's grace. Neither sign and seal nor benefits and representation, in other words, are to be separated.[49]

Nevin believes that the liturgy, rightly understood, provides for more than the mere possibility of God's grace in sacrament. "It affirms that God, on his part, makes it to be always objectively just what it means. In other words, it teaches sacramental grace." Baptism in this context does not regenerate people as if it were in some sense magical. Nevertheless, it retains an intrinsic value as a divine gift and a means of God's grace whereby the sign is truly accompanied by that which is signified.[50] He further explains,

> Our spiritualists admit that God *may* make baptism the channel of His grace—may cause the thing signified to go along with the outward sign, when He is pleased to do so; only they will not have it that His grace is in any way bound to the ordinance. Will they not admit then also, that the sacrament ought to be so used as to carry with it the benefit it represents; that God designed it to be in this way more than an empty form; and that it is the duty of all, therefore, to desire and expect through it what it thus, by Divine appointment, holds out to expectation? Who will be so bold as to say, in so many words, that baptism means no deliverance whatever from the power of sin, and that it is superstition to come looking for anything of this sort from it? Why then quarrel

---

49. See also Littlejohn, *Quest for Reformed Catholicity*, 98–102.
50. Nevin, "Theology of the New Liturgy," 61.

with the Liturgy for making earnest with the objective force of the sacrament in this view?[51]

As was the case with the doctrine of sin, Nevin and Bushnell differ with respect to baptism in the origin and nature of Christian nurture. Bushnell is primarily concerned with the enculturation of the faith at the familial and natural levels, and, from Nevin's point of view, he is all too willing to conflate the divine source and work of baptism into this natural scheme. The divergence between the two theologians is clearly seen in the following words of Bushnell:

> With the former class I certainly agree, so far as to admit that baptism, as an operation, can do no good to your child; but, if it has no importance in what it operates, it has the greatest importance in what it signifies; and, what is more to be deplored by you, the withholding it signifies as much, viz.: that you yourselves have no sense of the relation that subsists between your character and that of your child, and as little of the mercy that Christ intends for your child, by including him with you in his fold, to grow up there by your side in the same common hopes.[52]

Bushnell's situating baptism within the framework of familial and moral relations is a far cry from Nevin's doctrine of baptism, wherein an affirmation of objective sacramental efficacy is in view. In the case of infants, for instance, "The mystical union must be regarded as originating in the divine mind, but not as something abstract; so, also, the justification of infants who die. They cannot realize the mystical union. Yet, if we grant that children are saved, then there is an objective justification before the infant can embrace it."[53]

What stands out in Nevin's view of sin is his insistence that the entire race is included in Adam's very being and that Adam likewise lives in the general life of humanity.[54] The union between Adam and the human

---

51. Ibid.

52. Bushnell, *Christian Nurture*, 41.

53. Erb, *Dr. Nevin's Theology*, 294. Evans, *Imputation and Impartation*, 177–78, is right to point out that Nevin's "concern for objective efficacy created friction at two closely related points—the necessity of faith and the central importance of union with Christ as the mediator of salvation. Here the problem is simple: given the Reformed insistence on faith for regeneration, union with Christ, and justification, what is the efficacy of infant baptism?"

54. Nevin, "Anxious Bench," in Appel, *Life and Work*, 171. Bonomo, *Incarnation and Sacrament*, 72, perceptively comments that "the connection Nevin draws here

race is so intimate that "Our participation in the actual unrighteousness of his life forms the ground of our participation in his guilt and liability to punishment."[55] This way of thinking flows naturally from Nevin's emphasis on universal humanness and the necessity of being united to Christ, who as the second Adam, gathers all of humanity into his person and transforms the race. The distinction can be seen most clearly in Nevin's views on imputation, particularly in contrast to the Federal Headship models espoused by Hodge and the Princeton tradition. As Nevin contends,

> Men have been one before they became many; and as many, they are still one. We have a perfect right then to say that Adam's sin is imputed to his posterity. Only let us not think of a mere outward transfer in the case. Against such imputation the objection commonly made to the doctrine has force. It would be to substitute a fiction for a fact. No imputation of that sort is taught in the Bible. But the imputation of Adam's sin to his posterity involves no fiction. It is counted to them simply because it is theirs in fact.[56]

For Nevin, humanity was guilty of sin not only by virtue of inherited guilt from its representative, Adam, but because humanity *really* and *actually* sinned in Adam. "How can that be imputed or reckoned to any man on the part of God which does not belong to him in reality?"[57]

> The judgment of God must ever be according to truth. He cannot reckon to any one an attribute or quality which does not belong to him in fact. He cannot declare him to be in a relation or state which is not actually his own but the position merely of another. A simply external imputation here the pleasure and purpose of God to place to the account of one what has been done by another will not answer . . . A merely outward constitution, making

---

between Adam's first sin and the corruption of the race is one of the key elements of his thought that distinguishes it from the system of Schleiermacher. Schleiermacher held that no significant change took place within human nature on account of the first sin committed (and whether or not Adam and Eve were really historical figures was of little importance to him). For Schleiermacher, original sin is the tendency rooted deep within all men for the passion of the flesh—which was present within humanity even before the first sin was committed—to overcome and drown out the potential for God-consciousness. Christ therefore, according to Schleiermacher, came as the ideal man in order to restore this God-consciousness in humanity."

55. Nevin, *Mystical Presence*, 189.
56. Ibid., 155.
57. Ibid., 189.

him to be one with us in law simply, and giving us an interest in his righteousness only as if it were our own, while it is not our own in fact, cannot satisfy our sense of truth and right . . .[58]

Hodge objects, "We had no being before our existence in this world; and that we should have acted before we existed is an absolute impossibility."[59] The contrast here between Nevin and Hodge is helpful not only to show divergence in views regarding guilt's transmission or imputation to the human race, but also to reiterate the fundamental differences between the idealist Nevin and his nominalist contemporaries. For Hodge and the majority of the Princeton tradition, the fall of man (and indeed the redemption of man) starts with the individual, Adam. Adam serves in this capacity as a representative for the whole race, which, by virtue of imputation, now bears the guilt that he incurred. By contrast, Nevin proposes an ontological, participatory link between Adam the individual and the human race as a whole. In the case of Adam and Christ, Nevin says in effect that an insistence upon "imputation" should take into account the whole Adam and the whole Christ, not merely their respective legal statuses.

Both Hodge and Nevin are consistent in their application of the doctrine of imputation. Hodge follows his forensic view whereby believers are declared, by divine fiat, righteous on account of the verdict pronounced over Christ. Christ's righteous verdict is thus imputed to the believer apart from his or her own righteousness. The relationship is representative and legal, not ontological. Nevin stood in determined opposition to this view, arguing, "The imagination that the merits of Christ's life may be sundered from his life itself and conveyed over to his people under this abstract form on the ground of a merely outward legal constitution is unscriptural and contrary to all reason at the same time. The legal union to be of any force for the imputation that is here required must be a life union in the very act of our justification by which the righteousness of Christ is accounted to be ours it becomes ours in fact by our actual insertion into Christ himself . . ."[60]

Nevin, therefore, offers an alternative view of imputation and indeed of justification to his reformed contemporaries and the majority of

---

58. Ibid., 189.

59. Hodge, *Systematic Theology*, 2:222–25. Cited also by DiPuccio, *Interior Sense*, 174.

60. Nevin, *Mystical Presence*, 190.

his predecessors. While the degree to which Nevin is within the boundaries of Reformed orthodoxy on this point needs attention, the intended focus here is upon the social, anthropological, and ecclesiological implications of Nevin's project.[61] Seemingly without fail, Nevin is adamant in his emphasis upon the ideal and the whole, whether with respect to the church, its sacraments, or the finer tenets of Reformed soteriology. It is important to remember that the more pivotal shifts in these areas of theology not only represent drastic implications for Christian worldview, but had, in fact, resulted in earth shattering societal transformation at the time of the Reformation. So how is Nevin to be discussed in relation to his reformed predecessors? Where do his views overlap with other theologians and traditions? To these questions we now turn.

---

61. On the comparison of Nevin's soteriology with that of others in the broader Reformed tradition, see Evans, *Imputation and Impartation*.

5

Nevin in Conversation, Part One—
Nevin and the West

Liturgy, Natural Law, and the Two Kingdoms

ONE OF THE MORE intriguing aspects of Nevin's theology is its unique way of penetrating not only the methods and content of his own Calvinistic tradition, but also traditions beyond the scope of his Reformation heritage.[1] For this reason, it is always instructive in the case of Nevin to consider whether and to what degree he can be located within various streams of intellectual and theological expression. A brief consideration of the political theology of the Reformation, for example, provides yet another way to examine the extent to which Nevin takes up or discards the tradition of his forbears. In addition, Nevin can be appropriately implicated (to varying degrees) in the tradition of Aquinas, Eastern Orthodoxy, and the more recent Radical Orthodoxy. The present chapter, constituting part one of this discussion, will principally focus on Nevin and the Reformation tradition. The following chapter will consider points of engagement with those traditions which have something to add to the discussion, but which do not so easily come to the fore.[2]

NEVIN AND THE REFORMATION

Nevin, reared a Presbyterian and having served for many years in the German Reformed Church, would seemingly fit well into the American

---

1. Littlejohn, *Quest for Reformed Catholicity*, demonstrates this point remarkably well.

2. I would like to thank Robbie Crouse for offering a detailed review and constructive criticism of an early draft of this chapter. His comments proved to be indispensable in developing the final product.

Reformed tradition, and certainly within the boundaries of Reformed orthodoxy. And yet, such cannot be so easily assumed. From the outset, the influence of German idealism upon Nevin and the Mercersburg tradition resulted in what was not only a marked difference from Hodge and other theologians immersed in Common Sense Realism, but also a departure from Reformed scholasticism and, on some matters of import, the earliest of Lutheran and Reformed theological expression.

At the close of chapter four, one of the crucial differences between Nevin and his predecessors was noted, namely, their respective approaches to the doctrine of justification.[3] But what of the remaining principles of the Reformation? If shifts in the doctrine of justification, as well as in liturgy, sacraments, and ecclesiology were so earth-shattering in their societal effects at the time of the Reformation, how far reaching are the implications of Nevin's idealist theological hermeneutic?[4]

Eucharist and "Social Body"

In his remarkable study, *The People's Work: A Social History of the Liturgy*, Frank C. Senn describes what happened to the Eucharistic liturgy at the hands of the reformers as "the dissolution of the social body in the reformation communion."[5] Simply put, despite the fact that the reformers were building on a long tradition of Eucharistic ritual fellowship, they were unable to maintain the social bonds through Eucharistic communion that had existed in the medieval church. For one, that the Lutheran, Reformed, and Anabaptist could not agree on the nature of the sacramental elements was no mere matter of theory or abstract speculation,

---

3. Along with revolutionary shifts in ecclesiology and the sacraments, the early Lutheran and Reformed doctrines of justification resulted in a new sense of freedom and individualism. No longer would the layperson be reliant solely upon the visible church for his salvation; rather, justification by faith meant a personal assurance previously unknown to the Christian in most parts of the world. The assertion, moreover, that all Christians share in Christ's priesthood and the accompanying erasure of the notion that the clergy retained a position superior to the laity had radically and irrevocably changed the face of the Christian church. See Burns and Goldie, *Cambridge History*, 166.

4. As Bradstock, "The Reformation," 62, comments, "Luther's rediscovery of the doctrine of justification through faith may well be understood as a 'spiritual experience,' yet any appreciation of its impact will be at best partial if it takes no account of its political and ecclesiological repercussions."

5. Senn, *People's Work*, 183.

as the relationship between the sacramental and ecclesial body had had profound implications for how and why the church assembled.

Along these lines, especially among the Anabaptists, the Reformation saw the emergence of a type of memorialism that made participation in the eucharistic assembly of less consequence, as the bread and wine were now treated as ordinary elements. Lutherans were not immune to the dissolution of the body either, however, as Luther's expectation that greater availability of sacrament to the public would foster stronger communal fellowship had not worked out as planned.[6] No doubt in frustration, he suggested that a third communion service be held besides the Latin and German masses—one not "held in a public place for all sorts of people."[7] At Geneva, Calvin attempted to remedy this problem (among others) by pushing for frequent communion, but could not budge the civil magistrate beyond authorizing quarterly celebrations. Senn sums up the Reformation circumstances well: "The connection between Communion and community in popular thinking was undermined by the more individualistic piety inherited from the late Middle Ages combined with practices espoused by the Reformation, including failure to ritualize public reconciliation, fencing the table, an emphasis on hearing the word and its architectural requirements, and the sanctification of civil government."[8]

It is important to note how Nevin shares with the architects of the Reformation this concern for sacramental and ecclesiological unity. He shares this sentiment not only by virtue of his desire for the church to be a community governed by the wholeness of incarnation and Eucharist,

---

6. Wannenwetsch points out the political nature of Luther's eucharistic theology in Luther's "Concerning the Blessed Sacrament of the Holy and True Body of Christ and Brotherhoods." In this 1519 treatise, Luther does not argue as much as he assumes that the eucharistic liturgy has vast political implications: "The significance or purpose of this sacrament is the fellowship of all saints, whence it derives its common name *synaxis* or *communio*, that is, fellowship; and *communicare* means to take part in this fellowship, or as we say, to go to the sacrament, because Christ and all saints are one spiritual body, just as the inhabitants of a city are one community and body, each citizen being a member of the other and a member of the entire city. All the saints, therefore, are members of Christ and of the Church, which is a spiritual and eternal city of God, and whoever is taken into this city is said to be received into the community of saints, and to be incorporated into Christ's spiritual body and made a member of Him." Luther, "The Blessed Sacrament," 2:743.7–22, cited by Wannenwetsch, "Liturgy," 85.

7. Martin Luther, "German Mass," 53:64. See Senn, *People's Work*, 184.

8. Senn, *People's Work*, 185.

but also in the way that he draws out the societal implications of eucharistic wholeness versus that of "party spirit" and the "spirit of sect." In the same way that the reformers—and Luther in particular—feared the dissolution of the *ekklesia* at the hands of over-zealous Reformation accomplices, Nevin lamented the way in which American Christians had blindly adopted liberal democracy and republicanism. In both cases, the theological and pastoral difficulty lay in addressing the over-reaction and over-indulgence with respect to the novel principles that had come to the fore.

Calvin, no less, almost certainly had in mind the unity of Christ's body in his efforts to create in Geneva a society which reflected the Apostle Paul's depiction of the church as an organic, life giving body, from which the world's nourishment poured forth. Anticipating Nevin, Calvin sought a model of civil society that was built upon mutual dependence, cooperation, and intercommunion. Earthly citizenship, he believed, should be patterned after heavenly citizenship. For Calvin and Nevin, the social body constitutes a whole from which each part or member finds significance.[9]

The enduring war waged by Nevin in the name of reformed catholicity did not therefore constitute a cultural or theological *novum*. While it was in many ways a revolutionary theological advance for his time and place, the history of the Reformation demonstrates quite clearly that Nevin was well within the broader concerns of his Reformation ancestors. Were the causes, circumstances, or conflicts identical? Of course not. But the desire for a unity in the body of Christ that would necessarily and inevitably reorient the way that society understood its relationship to Christ and his church marked an instance of profound concurrence. The reforms of the liturgy in the sixteenth century resulted in massive societal shifts, particularly in the way of education, welfare, and public vocation. One cannot help but wonder what effects the incarnationally—and to be sure, eucharistically—oriented approach of Mercersburg would have had in the early American republic had Nevin acquired more literary, intellectual, and cultural clout.

---

9. Ronald Wallace, *Calvin, Geneva*, 117.

Natural Law

Despite the fact that Calvin never set out to develop a systematic formulation of natural law, the doctrine remained an important feature of his theology.[10] Calvin believed that natural law had been present in creation prior to the fall of mankind, and though in his fallen state mankind is unable to entirely comprehend this natural law, he is still bound to obey it since there is still a universal knowledge of the creator:

> As to the will, its depravity is but too well known. Therefore, since reason, by which man discerns between good and evil, and by which he understands and judges, is a natural gift, it could not be entirely destroyed; but being partly weakened and partly corrupted, a shapeless ruin is all that remains . . . Since man is by nature a social animal, he is disposed, from natural instinct, to cherish and preserve society; and accordingly we see that the minds of all men have impressions of civil order and honesty. Hence it is that every individual understands how human societies must be regulated by laws, and also is able to comprehend the principles of those laws.[11]

Nevin ostensibly verifies a natural law theory similar to that of the reformers, not least in his essay, "The Wonderful Nature of Man," in which he writes, "the actual structure of the world . . . is plainly a single system throughout, subject everywhere to the presence of a common law, pervaded universally by the power of a common idea or thought, and reaching always, with inward restless nisus, toward a common end."[12] The teleological thrust Nevin uses is particularly reminiscent of Calvin, though, as will become clear, it also constitutes a significant departure when understood in the broader context of Nevin's thought. DiPuccio characterizes Nevin's "natural law" as follows:

> Natural law, then, constitutes the ground of all phenomena. So, for example, all trees are in fact manifestations (that is, "instantiations") of one archetypal law or idea we call "tree." This, in turn,

---

10. See Grabill, *Rediscovering the Natural Law*, 91. Grabill adds, "Calvin's understanding of the faculties of intellect and will in both their pre- and post-lapsarian states, taken together with the importance attributed to conscience as an intellectual habit that grasps and acts upon the precepts of the moral law, places his discussion squarely within the scholastic natural-law tradition, and . . . quite possibly even in the realist trajectory of that tradition." Ibid., 92.

11. Calvin, *Institutes*, 2.2.12–13.

12. Nevin, "Wonderful Nature of Man," 516.

is part of the vegetable kingdom, which is subsumed under the idea of organic matter, etc. Natural laws, therefore, are not only objective realities, but the unified source of natural phenomena. The unity implicit in the ideal is bodied forth by a corresponding unity in nature. There is a difference between the ideal and nature however: Whereas the ideal includes all *potential* phenomena, nature includes only *actual* phenomena.[13]

It is, therefore, difficult to draw a direct line from the reformers to Nevin on the issue of natural law. Part of this difficulty lies in the fact that the debate over which tradition of American theology marks the true heirs of Reformed theology is far from settled. While Nevin's heavily romanticized emphasis on the will, the emotions, and the organic relationship of mankind to the natural world necessarily opposes a rationalism that Calvin would have likewise opposed, this is far from saying that the two theologians advanced a common view of natural law. Paul Helm's description of how Calvin fit into the natural law tradition of Aquinas is analogous to how one might understand Nevin in relation to Calvin, namely, as "a contented occupant of a general climate of thought of which [Calvin] was a distinguished member, but also someone who did not hesitate to depart from elements in this climate of thought when he judged this to be necessary."[14]

More specifically, Nevin is reticent to articulate the relationship of natural law to sin and to temporal rule in strictly metaphysical terms. He is unwilling, in other words, to stipulate a point of reference for understanding natural law that is not in some sense rooted in the continuous, organic development of history and mankind. This is undoubtedly in part due to the influence of Nevin's hermeneutical categories, particularly his idealist, hierarchical view of reality, in this case deriving from Kant as much as his other more traditional predecessors.[15] Such prompts Nevin to place an inordinate emphasis on the will and the subjective dimension of human existence in relationship to the perceived natural world.

---

13. DiPuccio, *Interior Sense*, 168.

14. Helm, "Calvin and Natural Law," 10. (I have replaced "Aquinas" with "Calvin" in brackets.)

15. See, for example, the notes compiled from Nevin's "Ethics" lectures in Appel, *Life and Work*, 689.

It is thus with respect to the role of the human mind and will that Nevin either departs from or redirects the Reformed understanding of natural law. This redirection can be seen throughout various tenets of Nevin's theology, but in the present case emerges once again in his "Wonderful Nature of Man":

> But the very conception of will implies and involves the contrary of this. It is, by its very constitution, a self-determining power. It is no blind, necessary force, like the laws of nature, but a free, spontaneous activity, which knows itself, and moves itself optionally its own way; giving rise thus to a whole universe of relations, interests, actions and systems of action, which but for such origination could have no existence whatever, and which, however it may be joined with the constitution of nature, and made to rest upon it in some sense as a basis, is nevertheless in fact a new world altogether of far higher and far more glorious character.[16]

While the Calvinist underpinnings of Nevin's thought provide the necessary structures for constructing a version of Reformed natural law theory, Nevin instead opts to emphasize mankind's moral and spiritual role in relation to the natural world. To be sure, it is not clear as to what degree Nevin's language of "natural world" or "law of nature" can even be implicated in terms of an earlier Reformed natural law theory. What is more, while Calvin viewed the spiritual and temporal spheres as conterminal and the visible church as a mixed body of these spheres, Nevin's *telos* for these spheres is in fact the visible, albeit eschatological, church. Therefore, Nevin's model, in which the state finds its completion in the visible church, resonates with Calvin's eschatology at points but in the final analysis retains too much of a Hegelian tone. Nevin, in this way, (perhaps inadvertently) joined other Romanticists by challenging the metaphysical foundation of natural law, replacing analogies between the physical and the moral world with a newfound emphasis on humanity's subjective freedom and power, principles which he believed would alter the very course of nature's "laws."[17]

The Two Kingdoms

In many respects anticipating the thought of Calvin and other reformers, Luther combated the assumptions of Rome by advocating for a

---

16. Nevin, "Wonderful Nature of Man," 525.
17. Steuer, "Nature," 793.

distinction between the spiritual and temporal kingdoms.[18] "These two kingdoms must be sharply distinguished," he wrote, "and both be permitted to remain; the one to produce piety, and the other to bring about external peace and prevent evil deeds; neither is sufficient in the world without the other."[19] Luther's doctrine of the two kingdoms re-

18. For Luther, Calvin, and the majority of the early Reformed theological tradition, it was understood that the Christian occupies both spiritual and temporal kingdoms as one whose citizenship is simultaneously in heaven and on earth. The visible church, moreover, was understood as being under jurisdiction of the visible, temporal kingdom and thus the protection of the magistrate. This is evident, among other instances, in the case of the Schmalkaldic League and in Calvin's calling upon the King of France for protection of the church. It is important to understand, however, that for the majority of the early reformers, the development of a two kingdoms theory does not correspond to the modern church-state paradigm as neatly as one might suspect. Rather, a more accurate account of the theory distinguishes between the invisible, spiritual kingdom of heaven and the visible kingdom of earth.

19. Luther, "Secular Authority," 371. Luther's "two kingdoms" theory was in some measure rooted in Augustine's political theology. Such is evident in Luther's "Secular Authority," a treatise in which the reformer advances an Augustinian approach that, while anticipating his reformed heirs, demonstrates Luther's willingness to draw clearer lines between the two kingdoms: "We must divide all the children of Adam into two classes; the first belong to the kingdom of God, the second to the kingdom of the world. Those belonging to the kingdom of God are all true believers in Christ and are subject to Christ . . . All who are not Christians belong to the kingdom of the world and are under the law . . . For this reason God has ordained two governments; the spiritual, which by the Holy Spirit under Christ makes Christians and pious people, and the secular, which restrains the unchristian wicked so that they must needs keep the peace outwardly, even against their will." Luther, "Secular Authority," 368, 370. One of the difficulties encountered when trying to understand Luther's view of church and state and the two kingdoms theory in particular is the fact that his thinking on the subject seems to shift over a short period of time. In his 1520 "Address to the Christian Nobility of the German Nation," Luther counters the subordination of secular authority to spiritual authority as well as the primacy of papal jurisdiction over secular jurisdiction. He does so by insisting that all Christians are priests by baptism, the radical implication being that the spiritual/temporal distinction is only in terms of vocation; the clergy has no unique ontological status and is thus subject to temporal, civil law just like everyone else. In his 1523 "On the Limits of Secular Authority," Luther further nuances his approach to the temporal/spiritual distinction by seeking to divide those who belong to the Kingdom of God from those who are of the Kingdom of the World. "All those who truly believe in Christ belong to God's kingdom . . . Now: these people need neither secular sword nor law." Here, the shift in Luther's two kingdoms paradigm lies in the fact that Kingdom of God is conceived as an ideal society which has not been perfectly realized in the temporal world. This is conducive to his doctrine of *simul iustus et peccator* because the human being is understood as not requiring worldly authority but submitting to it nonetheless while living simultaneously in both kingdoms. See Hoelzl and Ward, *Religion and Political Thought*, 66–67.

sulted in a system in which princes were not to personally involve their office in crafting doctrine or worship, but they surely were involved in financing, defending, and promoting certain visible churches to the exclusion of others.[20]

In Luther's judgment, then, God has ordained different means for each of the two "kingdoms" in order for them to perform and fulfill their respective roles. The temporal kingdom is enacted through princes, magistrates, and legislation ensured by the sword. Those in positions of secular authority are therefore administrators of divine origin, despite their personal piety or relationship to the visible church. To be sure, for Luther, the temporal kingdom operates on different principles from that of the spiritual kingdom since the sword ought not to be used to enforce the Christian's obedience to God. God's word, rather, speaks for itself and demands its own allegiance. This dynamic is possible because the Christian is indwelt by the Spirit and therefore led to act righteously. "A good tree," writes Luther, with an organic metaphor that Nevin would have appreciated, "brings forth good fruit by nature, without compulsion; is it not madness to prescribe laws to an apple-tree that it shall bear apples and not thorns?"[21]

Calvin's two kingdoms theory, while sharing with Luther the basic spiritual/temporal division, undoubtedly eventuated in a different overall approach to church and state. Luther's approach eventuated in a view where the church is to be regarded as mostly, if not entirely, distinct from the state, even taking a passive disposition.[22] This had perhaps not been the intention of Luther's earliest formulations, but it nevertheless became the prevailing Lutheran paradigm. Calvin's view lacks the apparent passivity and cynicism of both the Lutherans and Anabaptists with respect to the church/state relationship, opting rather for a scheme in which both the spiritual and temporal orders work toward a common end.[23]

---

20. A corollary to this is the fact that since all Christian laypersons were priests, the Reformers saw no problem with allowing princes to function as Christians in their particular vocation and to make use of their superior ordering abilities in the visible church.

21. Acton, *History of Freedom*, 120.

22. "At the level of church response to the state he has often been blamed for encouraging 'quietism' on the part of Christian, even if in the face of tyranny and injustice." Bradstock, "The Reformation," 66.

23. As Schaff explains, Calvin affirms "the supremacy of Christ over both Church and State. Calvin united the spiritual and secular powers as the two arms of God, on

Calvin likewise distinguishes between the spiritual and political kingdoms and follows Augustine and Luther by conceiving of the two kingdoms as overlapping in the life of man. The spiritual kingdom lays claim insofar as one's conscience is prompted toward piety and obedience to God. The political kingdom instructs man for the sake of his just living in society. As Calvin explains, "These are usually called the 'spiritual' and the 'temporal' jurisdiction (not improper terms) by which is meant that the former sort of government pertains to the life of the soul, while the latter has to do with the concerns of the present life ... For the former resides in the inner mind, while the latter regulates only outward behavior. The one we may call the spiritual kingdom, the other, the political kingdom."[24] Calvin is careful to insist that the two kingdoms not be confused, even in theory. They should be "examined separately," so much so that "while one is being considered, we must call away and turn aside the mind from thinking about the other." Both realms of authority reside in man and are simultaneously submissive to "different kings."[25]

However, while the kingdoms ought not to be confused, it does not follow for Calvin that the kingdoms have no relationship. "They are quite distinct," he writes, "but in no way incompatible with each other."[26] This principle is most profoundly demonstrated in the prefatory address to Calvin's *Institutes of the Christian Religion*, where he calls upon the king's protection of the church: "The characteristic of a true sovereign is, to acknowledge that, in the administration of his kingdom, he is a minister of God."[27] Calvin implemented his approach in Geneva, where it became clear that Calvin acknowledged and promoted the necessary, if not inevitable, confluence and interdependence of the temporal and spiritual kingdoms. He was guided by the concept of covenant, by which the relationship between God and man as well as man and man was to be understood. Thus, both tables of God's law were to be respected by

---

the assumption of the obedience of the State to the law of Christ ... In the nineteenth century, when the State has assumed a mixed religious and non-religious character, and is emancipating itself more and more from the rule of any church organization or creed, Calvin would, like his modern adherents in French Switzerland, Scotland, and America, undoubtedly be a champion of the freedom and independence of the Church and its separation from the State." Schaff, *History of the Christian*, 7:263.

24. Calvin, *Institutes*, 3.19.15.
25. Ibid.
26. Hopfl, *Luther and Calvin*, 49. See also Bradstock, "The Reformation," 72.
27. Calvin, *Institutes*, Prefatory Address.

the temporal sphere.[28] In Geneva, the governing role was relegated to the consistory and elected body of civic and religious officials. This body exercised jurisdiction over a number of matters pertaining to morality, charity and social welfare, and worship.[29]

Nevin acknowledges the existence of "two kingdoms," but would have criticized the Reformation view as one in which the model of society is unnecessarily flattened out (particularly as in Luther's view). For Nevin, to the contrary, the church is fundamentally and ontologically "above" the state, a view that does not emerge among Lutherans or the Reformed. To be sure, Calvin does retain a hierarchical view of church and state insofar as the state's obedience to the "law of Christ" is concerned, but Nevin is perhaps more inclined to see this law of Christ embodied in the visible church than Calvin. In this way, while Nevin's view is too idealist and eschatologically-oriented to be in line with Roman Catholicism, it is still one which subtly but surely diverges from Reformation formulations. Calvin, after all, does not appear to believe, as Nevin does, that the state will be "vanished away in the church."[30] This common affirmation among Mercersburg theologians, therefore, marks a slight departure from their Reformed predecessors in a number of ways, not least with respect to the theoretical basis of the church/state relationship.

The state, in Nevin's judgment, cannot be understood according to its "external form." Such only provides clues or symptoms to its internal life, the principles which serve as fundamental to its constitution. The internal life of the state—that is, its organic constitution—is only properly understood when considered through the lens of the church, the end for which the state was created. In this way, Nevin understands the relationship between the state, mankind, and the church to be one

---

28. Amos, "Reformation as a Revolution," 233.

29. See Gamble, *Calvin's Thought on Economic*. See also Witte, *God's Joust, God's Justice*, 219. Thus, Calvin presumed that the magistrate retained significant—thought not total—jurisdiction with respect to the church, namely, by providing for their safety, freedom, and protection from heresy. God's design for the civil sphere, he wrote, is "to cherish and protect the outward worship of God, to defend sound doctrine of piety and the position of the church, to adjust our life to the society of men, to form our social behavior to civil righteousness, to reconcile us with one another, and to promote general peace and tranquility." Calvin, *Institutes*, 2.2.13.

30. See extended quote below. Nevin, "Early Christianity, Article III," in Yrigoyen, *Catholic and Reformed*, 297.

which turns the Hegelian scheme on its head. This reversal is noted by Nevin in his repudiation of Rothe, who, with Hegel, believes that "The ultimate and only fully normal order of man's existence is the state, the organism of his moral relations . . ."[31] Contrary to Hegel and especially Rothe, Nevin insists,

> The overshadowing embrace of a higher economy—the absolutely supernatural—we must believe rather to have been needed from the first to complete its process in the life of man . . . The church, as the medium of its work, is more than a provisionary institute simply for perfecting the scheme of the state, the highest form of man's life on the basis of nature as now stands. The true destination of this lies beyond the present economy of nature in the sphere of the supernatural, in an order of things that fairly outleaps and transcends the whole system out of which grows now the constitution of political kingdoms and states . . . The church will not lose itself in the state; but it will be the state rather that shall be found then to have vanished away in the church.[32]

This sentiment is clearly witnessed to by the broader Mercersburg tradition. In a very Nevinesque passage of the *Mercersburg Review*, Moses Keiffer wrote, "It is only possible, however, for the State to attain a full consciousness of her dependence through that medium in which God has given the fullest revelation of himself to the world, i.e., the Church."[33] He continued, moreover, "It is in the Church, and in the Church alone, that the State can reach her ideal perfection. Christianity being the highest form of humanity, we may safely say, that the Church is the perfection of the State."[34]

Nevertheless, with regard to temporal authority, commonality can be found among Nevin and his Reformed tradition. Nevin believes that the organic relation between the state and the inner life of humanity, in order to be sustained as a consistent system, necessitates that office bearers of the state be vested with a sacred responsibility. Aligning himself with Calvin, he explains,

> Institutions and efforts, which propose to do something towards a proper provision for this great religious and social interest, are

---

31. Ibid.
32. Ibid., 299.
33. Kieffer, "Church and State," 575.
34. Ibid., 577.

always entitled to respect; and so far as they may be found suitable and sufficient for their proposed end, they may well challenge the sympathy and support of all true patriots, as well as of all true Christians. They should feel, that in lending their help to efforts, which are made for providing and maintaining in this nation a competent and efficient Gospel ministry, they are rendering to their country and their race the highest kind of service of which they are capable.[35]

Nevin, in this respect, was not alone among his American idealist theological peers. As Keiffer wrote, "The civil ruler does not merely bear the sword of utilitarian, but of vindictive justice. Lawyers, whose office it is to unfold the hidden mysteries of law and truth, are oracles of God."[36] In this instance, among others, one finds affinity between Mercersburg and Reformed political theology, particularly in the Calvinist vein. Nevin, after all, having been raised in a conservative Old School Presbyterianism, was surely familiar with the Westminster Confession on this point, that the civil magistrate "hath authority, and it is his duty, to take order, that unity and peace be preserved in the Church, that the truth of God be kept pure and entire; that all blasphemies and heresies be suppressed; all corruptions and abuses in worship and discipline prevented or reformed; and all the ordinances of God duly settled, administered, and observed."[37]

Nevin's hierarchical ontology marks a departure from the traditional two kingdoms model, but this does not mean that the two models are entirely incompatible. Nevin's theology of incarnation, and specifically the union of the two natures of Christ, renders the possibility of a viable avenue for the entry of two kingdoms theory into Nevin's church/state philosophy and vice versa. On this point, O'Donovan is especially helpful.

> ... as in speaking of the Incarnation itself we cannot affirm the hypostatic union without the two natures, so with the Kingdom of God we cannot conceive the *henosis* of political and spiritual without the duality of the two terms held together in it. That is why those who have asserted that a conception of Two Kingdoms is fundamental to Christian political thought have spoken truly, though at great risk of distorting the truth if they simply leave it

---

35. Nevin, "German Character," in Appel, *Life and Work*, 111.
36. Kieffer, "Church and State," 575.
37. *Westminster Confession of Faith* (1646), 23.3.

at that. The unity of the kingdoms, we may say, is the heart of the Gospel, their duality is the pericardium. Proclaiming the unity of God's rule in Christ is the task of Christian witness; understanding the duality is the chief assistance rendered by Christian reflection.[38]

Insofar as the duality of the two kingdoms can be rooted in the language of the incarnation, Nevin would appreciate the sentiment of this Augustinian-via-Reformation doctrine. Nevin is certainly not a monist when it comes to church and state, and he recognizes that Christians simultaneously occupy different spheres of life. Again, however, despite appreciation for the hypostatic tone of this two kingdoms theory (if it were in fact to be proposed in this way), Nevin would adamantly maintain a greater emphasis on the visible church, thus rendering the *simul* of Christian existence in a slightly different light, emphasizing the hierarchical and ontological dimensions of this existence more than the forensic and moral.

OUTLIERS: NEVIN THE THOMIST? NEVIN THE NEOCALVINIST?

Nevin the Thomist?

Though certainly situated more firmly in Platonic idealism and Calvinistic eschatology, and despite his rejection of any sort of "static" ontology, Nevin's hierarchical version of reality nevertheless resonates with several aspects of Thomas Aquinas's approach to the natural and supernatural. Following Aristotle, Aquinas held that all things have an immanent purpose that has its origin in the divine: "God not only causes creatures to be. He causes them to be in the specific ways in which they exist and orders them to their specific goals."[39] Accordingly, everything is to be understood according to its participation in the divine, finding its fulfillment when it is "copying God in its own manner, and tending to existence as knowledge in the divine Mind."[40] The goals of humanity in this model constitute an adumbration from lower to higher, that is, the

---

38. O'Donovan, *Desire of the Nations*, 82.

39. Kelly, "Influence of Aquinas' Natural," 108. Cited by Kent Van Till, "Subsidiarity," 613.

40. Milbank and Pickstock, *Truth in Aquinas*, 9. See Leithart, "Medieval Theology," 164.

creaturely level of humanity in its relationship to the rest of creation is raised up by rational ability, faith, and so on.[41]

Despite the fact that Aquinas's ontology is too Aristotelian for Nevin's full appreciation, his insistence upon human freedom and participation in the divine accompanies well Nevin's participationist ontology, particularly insofar as this participation is by way of the church and its sacraments. Following closely his theological anthropology, Nevin insists that it is the life—and here more specifically the will and the mind—of mankind that serves as the avenue for the natural world's redemption. He continues in "The Wonderful Nature of Man,"

> Let it be considered only, for a moment, what this *hyper-physical* economy—the moral world as distinguished from the world of nature—is found to comprehend and contain. It comprises in itself all the powers, functions, and operations of mind; the thinking of men; their purposes and aims; their affections, emotions, and passions; their acts of whatever kind, whether inward only or extending out into the surrounding world; the full unfolding and putting forth, in one word, of all that is involved in their spiritual being. In it are embraced, at the same time, the idea of society, the order of the family, the constitution of the State, the organization finally of the Church; all social, political, and religious relations; all virtues and opposing vices; all human privileges, duties, and rights.[42]

The law of nature is a proleptic type of the true law of human freedom in Christ—the law of a "higher sphere." This lower law of nature anticipates and adumbrates the presence of the higher law. Nevin, to this point, suggests that such was in the mind of the psalmist when he exclaimed, "Forever, O Lord, Thy word is settled in heaven! Thy faithfulness is unto all generations; Thou hast established the earth, and it abideth." He likens this sentiment of the psalmist to those who he believes have sensed "God's glorious moral government mirrored upon them from the contemplation of the natural world."[43]

---

41. As a corollary to this model, Aquinas understands natural law as being prompted by human participation in the eternal law. "By assigning a participatory role to human beings in legislating the eternal law for and to themselves, (he) recognizes the necessity of personal autonomy for authentic moral decisions." Baumgarth and Regan, *Aquinas: On Law, Morality*, 24.

42. Nevin, "Wonderful Nature of Man," 525–26.

43. Ibid., 526–27.

Nevin's "social principle" is also hinted at by the medieval theologian, as Aquinas believes that any social body, whether secular or sacred, necessarily includes another naturally smaller one in a succession of concentric circles.[44] This concentric ring of lesser societies grows naturally from one to the next, each building upon or supporting the other. Aquinas uses the example of a family growing to a village and then to a city and a principality. When functioning harmoniously, this ordering of society permits each person to fill his or her particular goals at appropriate levels. This set of relationships is discernible via the natural law.[45]

The risk of inapt anachronism makes the comparison of Nevin to Thomas Aquinas a difficult one. Yet, despite some important differences in the conclusions of the two theologians, there are some striking hermeneutical similarities. For one, Aquinas would have shied away from Hegel for similar reasons that Nevin did, rejecting Hegel's identification of the real or actual with the rational. For both Aquinas and Nevin, what makes a thing knowable is its universal form. The knowable thing is real and not just phenomenal, escaping pure intellect. The temptation here to align Aquinas and Nevin with Kant is avoided in the fact that both theologians reject Kant's skepticism, insisting rather that what is real and objective can in fact be known.[46]

Nevin the Neocalvinist?

If not two kingdoms theory, perhaps Nevin's approach is more akin to the "sphere sovereignty" doctrine developed by the Dutch reformer Abraham Kuyper.[47] James D. Bratt, who has written extensively on the Dutch Reformed theological tradition, has made this very case. His argument proceeds from the fact that both theologians were indebted to modified German philosophy and that this is particularly evident in their approach to church and state.[48]

---

44. Mueller, "Principle of Subsidiarity," 147.

45. Kent Van Till, "Subsidiarity," 614, citing Thomas Aquinas, *Summa Theologiae* 3, q. 8, q. 1, ad 2.

46. Peterson, *Aquinas: A New Introduction*, xii.

47. This doctrine is conventionally—though not without opposition—located within the legacy of the two kingdoms theory of Reformed theology. VanDrunen, *Natural Law*, 302.

48. See Bratt, "Christian Reformed History," 9–32, esp. 21–25.

In Kuyper's view, each sphere of life has its own legitimacy and its own nature; no sphere is more spiritual or worldly than any other. Whether in family life, economic life, churchly life, sports, or any other sphere, each person can fulfill the "cultural mandate" to "till the earth and keep it."[49] With Nevin and the majority of nineteenth-century American theologians, Kuyper eschewed the notion that society ought to be ordered by a secular, pragmatic politics. The character of local communities and the fabric of the society at large, rather, are inextricably bound to theological and moral issues.[50]

Nevin almost certainly would have agreed with Kuyper's famous dictum that there was "not a square inch in the whole domain of human existence over which Christ ... did not pronounce, 'Mine!'" However, this does not correspond with Nevin's "catholicity" nearly as much as Bratt indicates.[51] As is the case with respect to his earlier Reformed predecessors, Nevin's hierarchical model of reality marks a significant departure from Kuyper. First, Nevin's notions of catholicity and organic unity hardly correspond to the Dutch theologian's insistence upon Christ's lordship over the various spheres found in creation. Additionally, Kuyper employs the term "organic" in relation to "spheres" as a way of positing the mutual dependence and preservation of institutions in society. Each sphere is equally legitimate and equally important.[52] The church, in this model, does not retain the ontological priority that it does or Nevin, who not only believes that Christ pronounces "mine," but also that Christ, in his pronouncement, reconciles all "spheres" to himself through the church.

---

49. Henry Van Til, *Calvinistic Concept of Culture*, 29–30. See also Kent Van Til, "Subsidiarity," 624. I am drawing generously from Kent Van Til, "Subsidiarity," in what follows.

50. Kent Van Til, "Subsidiarity," 620. See also Stackhouse, Preface to *Religion, Pluralism*, xi–xviii, esp. xiii.

51. Bratt, "Christian Reformed History," 24, comments, "Nevin's high-church version stated that 'Christianity is Catholic ... inasmuch as it forms the true and proper wholeness of mankind, the round and full symmetrical cosmos of humanity ...' Anticipating Kuyper's idiom no less them his substance, Nevin said that all the individual conversions wrought by the artificial mechanisms of revival would remain incomplete in themselves until absorbed in the redemption of the organism of humanity as such; which humanity, furthermore, 'includes in its general organization' 'certain orders and spheres of moral existence,' especially the family, the state, and 'the various domestic and civil relations that grow out of them.'"

52. Skillen, *Introduction to Abraham Kuyper*, 21. See Kent Van Til, "Subsidiarity," 621.

Nevin, rather than advocating a model of spheres of church, state, and family, refers more often to lower and higher spheres of existence. The church, for Nevin, holds a unique redemptive role in the world's constitution, and is not merely another institution under Christ's Lordship—it is the very embodiment of Christ's lordship, the "sphere" of salvation, designed to reconcile all other realms of existence unto God.[53]

CONCLUSION

One of the most significant and enduring contributions of early Reformation theology was the necessary development of a new political theology. It is not an overstatement to say that the reformers' rethinking of how various institutions of society should relate to each other has had profound implications for the last half millennium of western civilization. For this reason, if Nevin is to be taken seriously as a theologian in the Reformed tradition, it is important to consider how Nevin both draws from and departs from the various strands of his Reformation heritage on this theme. Nevin, while agreeing with Luther, Calvin, and even the likes of Kuyper that the state exists in order to guarantee freedom and justice for the natural order, does not do so without trying to improve upon this basic conclusion. Nevin found the Roman Catholic doctrine of church and state wanting, but he also sought to infuse the Reformation doctrine with an organicism, historicism, and, accordingly, a romanticized eschatology that is not so clearly assumed among his theological predecessors. The result, as indicated above, is that through the church, "the constitution of grace fulfills and glorifies what the constitution of nature aspires to and dimly recognizes."[54] Therefore, nature (including the state) and the church are not to be seen as developing along parallel trajectories with distinct ends. Redemption, as Nevin explains, "is more than the carrying out of the natural order of the world to any merely natural end;"[55] it is, rather, the fulfillment of the church's mission to raise the natural world into a "higher order of existence" by appropriating it into the new creation through the ministry of word and sacrament.

53. Despite following Kuyper to a great degree, Dooyeweerd may actually serve as a more appropriate neo-Calvinist counterpart for Nevin by insisting on the "inner connection" and "inseparable coherence" of societal structures. As Smith comments, "... this insight implies that the gradual differentiation of distinct institutions and sectors can go wrong if it is not accompanied by their integration into a larger societal cohesion." Smith and Olthuis, *Radical Orthodoxy*, 139.

54. Wentz, *American Theologian*, 76.

55. Nevin, "Early Christianity, Article III," 43.

6

Nevin in Conversation, Part Two— What Has Mercersburg to Do with Moscow and Cambridge?

NEVIN AND SOLOVYOV ON HISTORY, POLITICS, AND INCARNATION

ONLY RECENTLY HAVE INTERPRETERS of Nevin begun to more fully develop the striking resemblance between his theological trajectory and that of Eastern Orthodoxy.[1] The emphases of the Mercersburg theology, including the Incarnation as well as participationist, ontological, and soteriological categories, resonate well with the tenets of Eastern Orthodox ontology and the doctrine of theosis. That this is the case has been demonstrated remarkably well by Littlejohn.[2]

Nevin's Orthodox leanings are quite conspicuous, but are perhaps not entirely coincidental. Over the course of his theological career, Nevin developed a deep interest in Patristic theology, not least the Cappadocians, Athanasius, Cyprian, and Irenaeus. Thus, while evidence is insufficient to suggest that Nevin was directly influenced by (or even significantly exposed to) modern Orthodox theology, it is perhaps not so difficult to see where a common Patristic seed had been sown among him and his Orthodox contemporaries.

---

1. Nevin's theological affinity with the East had been initially noted by one of his contemporaries, Isaac Dorner, in 1868, but it was perhaps due to the lack of resources and engagement with Eastern Orthodoxy among American theologians that this correlation was not more closely examined during Nevin's lifetime. Isaac Dorner, *Liturgical Conflict*, 21, cited by Nichols, *Romanticism*, 159. Nichols is right to point out that Nevin's conception of development would not have been well received by the Orthodox.

2. Littlejohn, *Quest for Reformed Catholicity*, 124–46.

In addition to the common Patristic theological influence, the predominance of German idealism in much of Eastern Orthodox thought in the nineteenth century poses some interesting possibilities for a connection between Nevin and the East. During the nineteenth century, Russia was the recipient of a major influx of German philosophy and theology. German idealism, among other trends, gained a strong foothold in what would become known as the "Russian school." Proving to be one of the most influential thinkers of this school, Vladimir Sergeevich Solovyov, emerged as a brilliant philosopher and Orthodox theologian. Regarded by many as the father of sophiology, it has been said that the whole of Russian religious thought is but a footnote to Solovyov.[3]

The central tenets of Solovyov's theology are Sophia and the humanity of God, the latter of which he understood in terms of divine-human union in the incarnate Christ. Notably, he rendered the principle of the Incarnation in idealistic categories that had been espoused by none other than F. W. J. Schelling, the same philosopher who had likewise provided categories for Nevin's theology. Like Nevin, moreover, Solovyov insisted on tempering German idealism in his affirmation of the divine-human principle of the Incarnation. The two theologians also shared concerns over materialism and rationalism.[4]

Solovyov's approach to theology, history, and politics bears striking resemblance to that of Nevin. Although the two theologians worked completely independent of each other, and in quite different political contexts, the categories in which they thought and the language they employed are remarkably similar. A brief survey of Solovyov's work in relation to Nevin's has two aims for the present study: (1) To more firmly establish Nevin in his intellectual tradition and context, and (2) to offer additional conjecture concerning Nevin's understanding of history and politics in light of the Incarnation.

An insightful essay by Matthew R. Johnson discusses Solovyov's combination of Orthodox theology and Hegelian dialectics.[5] Johnson deals more specifically with the issue of nationalism and the role of the state in light of Solovyov's notion of the transfiguration of the human person and the human community. "For Solovyov," Johnson writes, "the transformation of humanity under the Christian ideal, made manifest

3. Papanikolaou, "Orthodox Christianity," 414–18.
4. Ibid., 414.
5. Johnson, "Nation," 347–55.

through the Incarnation, is a gradual process." In the Incarnation, "the process of human perfection became the world historical task transcending all others; it became the substance of history."[6]

Solovyov's concerns over nationalism, a principle he believes to be most clearly manifest in imperialism, echo Nevin's concerns for "Party Spirit." He writes, "The politics of interest, the aspiration to one's enrichment and to empowerment, which is characteristic of the natural man—is a pagan concern, and resting on this ground, Christian nations return to paganism."[7] The dialectic of nationalism is found in its simultaneous insistence upon both self-determination and the subjugation of others. For both Solovyov and Nevin, the operative principle at work in nationalism and party spirit is materialism.

Such materialistic tendencies in humankind need to be transformed—they need to be, in Nevin's terms, redeemed into a higher order of existence. Although Solovyov employs the language of "deification" to describe this process, Nevin would essentially agree with him that "both material property and self consciousness of the national spirit themselves become positive forces in subordination to higher considerations of Christian duty—real means and tools of the moral good, because the acquisitions of this nation then really go for the use of all others, and its greatness really extols all humanity."[8]

In its restoration of the true humanity, through whom politics can be united to the supernatural order, the Incarnation resolves and transforms social and political existence into a universal. It is important to note that for Solovyov as well as Nevin, this universal does not overthrow human freedom or, for that matter, material particulars. Such principles must persist if there is to be integrity to the union between humanity and divinity. This is, after all, precisely what was demonstrated by the Incarnation. As such, to ascend into the life of the divine, humanity must remain humanity. Solovyov writes,

> A truly Christian culture establishes in all human society and in all its activities the same relationship of the three principles of humanity's being that was realized individually in the person of Christ. As we know, this relationship consists in the free harmonization of the two lower principles (the rational and the mate-

---

6. Ibid., 347–48.
7. Solovyov, "Morality and Politics," 11. Cited by Johnson, "Nation," 350.
8. Solovyov, "Morality and Politics," 13. In Johnson, "Nation," 351.

rial) with the higher, divine principle through their voluntary subordination to it, through their subordination to it not as to a coercive force but as to the good. For such a *free* subordination of the lower principles to the higher one, in order that they may *of themselves* come to recognize the higher principle as the good, requires them to be independent.[9]

And furthermore in "Law and Morality," he explains,

If human society as a union of moral beings cannot only be a natural organism but essentially a spiritual organism, then the development of society, that is, history cannot only be a simple organic process but is also essentially a morally free process psychologically as well, that is a series of individual, conscious, and responsible actions.[10]

The organic process of history is revealed in the Incarnation. History, through this event, comes to terms with the fact that its essence is not to be found in the "mere clashing of individual material interests or vulgar power politics."[11] Rather, it is to be found in the liturgical and sacramental ethics of the church, the presence of the Incarnation in history.

Solovyov, then, rejects dualism in favor of a hierarchy of love, justice, and material welfare. He insists that the "parts" of the hierarchy are in fact part of a greater divine whole, which is the supreme good. The procession within the hierarchy is as follows. From the divine whole, love (in anticipation of its return to the whole) proceeds and finds its expression in the church. Next, justice is expressed in the state rule by law, insisting upon the freedom and rationality of human beings. Finally comes material welfare, manifest in economic initiative. These steps within the hierarchy, Solovyov insists, do not represent authoritarianism, but a dynamic expression of relatedness. This, he believes, is the ideal theocracy.[12] In Paul Valliere's description, "Theocracy is the social and political reflection of the whole of things, but a free, rational being must participate in the whole of things *as* a free, rational being; otherwise he or she strictly speaking does not participate in it."[13]

9. Solovyov, *Lectures on Divine Humanity*, 171.
10. Solovyov, "Law," 150–51.
11. Johnson, "Nation," 347.
12. Valliere, *Modern Russian Theology*, 132–33.
13. Ibid., 134.

The extent to which Solovyov's hierarchical scheme or broader approach in general can assist scholars in their interpretation of Nevin is indefinite. A couple of observations, however, should be made. First, Solovyov's broader theology reflects a hierarchy similar to Nevin's. Where Solovyov implicates welfare, justice, and love, Nevin employs the natural, humankind, and the Incarnation. Solovyov, in this respect, has demonstrated quite clearly what is perhaps more implicit in Nevin's thought, namely that the church is in a sense above the political realm, not beside or parallel to it. Generally, modern interpreters of Nevin have not made this point clearly enough, emphasizing what God does in the world through the church and the state (by virtue of the Incarnation) without recognizing the church's distinct, transcendent role as a medium of salvation, the very embodiment of the Incarnation.

Second, Solovyov's rejection of strict dualisms, on account of the uniting principle of the Incarnation, marks yet another example of a theologian who rejected substance dualism despite his indebtedness to German idealism. Scholars who question whether or not Nevin did in fact eschew dualism have another example in Solovyov of how this feat is approached theologically. Solovyov insisted that the material is in fact necessary for the embodiment of the divine. In political-theological terms, a theocracy that adequately represents the whole of things, by contrast, will achieve "the mutual spiritualization of matter and materialization of spirit, or the inner agreement and balance of both principles."[14] Nevin likely could not have put it better himself. This necessary mutual union of matter and spirit is precisely why, for both theologians, the Incarnation was such a profound event. It is an event which casts light upon all the seemingly contradictory principles of history, bringing them all into union in the life of God himself. This is not to say, of course, that both theologians are completely innocent of a dualistic tendency at various points in their theology. It is to say, rather, that theologians ranging from Russia to Mercersburg, Pennsylvania, were fully aware of their Hegelian tradition and the pitfalls therein, and that Nevin and Solovyov, among others, were able to modify this tradition by implicating the Incarnation of Jesus Christ as paramount in their theological systems.

---

14. Ibid., 134.

IS NEVIN RADICALLY ORTHODOX?

The chiefly Cambridge-driven theological movement (or perhaps more appropriately, "theological sensibility"[15]) known as Radical Orthodoxy seeks to deploy a vision "to criticize modern society, culture, politics, art, science and philosophy with an unprecedented boldness."[16] The framework employed to this end is "'participation' as developed by Plato and reworked by Christianity, because any alternative configuration perforce reserves a territory independent of God."[17] This project has prompted a number of alarming concerns among those of Reformed theological persuasion, especially what is viewed by many as Radical Orthodoxy's subtle shifting of participationist categories away from a Christological center.[18] Nevertheless, the effort towards meaningful engagement between these two groups ensues, most notably in *Radical Orthodoxy and the Reformed Tradition* and, to a lesser degree, in Smith's *Introducing Radical Orthodoxy*. Though these efforts have been instructive and beneficial, the Reformed and Radical Orthodoxy camps have largely been unable to find common ground via the likes of Augustine, Calvin, Kuyper, and associated theologians. Finer points of convergence have been established, and such has led to fruitful scholarship, but the fundamental departure of Reformed orthodoxy from the type of metaphysic and ontology to which Radical Orthodoxy adheres has stifled much of the dialogue.

My interest in this theological dialogue between Radical Orthodoxy and the Reformed is piqued largely by my belief that John Nevin has much to offer to the enduring conversation between these two camps. To be sure, Nevin is not to be counted among those firmly within the

---

15. This insight was offered by James K. A. Smith during a forum at the American Academy of Religion in Atlanta, GA, Oct 30, 2010.

16. Milbank, et al., *Radical Orthodoxy*, 2.

17. Ibid., 3.

18. For instance, Holcumb insists that "For both John and Paul . . . creation's participation in the divine has its center of gravity *in* Christ. According to Reformed theology, we do not just participate, we participate *in him* . . . Radical Orthodoxy strongly emphasizes what is universal, general, and speculative at the expense of affirming and defending the particularity of divine redemption in Christ. The scope of participation is wide, but the center is unfocused." Holcomb, "Being Bound," 250. Horton concludes that Reformed theology and Radical Orthodoxy "operate in different universes of discourse," that is, "Reformed theology inhabits an ethical-historical-eschatological rather than a metaphysical-ontological-speculative atmosphere." Horton, "Participation," 132.

stream of Radical Orthodoxy. Most significantly, Radical Orthodoxy lacks the confessional and ecclesiological boundaries upon which Nevin was so insistent. Nevin would not go as far as some advocates of Radical Orthodoxy in saying that there is no such thing as the "secular."[19] Granted, the boundaries between "sacred" and "secular" are far more permeable in Nevin's theology than most of his contemporaries would allow, but to eschew the possibility of the secular is a notion quite foreign to Nevin's theology.

This is not to say that the Reformed tradition does not also have its qualms with Nevin. To the degree that the Reformed have followed the tradition of Hodge and his scholastic predecessors, there remains a trenchant criticism of Nevin's soteriological categories, principally concerning his rejection of both Calvinist predestinarianism and imputation, his unwillingness to adopt strictly forensic categories as advanced by scholasticism (his forensic categories are framed within a greater emphasis on ontology), and his "high" view of the visible church and its sacraments in relation to salvation.

The basic tenets of Radical Orthodoxy's critique of modernity insofar as they relate to Nevin's theological project may be summarized as follows: Radical Orthodoxy, via critique of modernity's adaptation of the univocity of being, rejects an atomistic ontology of immanence in favor of a participatory ontology. This metaphysic is constructed in terms of an analogy of being in which materiality finds itself suspended from the transcendent, so as not to dissolve into nothingness. With respect to the church, Radical Orthodoxy builds upon this metaphysic of participation in an effort to reestablish the church's sacramental identity and power as a means to incorporating the life of the world into the life of the di-

---

19. Horton rightly points out that Radical Orthodoxy's "account of participation at many junctures blurs the distinction between Creator and creature, redeemer and redeemed, cult and culture . . . With its focus on the mystical union with Christ, Reformed theology is able to avoid the particular version of extrinicism that Milbank criticizes and caricatures without surrendering important distinctions between Christ and the believer, the believer and the church, the church and the cosmos." Horton, "Participation," 132.

vine.[20] The result is a view towards a sociality and a polis where the true humanity finds itself in communion, not in autonomy.[21]

While heterodox with respect to both Reformed and Radical Orthodox perspectives, Nevin advances a Christianized platonic metaphysic, insisting upon a hierarchical ontology that not only stipulates a doctrine of participation for all of creation, but a doctrine of participation that unwaveringly and staunchly insists upon a participation *in Christ*. As such, Nevin's idealist, Christocentric hermeneutic indicates that he may be a viable, palatable alternative for Reformed theologians who desire to engage Radical Orthodoxy, but who have yet to find the most appropriate avenue for doing so. Here, then, my aim is to simply introduce John W. Nevin to the conversation with hopes that he might be included in the ongoing dialogue.[22]

Platonism, Incarnation, and the Goodness of Creation

Radical Orthodoxy aims to articulate an ontology that is at once "more incarnate" and "more platonic," themes which, as Smith rightly notes, appear to be at odds in the eyes of those in the Reformed tradition.[23] Unquestionably, the Reformed tradition has consistently criticized the apparent dualisms of Platonism. Thus, if the Reformed tradition is to

---

20. As Yong explains, Radical Orthodoxy maintains (1) A rejection of modernist notions of autonomous reason; (2) accordingly, the removal of dualistic boundaries (i.e., between faith and reason as well as sacred and secular) that prohibit religious engagement with politics, economics, and social life; (3) the reestablishment of the church's sacramental identity and power as a means to incorporating the life of the world into the divine life and work of God. These points of emphasis have been selected from among those set forth by Yong, "Radically Orthodox," 233–50. James Smith, in his introduction to Radical Orthodoxy, attempts a Reformed rendition of the movement. To this end, he begins by presenting five themes of Radical Orthodoxy: A critique of modern Liberalism; post-secularity; participation and materiality; sacramentality, liturgy, and aesthetics; and cultural critique and transformation. James Smith, *Introducing Radical Orthodoxy*, 70–80.

21. As Cavanaugh writes, "Humankind was created for communion." Cavanaugh, "The City," 182.

22. The current study is not designed for rigorous engagement with Radical Orthodoxy. Such an engagement, as shown by the critics of the movement, requires an in depth and rather incisive analysis of a wide range of topics. As such, few have been able to capture the far-reaching implications of Radical Orthodoxy's project. The goal here, rather, is to introduce Nevin and his thought in light of the basic principles and intentions behind Radical Orthodoxy.

23. James Smith, *Introducing Radical Orthodoxy*, 197.

constructively engage with Radical Orthodoxy, the viability of Platonic metaphysics and ontology must be carefully considered. Are the fundamental tenets of Platonism compatible with a traditional Christian incarnational or sacramental ontology?[24]

Nevin's appreciation for Platonism, paired with his decisively incarnational and sacramental theology, raises rather interesting points of consideration for this apparent impasse. Nevin clearly adopts the principle features of Plato's idealism and is explicit in his sympathetic engagement with Platonism at several points.[25] Platonism, particularly by way of the English divines and mediating theologians, was conducive to Nevin's mystical inclinations and provided Nevin with the necessary raw philosophical material for articulating the objectivity of the ideal. "It had to do with *ideas* at least," he wrote, "which were held to be of objective force, and not merely subjective notions and fancies."[26]

Nevin's incorporation of Platonic thought can be viewed along the trajectory of a distinctly American adoption of idealism. DiPuccio is particularly insightful on this point. Instructively, he compares Nevin with the Edwardsean tradition of appropriating Platonic philosophy. The synthesis of American philosophy with idealism, he writes, meant for Edwards a synthesis of Lockean empiricism with puritan Platonism. For Nevin, the synthesis entailed a "hybrid of common sense realism, puritan and post-Kantian Platonism, and German Idealism."[27] In this

---

24. Ibid., 199.

25. Nevin, *Party Spirit*, 125.

26. Nevin, "My Own Life," 122. See DiPuccio, *Interior Sense*, 10. In his address on party spirit, Nevin explains, "Even apart from revelation, such philosophy, as it meets us in the towering thoughts of the Grecian Plato, may well be denominated the mistress of an immortal mind. With him all inward illumination and stability are found in communion with the *In onta* as opposed to the *to phainomena*, and nothing less than the *to agathon*, the self evidencing light of the Truth itself, will serve as the medium by which this communion is to be maintained. Conversing only with the world of time, through the medium of the senses, the soul is represented as reeling in a sort of drunken delirium, with the fluctuating show on which it looks; but in the use of its own higher vision, it becomes itself again (Phaedo, 1:126, Ed. Tauchnitz.) Thus exercised, as he tells us in another place, it cannot afford to stoop to the trivial interests with which men are commonly employed, so as to be filled with all malignant affections in struggling with them for such things; but aims rather in the steady contemplation of what is always the same and always right, to be transformed into the same image. De Republica, Vol. V. p. 230." Nevin, *Party Spirit*, 125.

27. DiPuccio, *Interior Sense*, 195.

way, slightly deviating from Edwards, Nevin fell into line with Rauch, Coleridge, and the mediating theologians. As DiPuccio explains,

> This restoration of metaphysical optimism was accompanied by the corresponding recovery of a Platonic-Augustinian epistemology in religion. The Cartesian dualism of mind and matter, appropriated by the Scottish philosophy, was discarded like an obsolete hypothesis. Participation, communion, and immediacy took precedence over detachment, observation, and objectivity. The cold and sterile methods of the Enlightenment (that is, evidences and outward authority) and the ecclesiastical authoritarianism found in some forms of Roman Catholicism, were subordinated to intuition and religious feeling. This is not, of course, a total rejection of evidences or authority, but an attempt to show that by themselves such objective methods can never unite nature and supernature, subject and object, the ideal and actual.[28]

Nevertheless, Nevin departs from Plato's static version of the ideal and the actual, rejecting the sheer abstraction of the former. For Nevin, the Incarnation of Jesus Christ requires a Christianized version of Platonism that rethinks the good, the true, and the beautiful, as well as the relationship between the ideal and actual. Rather than a static version of reality, Nevin insists upon a dynamic, organic view in which the ideal is understood as organically embodied in the temporal, reconciling all things unto God in Christ.[29] He writes,

> The Bible knows nothing of that abstract separation of soul and body, which has come to be so widely admitted into the religious views of the modern world. It comes from another quarter altogether; and it is as false to all true philosophy, as it is unsound in theology and pernicious for the Christian life. Soul and body, in their ground, are but one life; identical in their origin; bound together by mutual interpenetration subsequently at every point; and holding for ever in the presence and power of the self-same organic law. We have no right to think of the body as the prison of the soul, in the way of Plato; nor as its garment merely; nor as its shell or hull. We have no right to think of the soul in any way as a form of existence of and by itself, into which the soul as another form of such existence is thrust in a mechanical way. Both form *one* life. The soul to be complete to develop itself at all

---

28. Ibid., 145.
29. See especially Nevin, "Natural and Supernatural." Also, *Party Spirit*, 125.

as a soul, *must* externalize itself, throw itself out in space; and this externalization is the body.[30]

Nevin's modified idealism, then, might also be described as a Christian Platonism that, while providing the framework for Nevin's critique of materialism, was eventually "swallowed up by his incarnational theology." Nevin's contention that the "whole constitution of the world is sacramental . . ." is indicative of this particular strain of development in his thought.[31]

One of the corresponding impetuses for Nevin's thought, already noted in the introduction of this study, is the neoplatonic concept of the analogy of being. It is important to recall this concept at this point given Smith's caution towards Radical Orthodoxy's doctrine of creation. He affirms that both Reformed and Radical Orthodoxy affirm the goodness of creation, but he remains concerned that Radical Orthodoxy may be erecting a "hierarchical and oppositional bifurcation between the immaterial and the material, the soul and the body, the invisible and the visible" and that such would necessarily lead to the denigration of creaturely life, including sociopolitical engagement.[32] Smith proceeds by critiquing Catherine Pickstock's reading of Plato's *Phaedrus*, insisting that despite her efforts to affirm the "positive account of physicality," it is nevertheless "difficult not to see Plato suggesting that the body and time are indeed ladders that are kicked away once the ascent has been completed."[33]

Whether Smith is correct in his criticism of Pickstock on this point is not of immediate concern. What is important is that such presents a particular instance in which Nevin may prove instructive. Nevin is careful to affirm the goodness of creation, namely because his version of the analogy of being demands that God's imprint be actualized in the created order.[34] He rejects, moreover, the dualistic version of creation advanced by Newtonian physics and common sense realism. Creation is not static or merely passive, but a system of organic dynamism, yearn-

---

30. Nevin, *Mystical Presence*, 171.
31. DiPuccio, *Interior Sense*, 131; Erb, *Nevin's Theology*, 373.
32. James Smith, *Introducing Radical Orthodoxy*, 198.
33. Ibid., 201.
34. DiPuccio, *Interior Sense*, 35.

ing for its redemption.³⁵ The question is raised, to what degree is this analogical notion of God's presence in creation sufficient for a Reformed doctrine of creation? Answers to this question among the Reformed will vary. To be noted here, however, is that Nevin emerges as a theologian who is at once opposed to the very dualisms which Reformed theology has adamantly rejected while also maintaining a participatory ontology that demands the goodness of creation.

Nevin in Conversation with Milbank, Cavanaugh, and Ward

In his seminal work, *Theology and Social Theory*, Radical Orthodoxy theologian John Milbank insists upon the continuing relevance of the following Hegelian tasks: a theological critique of the enlightenment; a historical narration of the interconnection between politics and religion; a self-critique of Christian historical practice; and finally, the transformation of the Greek *logos* through encounter with the Christian *logos*, so that thought essentially becomes "beyond secular reason."³⁶ His overarching thesis combats the trends of enlightenment modernity by insisting that theology, rightly understood, is itself a social science and that, as such, it will necessarily have to give an account of society and history that is based on faith. According to Milbank, true sociology is "first and foremost an *ecclesiology*, and only an account of other human societies to the extent that the Church defines itself, in its practice, as in continuity and discontinuity with these societies." He believes, moreover, that the church must necessarily approach this task with rigorous concern with the "actual genesis of real historical churches." In order for all theology to become an ecclesiologically-driven sociology, he explains, it must not treat reason and morality like ahistorical universals. Instead, it "turns to

---

35. Ibid., 38.

36. Milbank lists these tasks in the opening paragraph of his chapter entitled "For and Against Hegel." Milbank, *Theology and Social Theory*, 147. Perhaps most fundamental to Milbank's approach is his insistence that "scientific" social theories are in fact theologies or anti-theologies in disguise. This union of theology and modernist social theory, he claims, was formed in the nineteenth century and has profoundly affected both the social theorist and the theologian who, as a product of this union, now seeks to affirm the "scientific" and "humanist" discourses of modernity. Milbank suggests two reasons for the development of such trends: First, humanism has become a substitute for transcendent faith. Second, it is believed that Christian moral values should play a role in society without upsetting non-Christian citizens. Milbank, *Theology and Social Theory*, 2–3 (italics his).

the Church Fathers, and indeed goes beyond them, in seeking to elaborate a Christian *logos*, or a reason that bears the marks of the Incarnation and Pentecost."[37]

Nevin would find odd Milbank's insistence that theology is a social science but would nevertheless resonate with the notion that ecclesiology is the standard of true sociology. This is evident not only in the way that Nevin articulates what he calls the "social principle," but also in the way he employs ecclesiological themes in his critique of antebellum culture and politics.[38] Nevin's rhetoric in such instances is designed to constructively criticize both church and state for not constructing the type of society that God desires, namely, one that is whole and communal, not privatized and sectarian. Like Milbank, Nevin seeks an historical delineation of these concepts, one which incorporates the mind, the will, and human nature, viewed through the lens of the Incarnation. In this way, both theologians offer historicist accounts of the church, albeit along different lines of thought and with different objectives in view. Nevin, moreover, goes to great lengths to "re-narrate" the historical relationship between politics and religion in America, something which sets him apart from the vast majority of his fellow American theologians.[39]

In his essay, "The City: Beyond secular Parodies," William T. Cavanaugh recognizes the assumptions of modern political philosophy and attempts to reclaim a pre-capitalist, ecclesiocentric view of society. He argues that the state is but a false copy of the body of Christ and that the church should overcome the state's inherent trend of privatization, not through the acquisition of political clout, but by insisting upon the Eucharist as the heart of a "practice which . . . challenges the false order of the state."[40] Nevin does not go as far as to label nature or the state

37. Ibid., 380–81.
38. See Nevin, *Party Spirit*; also Nevin "Catholicism."
39. See Nevin, "Early Christianity," *Party Spirit*, and "The Sect System."
40. Cavanaugh, "The City," 194–95. Cavanaugh's assertion that the state is a "false" copy of the church is an odd one, particularly to Reformed readers. Reformed theology is careful to affirm the legitimacy of the state as an institution created and sustained by God for the sake of justice in society and protection of the church's freedom and well-being. Although Nevin believes that the state will be "swallowed up" in the church, he would nevertheless ascribe legitimacy to the state. He neither indicates that the state is a "false" copy of the church, nor that it is a "copy" of any sort in the first place. Cavanaugh proceeds to demonstrate the ways in which the Eucharist addresses the "mythos" of the state. Most significantly, in Cavanaugh's view, in contrast to the Lockean state in which property is commoditized and relationships revolve around contract and the exchange

as a false copy, but nonetheless suggests that "nature is only relatively true and real."[41] His criticism of societal fragmentation, moreover, is echoed in Cavanaugh's sentiment that "the church, as body of Christ is called to be an alternative to the atomization of U.S. society promoted by individualism, the market, and the state. As an alternative social body, the church realizes the eucharistic imperative to be what we receive, to become the body of Christ and allow others to feed on us."[42] Thus, for Cavanaugh, "The possibilities of a participatory or creational ontology and its attendant account of sociality are unfolded in and by the formation of the liturgy and practice of being the community of God."[43]

Nevin shares with Cavanaugh an insistence that the unity and wholeness of the Eucharist serves as the ideal for which all of reality, including fragmenting society, should strive. Certainly Nevin implicates the Incarnation to a great degree in this respect, more so than Cavanaugh,

---

of abstract labor, the Eucharist constitutes a means by which the gift and giver are intimately related. In this way, "the foundational distinction between mine and thine is radically effaced ... and the dualism of giver and recipient are collapsed." Similarly, one of Milbank's theses in *Theology and Social Theory* is that the enlightenment's attempt to regulate "competition" among individuals was in fact "heretical" in nature, ultimately reinforcing nominalistic and voluntaristic tendencies in society. He has explained that "The abstract opposition between the individual and society, which is convenient to the church's modern self-understanding as a voluntary society which respects the independence of the secular order, is quite clearly a 'sociological' opposition." The more desirable alternative, he explains, follows Augustine, whose Christian ontology "implies both that the part belongs to the whole, and that each part transcends an imaginable whole, because the whole is only a finite series which continues indefinitely towards an infinite and unfathomable God." See Milbank, "Essay Against Secular Order."

41. Nevin, *Mystical Presence*, 195.

42. Cavanaugh, "Body of Christ," 170. In similar fashion to Nevin's critique of sectarianism and "party spirit," Cavanaugh blames privatization of religion for turning religion into little more than a mechanism for allowing "to fit into the state and market without conflict." "Private religion," he adds, "is meant as a refuge, a solace for tired shoppers and harried office workers. Religion helps us escape from or cope with, but not change, the frenetic pace of life in consumer society." Cavanaugh, "God is not Religious," 106. The Eucharistic event allows the individual to be incorporated into the Body of Christ, where they become nourishment for others. This leads to Cavanaugh's second point, that in the Eucharist, individuals are united both to God and to one another, and that this is a means of subverting the state's myth of protecting individuals from one another. From Cavanaugh's perspective, in the liberal political body, the center (God) seeks to maintain the independence of individuals from one another; the fascist body commits a similar sin by binding individuals solely through the center. Christ, rather, is to be found not only at the center, but at the margins. Cavanaugh, "The City," 194–95.

43. James Smith, *Introducing Radical Orthodoxy*, 232.

but he nevertheless insists upon the same basic principles in the midst of his sectarian context. More explicitly, Nevin, unlike the majority of his politically and theologically inclined contemporaries, shares with Cavanaugh distaste for the unchecked nominalist political philosophies. The voluntarism and ensuing contract theories of these traditions, Nevin cautions, would lead to the breakdown of social and ecclesiastical unity.[44] Nevin's frustration with this trend is articulated in a number of ways, not least in his view of Adam's sin in relation to the whole race. Contra Hodge, Nevin is unremitting in his organic, idealistic view of Adam and the human race, a view which advances an ontology that begins with the whole before proceeding to the parts. Cavanaugh agrees with Nevin in his affirmation, "The effect of sin is the very creation of individuals as such, that is, the creation of an ontological distinction between individual and group."[45]

One of the ways in which Nevin develops the implications of his idealist ontology is along the lines of anthropology. Traces of this anthropology can be found in Graham Ward's treatment of the body. In his *Cities of God*, Ward explains that "bodies here are frangible, permeable; not autonomous and self-defining, but sharing and being shared ... This is the ontological scandal announced by the Eucharistic phase—bodies are never simply there (or here)."[46] With Nevin, moreover, Ward affirms a sort of coextensiveness between Christ's body, the church, and human bodies (and indeed all of creation).[47] He insists that "all human bodies participate in this one body and this participation and belonging constitutes the ecclesial body the Church."[48]

Nevin's anthropology, though not as boundless as Ward's, is suggestive of a similar scheme, as the dialectic of individual and humanity ("bodies") is resolved in the church (Christ's body), the historic, physical extension of Christ's incarnation. As in his broader ontology, for Nevin, the "ideal" humanity, while taking priority in what it means to be human, has no reality unless it is actualized in the sphere of the natural; to be a

---

44. DiPuccio, *Interior Sense*, 170–71, summarizes well the nominalist political philosophy that Nevin encountered.

45. Cavanaugh, "The City," 184. See James Smith, *Introducing Radical Orthodoxy*, 235–39.

46. Ward, *Cities*, 91.

47. Ibid., 94.

48. Ibid., 225. See James Smith, *Introducing Radical Orthodoxy*, 258.

"true" human being, however, is to have one's constitution first in the ideal.[49] "He is a man," to recall Nevin's words, "the universal conception of humanity enters into him, as it enters also into all other men; while he is, besides, this or that man, as distinguished from all others by his particular position in the human world."[50] And furthermore, "the idea of man...in order that it may become actual, must resolve itself into an innumerable multitude of individual lives" who are to find their perfection in the "whole" constitution of mankind.[51] Nevin's idealistic, participatory ontology, then, while far from identical to Ward's anthropology, allows for the possibility of overlap at a number of crucial points.

Incarnation and Exclusion: The Question of Boundaries

The divergence between Nevin and Ward on the issue of boundaries points to a crucial point of departure between Nevin and Radical Orthodoxy. Ward writes, "Given an analogical world-view, I have no need to argue *for* a relationship between the ecclesial body and the civic. The relationship is already there; a participation already exists on the basis of the intratrinitarian community which causes other analogies of itself."[52] Appropriately, one of the recurring criticisms that the Reformed tradition has leveled at Radical Orthodoxy is the way in which themes such as "ontology of peace," "displaced bodies," and the state as "false copy" eventuate in and contribute to an apparent lack of ecclesial boundaries.[53] For Radical Orthodox theologians, this elimination of boundaries is often rooted in the doctrine of the Incarnation. As Milbank argues, "Above all, with the doctrine of the Incarnation, Christianity violates the boundary between created and creator, immanence and transcendence, humanity and God. In this way, the arch taboo grounding all the others is broken."[54] Milbank's view leads him to the following conclusion:

---

49 Nevin, "Human Freedom," 406.

50. Ibid., 406.

51. Nevin, "Moral Order of Sex," 551–52.

52. Ward, *Cities*, 36. Smith is right to point out the contrast here between Ward and Cavanaugh. Ward's "anti-realism" leaves him highly skeptical towards delineating any independence between entities such as church and state. James Smith, *Introducing Radical Orthodoxy*, 257.

53. James Smith, *Introducing Radical Orthodoxy*, 257–59.

54. Milbank, *Being Reconciled*, 197.

> One way to try to secure peace is to draw boundaries around "the same," and exclude "the other"; to promote some practices and disallow alternatives. Most polities, and most religions, characteristically do this. But the Church has misunderstood itself when it does likewise ... Christianity should not draw boundaries, and the Church is that paradox: a nomad city.[55]

Hans Boersma, among others, criticizes Radical Orthodoxy for what he sees as a failure to sufficiently account for critical boundaries and distinctions in Christian theology. His indictment is primarily aimed at Milbank. He explains,

> For Milbank, boundaries are inherently problematic. The Church has become boundaryless and so universal. In fact, he concludes that "none of this complex confusion (of the 'secular' sphere) is exactly 'outside' the Church." With the "counterpolity" of the Church refusing "the exclusionist logic of inside/outside," Milbank even ends up with a denial of the Creator/creature distinction: He bases the obliteration of boundaries in the Incarnation, that is to say, in the violation of the "boundary between created and creator, immanence and transcendence, humanity and God."[56]

Boersma does not stop with Milbank, leveling a similar criticism at Ward, whose critique of boundaries "results in a minimal sense of Christian identity and an expansion of Christ's displaced body—the church—which, in turn, leaves little or no space for political, social, and economic activities beyond the church, in the realm of the *civitas terrena*."[57] Boersma's concern over Radical Orthodoxy's postmodern allergy to boundaries is, as indicated above, shared by a number of Reformed theologians. Undoubtedly, Nevin would have shared similar concerns and offered comparable criticism.

Nevin's engagement with Bushnell, among others, is indicative of his caution toward conflating "boundaries," specifically boundaries between nature and supernature.[58] "Christianity can never resolve itself ... into the constitution of the world's life, as found beyond its own sphere," he writes. It is wrong, moreover, to "sink the conception of the supernatural

---

55. Milbank, "Postmodern," 269.
56. Boersma, "Rejection," 422.
57. Ibid., 424.
58. In what follows I am indebted to Layman, "Holistic Supernaturalism."

in Christianity into the sphere of mere nature."[59] This sort of distinction runs throughout Nevin's theology. The order or sphere of nature is understood appositionally to the supernatural.

In order to avoid a dualistic tendency (which Nevin sensed was present in Hodge's system), Nevin, like Radical Orthodoxy theologians, bases his ontology in the Incarnation of Christ. As Layman writes, "Thus, nature and supernature, body and spirit, are united in history; the Incarnation is a transforming energy in mundane existence that can be recognized as such in faith."[60] Nevertheless, Nevin maintains the boundaries of the *ecclesia*. Nevin is able to do this in two ways: First, he presents the objectivity of the church as a fundamental tenet of his theology and ontology. The church is a unique body created by God, logically prior to any human construct or collectivity and having a constitution of its own. He writes,

> If Christ be the principle of a new creation, the point in which the earth and heavens have been brought into permanent living conjunction as never before, it follows at once plainly that the Church in which is comprehended the power of this fact, and which of this very reason is declared to be his BODY, the fullness of Him that filleth all in all, must carry in itself a constitution of its own, as really objective and enduring, to say the least, as the course of nature, on which as a basis it is made supernaturally to rest.[61]

Second, while the Incarnation for Nevin removes the boundaries of nature and supernature, and thus the boundaries sacred and "secular," this reconciliation is understood as taking place historically and eschatologically. Nevin's dialectical historicism in this respect allows him to say that the "state will have vanished away in the church"[62] while simultaneously avoiding the "tendency in Radical Orthodoxy to conflate and confuse a particular direction of the state with the structure of the state as such."[63] Nevin recognizes the structure of the state as having a constitution of its own, even if it is one which will ultimately be swallowed up

---

59. Nevin, "Educational Religion," 24–58, cited in Layman, "Holistic Supernaturalism," 196.

60. Layman, "Holistic Supernaturalism," 201.

61. Nevin, *Antichrist*, 40.

62. Nevin, "Early Christianity," in Appel, *Life and Work*, 360.

63. James Smith, *Introducing Radical Orthodoxy*, 255.

by the church. The state, or for Nevin, the order of nature, was created good. This is attested to throughout the Nevin corpus, not least in the following: "The world was good, not in the light of a penitentiary prepared beforehand to suit the circumstances of his case in a state of sin, but as a fit theatre for the free harmonious development of his life in a state of innocence. How the fall wrought to disturb this original order, is of course a great mystery."[64] Nevin, then, ostensibly recognizes the "distinction between creation structure and postlapsarian direction."[65] To be sure, Nevin will find sympathy among Radical Orthodoxy theologians insofar as he sees the state being subsumed by the church, but his insistence upon the goodness of creation, the ontology of "mere" nature, sin, and the "lower orders" of existence, accompanied by his eschatological orientation, should give Reformed theologians pause before dismissing him outright.

So how does one reconcile Nevin's participationist ontology with his preservation of boundaries? The way in which Nevin distinguishes between the orders of nature, mankind, and the Incarnation, along with his historicist ontology suggests degrees of participation that, while organically related and inseparable, are nonetheless distinct parts of the created order. These orders, while finding their true essence in the eschatological body of Christ, are at present orders of existence that must be treated as such. Nevin's ontology remains idealist, but the ideals, paradoxically, must be embodied and made concrete in the actual. It would be appropriate then to think of boundaries in Nevin's theology as having to do with degree or intensity of participation. Smith inadvertently gives an apt characterization of Nevin's approach. He is worth quoting at length on this point:

> ... while a participatory or pneumatological ontology holds that *all* that *is* participates in the Creator, or all is animated by the dynamic presence of the Spirit, this does not mean that all participates *in the same way* or *to the same degree* . . . To put this otherwise, it is structurally the case that all that exists participates in the divine, but not all that exists is properly ordered or directed *to* the divine: to *participate properly* in the Creator is to also be directed to the Creator. This provides a framework for thinking about both Fall and Redemption: the effect of the Fall is the dis-

---

64. Nevin, "Natural and Supernatural," 200.
65. James Smith, *Introducing Radical Orthodoxy*, 155.

ordering and thus de-intensifying of creation's participation in the divine; Redemption is the re-ordering and reintensifying of creation's participation in the divine, including both "nature" (the biotic and physical) and "culture" (the "human layer" of social institutions, etc.).[66]

In Nevin's own words, "we must distinguish between what is human in history, and what is properly universal and divine. The first may be worthy of all reprobation, where we are still bound to adore the presence of the second."[67] It does not follow for Nevin, however, that what is of *mere* nature does have its completion—its telos and fulfillment—in the divine. Rather, through the lens of analogy, all orders of reality are seen to be foreshadowing a higher, distinct, but inseparable order of existence, ultimately finding their end in Christ.

Conclusion

It should be restated that the aim here is not to situate Nevin within Radical Orthodoxy or to suggest that Nevin is *the* reconciling force of the Reformed Tradition and Radical Orthodoxy. Rather, it has been to make a case for Nevin's inclusion in the ongoing discussion between these two camps. Nevin, seeking to be a true Calvin's Calvinist, deserves the attention of Reformed theologians, particularly those working in hermeneutics and philosophical theology. As has been shown, Nevin not only offers an intriguing hermeneutical approach within the Reformed tradition, but also one which has staying power within the arena of theological and ecumenical dialogue. Justin Holcumb optimistically states, "When Radical Orthodoxy and Reformed theology are seen as compatible, they offer a transcendental, participatory, and covenantal understanding of the theology that does not fear making ontological claims concerning Christian doctrine because the traditional, covenantal reading of Scripture establishes its foundation."[68] Nevin, it seems, would serve as additional warrant for such optimism.

---

66. James Smith, "Spirit," 256.
67. Nevin, "The Year 1848," 23.
68. Holcumb, "Being Bound," 262.

7

The World's Ascension into a Higher Order of Existence
The Implications of a Sacramental Hermeneutic

ENGAGING NEVIN ON HIS OWN TERMS

This study has in many respects served as an assessment of Theodore Appel's claim that, for Nevin, "philosophy and theology had no interest or value, apart from their actual bearings on the welfare of man and the progress of society."[1] Was Appel's estimation of Nevin's theology accurate? If the present study is any indication, then one must answer in the affirmative. However, what exactly Appel meant by this will remain a mystery as long as interpreters anachronistically read into Nevin's theology modern notions of parachurch ministry, voluntary societies, social agendas, and political activism.

And yet this anachronism persists. The lack of a sufficient account of the social and political dimensions of Nevin's theology in contemporary scholarship can largely be attributed to the seemingly conventional—and faulty—assumption that the church's vitality in history has always been measured by its relationship with the broader culture or by the relevance of her theology. This assumption leads scholars to the conclusion that Nevin's work is either inconsistent or simply deficient. D. G. Hart is therefore correct to point out the unfortunate tendency of scholars to "study the church to see how strong its standing is in society, whether it speaks with a respectably authoritative voice to the major questions of a particular time and place."[2] One interpreter, for example, has suggested

---

1. Appel, *Life and Work*, ix.

2. Hart has suggested that Nevin's interpretation of American Protestantism challenges conventional periodization of the nineteenth century, especially with respect

that the want of practicality in Nevin's theology could be attributed to his "preoccupation with getting the church straight," which in turn "left little time for concerns of application."[3] Such an interpretation, however, imposes a rather pragmatic definition of application onto Nevin's idealistic orientation. It is, simply put, a failure to understand Nevin on his own terms. For Nevin, "getting the church straight" was precisely the most applicable task at hand. The church is not to be measured by its relative performance in society, but by its integral identity as the body of Christ. "As such," explains Hart, "the work of establishing the kingdom of God, not through political muscle or classroom intelligence, but by engrafting people onto the vine of Christ, establishes a different criteria for evaluating Christianity."[4]

Nevin not only establishes different criteria for modern interpreters, but his decisively theological approach to antebellum society reveals a sharp divergence between his theology and the pervading ideologies of his day. American theological—and especially ecclesiological—assumptions had violently shifted in the direction of antiauthoritarianism

---

to religious history. Nevin's "articulation of the church question," he writes, "stands the periodization of American Protestantism on its head because Nevin's understanding of the church poses a different set of criteria than that of Schlesinger and the company of historians who followed his lead." Schlesinger and others rightly pointed out that after the Civil War, the United States faced a new set of sociological, political, and economic problems. The majority interpretation that has followed this trajectory has sought to analyze the church in its relation to the post-war culture, that is, how it was affected by the myriad shifts that took place during and after the war, its approach to Darwinism and the new scientific methods, industrialization, and so on. Hart, *High Church Calvinist*, 230–32. Hart cites the following advocates of the traditional periodization: Schlesinger Sr., "Critical Period," 302; Turner, *Without God, without Creed*; Kilick, *Churchmen and Philosophers*, 227–29; Marsden, *Soul of the American University*.

3. Bratt, "Antebellum Culture Wars," 13.

4. See Hart, *High Church Calvinist*, 233–34. Indeed, while most historians have assumed that the church should be evaluated in terms of its externals— its interaction with various cultural phenomena and factors—Nevin sought to evaluate the church first in terms of its internal life. As such, according to Nevin, American Protestantism had broken with its Reformation roots much earlier, suggesting a period beginning much earlier than the 1870s. Hart believes that Nevin's singular contribution was in his insistence that "The critical period for American Protestantism is not the time that the churches adapted to or resisted the new knowledge and social conditions of modern society that emerged after the Civil War. Instead, it occurred earlier, as Nevin argued, sometime when Protestants no longer regarded the church as a medium of grace but more or less as a voluntary society of Christian disciples." Hart, *High Church Calvinist*, 237.

and voluntarism, resulting in a wide range of benevolent societies and grassroots political movements.[5] While such trends had a number of positive effects on American society, Nevin worried about their long-term ecclesiological implications. His analyses and interpretation of American culture remained focused not upon the "inalienable rights" of the individual or the "relevance" of the church in society, but upon the viability and necessity of the church, its worship, and its sacramental character. Insofar as his discourse was "public," Nevin sought to challenge and reorient antebellum Christians to see the church as the sole ark and medium of salvation, not a mere collection of individuals who adhere to a given system of doctrine. To repeat Nevin's own words, "Here are to be met, and answered in some way, the tremendous politico-economical and social problems ... Above all in interest for us, here must be settled the great ecclesiastical issues, (that is), the Church Question."[6]

THE MERCERSBURG ALTERNATIVE

While American Protestantism from the pews to the Princetons wrestled with the assimilation of democratic Republicanism into their church polity, liturgy, and praxis, Nevin and the Mercersburg movement sought to retain the marks of the high-church tradition through liturgical renewal and the propagation of a philosophical theology that was largely alien to American thought. Nevin's theology indeed demonstrates a critique from within American culture, but the categories he employed and the questions he asked represent at best a minority view.

From the perspective of the Mercersburg theologians, conventional theories concerning the church-state relationship did little more than present false alternatives. Built on the nominalist political theories of common sense realism, such theories assumed that society's institutions were at their core essentially and fundamentally distinct, and thus their

---

5. In Nevin's judgment, while such trends appear to be "Christian" on the surface, they are in fact violating the basic constitution of the faith, namely the objectivity of Christ's body and its demand for unity. Far from being a voluntary society, the church is representative of the objective, divine whole to which individuals must connect themselves. Rather than exercising sovereignty within his own sphere of authority, the individual is to be within the sphere of God's sovereignty, the church. As humankind submits to the historical church, the mediate institutions created by the "secular" are likewise submitted to Christ, the only true mediator. See Nevin, "Moral Order of Sex," 551–52; "Human Freedom," 408; "Catholicism," in Appel, *Life and Work*, 377.

6. Nevin, "Lancaster Commencement Address," 644.

relationship to one another was understood to be either one of contract or protection from one another. Indeed, the state as a whole was to be viewed as a social compact entered into for the sake of property and rights. The members of this state, accordingly, are bonded merely by mutual interest and expediency, one immense civil voluntary association. While overlap on certain points between these principles and the idealistic philosophy of Mercersburg was recognized by Nevin, there was no doubt that the tradition of Locke, Hobbes, Rousseau, and even Roger Williams, in its broadest sense, had unquestionably prevailed.

Everyone agreed that the church had a responsibility to create morally upright citizens who would do their Christian duty with respect to their families and civic responsibilities. From the secularist to the Transcendentalist, the sectarian to the Calvinist, all could share in this sentiment. But even this notion, namely that the church's primary political function is to act as the provider of social and moral principles, was recognized by Nevin as a distinctly modern phenomenon and was not to be accepted at face value. A product of modernity and the European and American Enlightenment in particular, it "presupposes a unified, harmonious reason which will prevail both in the church's presentation of the principles and in the acceptance of these principles by society."[7] This modern schema, in its pursuit of a moral society by way of reliance upon reason, only works if the church adopts the same rationalist foundations. For this reason, as one theologian has explained, "The very notion that society can be molded through principles of this kind also involves a conformity *to* modern society through the adoption of the aspects which are constitutive for 'principle' ethics: the belief that general rationality will prevail of itself . . ."[8] Nevertheless, this very approach is, in fact, what seems to have been adopted in most cases, particularly in America where even the likes of Charles Hodge employed a nominalist and rationalist method of interpreting the Bible as a "store-house of facts."[9]

---

7. Wannenwetsch, *Political Worship*, 93.

8. Ibid., 103.

9. "The Bible is to the theologian what nature is to the man of science. It is his storehouse of facts; and his method of ascertaining what the Bible teaches, is the same as that which the natural philosopher adopts to ascertain what nature teaches." Hodge, *Systematic Theology*, 1:10.

Protestant sectarianism was part and parcel of this vast phenomenon since reason and private interpretation were viewed as more hermeneutically reliable than the communal wisdom or historical continuity of the church. The church is regarded as a voluntary association, a distinct institution among others, lacking any fundamental priority in society. In sum, the Protestant church "was transformed . . . into an influential *ad hoc* organization which obtained its power largely by taking its cues from the non-ecclesiastical culture on which it was dependent."[10] Concurrently, the relationships of individuals within the church in this system were likewise governed by mere social contract and voluntarism. They understood themselves as part of a mechanism, "held together by the force of external power; or, to say the most, it is merely of a moral character, as, for instance, the bond of friendship."[11]

The idealism of Mercersburg, despite the movement's lack of appeal beyond a small alcove of the nineteenth-century theological culture, prompted a striking, trenchant critique of the church's seemingly willy-nilly adoption of nominalism, rationalism, and other accompanying tenets of the Enlightenment. To embrace these principles could only result in further ecclesial disunity and schism, Nevin argued, since rationalism mixed with nominalism resulted in private interpretation rather than communal reason. Nevin's caution in this respect was not merely theoretical; rampant revivalism and its accompanying sectarianism had provided more than enough warrant.

Nevin, for one, recognized the importance of the church being a society built upon *fides quarens intellectum*, and more specifically an institution rooted in that which surpassed sheer reason, the incarnation of God in Christ. The history of the world, Nevin understood, found its culmination—that is, its *telos*—in the Incarnation. Thus there was no sphere or institution which could claim a neutral account of the way things were. Moreover, sacred cannot be opposed to "secular" in a way that these spheres or realms are presumed to be in separate orbits. It is not a stretch to suggest that Nevin would agree with theologian William Cavanaugh in this respect. Cavanaugh writes, "The problem is not simply that this separation leaves the church's liturgy begging for relevance to the 'real world.' The problem is rather that the supposedly 'secular' world invents its own liturgies, with pretensions every bit as 'sacred' as

10. Douglass, *Feminization*, 24.
11. Kieffer, "Church and State," 569.

those of the Christian liturgy, and these liturgies can come to rival the church's liturgy."[12]

Without denying that the republicanism and utilitarianism of common sense philosophy had benefited America to some extent, Nevin nevertheless believed that, ultimately, such ideologies and their accompanying principles are deeply, if not fatally, flawed. They were, as *Mercersburg Review* contributor Moses Kieffer put it, "one-sided, incomplete, outward, mechanical," and thus "contrary to the organic character of reality."[13] The nature of this flaw, according to the Mercersburg theology, is rooted in the problem of original sin. All of creation bears the burden of sin and the fall of man, and until the power of sin is eradicated, it is not possible for the state to reach its divine design. While modernity, chiefly by way of the Enlightenment, had conceived of a new confidence in the ability of mankind, the Mercersburg theologians were under no illusions that secular morality, literature, art, science, and Republican cultural mores were not the means by which the state could be raised into "a higher order of existence." Any state that was seen as an institution of human rather than divine regulation was fated for perpetual failure: "In the form of government called the Monarchy, it is but the will of the monarch with reference to his subjects; in the Aristocratic form of government, it is but the will of the few in reference to the many; and in the Republican form of government it is the will of the majority of the people expressed with reference to the minority or the whole."[14]

To be sure, republicanism was to be the preferred form of government; Nevin affirmed this much. The problem was not republicanism *per se*, but that in its mechanized, outward form, its fate was not much more promising than alternative forms of government. Representative democracy did indeed represent the next stage of development in the history of humankind, a crucial stage in the unfolding of God's providence. Nevertheless, those in power had not sufficiently acknowledged the organic constitution of reality and had, therefore, not understood the need for God's redemptive power to be woven throughout. In Nevin's judgment, because no sphere of life has its constitution apart from the generic life of humanity and thus sin and the fall, a political theory or social ethic that does not have the fabric of redemption running through

12. Cavanaugh, "Liturgies," 25.
13. Kieffer, "Church and State," 569.
14. Ibid., 571.

all spheres will always be inadequate. To its credit, modernity, and the American project in particular, had long recognized the inescapability—and indeed the value—of the fact that free individuals are able to occupy multiple spheres of life simultaneously. Therefore, as the church produces moral, just, and benevolent citizens, all other spheres stood to benefit. What the enlightened modernist seemingly did not anticipate was the way in which its radical individualism could not fully account for the complexity of institutions and corporate morality.[15]

That being said, the myriad social and political difficulties which plagued the antebellum era were not cause for the Mercersburg theologians to simply devise new efforts to "transform" society. In the midst of cultural turbulence, the church's most appropriate course of action, they believed, is to uphold its ministry and serve as the primary model of catholicity. In doing so, the lower sphere, in its sociopolitical expression, is organically raised into a higher order of existence. In this way, according to the Mercersburg theologians, the progression of history ought to lead the church to a point where it is able to effectively impact every sphere of society, thus returning the world to its intended, perfected state.[16] For Nevin's perspective,

> It is a libel on Christ, to say that his religion has nothing to do with politics, or the fine arts, or the sciences, or common social life. It must unite itself with all these, inwardly and profoundly, so as to transfigure them fully into its own image, before it shall have accomplished its mission in the world. For how else should it deserve to be acknowledged the universal truth of man's life?[17]

Thus, for Nevin, the church question is concerned more so with matters of objectivity and wholeness than it is cultural engagement in the voluntaristic sense. The church's role is to retain its purity as the ark of

---

15. Consider Niebuhr's thesis in *Moral Man, Immoral Society*, that different ethical imperatives are employed when evaluating and directing the collective behavior of groups than when evaluating and directing the behavior of individuals. With respect to the young American republic, this is perhaps best pictured in the conflicting cultural and ideological rifts that led to the Civil War, which in some ways could be characterized as a war over the relationship of collective and individual rights.

16. What made this proposal so scandalous was its corollary that the proper historical development would inevitably reunite Protestant freedom and subjectivity with Catholic authority and objectivity. See Holifield, *Theology in America*, 473.

17. Nevin, "Human Freedom," 38.

salvation, the means by which creation could be brought into harmony with the divine.

NEVIN'S LITURGICAL PROTESTANTISM: IMPLICATIONS FOR A "LITURGY AFTER THE LITURGY"

Nevin does not explain the precise course of action for the church to take in relation to art, science, commerce, or politics. Perhaps much to the chagrin of modern interpreters, he is not interested in providing a "to do" list for the church. His aim, rather, is to construct the proper ecclesiological and liturgical foundations that he believes are necessary for reconciling all spheres of life to God. Renewed by the power of the Holy Spirit, the Christian, by way of participation in the ministry of word and sacrament, is prompted to be a testimony to the Lordship of Christ in the world. Thus the mission of the church rests upon the transforming power of the liturgy.

This "liturgy after the liturgy" model of understanding the relationship between worship and mission is traditionally understood to be a principle of Eastern Orthodoxy, but one which has also been aptly used to describe the liturgical and societal reforms that took place in Europe during the Reformation. As Orthodox theologian Ion Bria explains,

> The mission of the Church rests upon the radiating and transforming power of the Liturgy. It is a stimulus in sending out the people of God to the world to confess the Gospel and to be involved in man's liberation . . . In what sense does the worship constitute a permanent missionary impulse and determine the evangelistic witness of every Christian? How does the liturgical order pass into the order of human existence, personal and social, and shape the life style of Christians? In fact the witness of faith, which includes evangelism, mission and church life, has always taken place in the context of prayer, worship and communion. The missionary structures of the congregation were built upon the liturgy of the Word and Sacraments . . . The liturgical life has to nourish the Christian life not only in its private sphere, but also in its public and political realm . . . Liturgy means public and collective action and therefore there is a sense in which the Christian is a creator of community; this particular charisma has crucial importance today with the increasing lack of human fellowship in the society.[18]

---

18. Bria, "Liturgy after the Liturgy," 365.

The renewal of creation, the reconciliation of mankind, and the restoration of social and political life, therefore, begins with the liturgical assembly of Christ's body, the church. This "work of the people" demands that individuals take their attention away from themselves and find their true identity in community, a community which seeks a higher order of existence for all spheres of life. Insofar as this takes place, the Christian is reoriented in such a way that an atomist view of reality, which results in sectarianism, partisanship, and privatization, is no longer acceptable. This reorientation redirects the Christian back to the wholeness of the church and the wholeness of humanity. It should perhaps be of little surprise, then, that we find some of the clearest expressions of Nevin's missiology in his essay "Catholicity," where he declares, "Art, science, commerce, politics, for instance, as they enter essentially into the idea of man, must all come within the range of this mission ... It is fully as needful for the complete and final triumph of the Gospel among men, that it should subdue the arts, music, painting, sculpture, poetry, (and) fill them with its spirit ..."[19]

For Nevin, the arts, politics, and all of culture are reconciled unto God as mankind comes to know his creator in Christ. In the liturgy, mankind discovers who he is truly meant to be, and as he is reconciled to God, he brings with him all of the ways he expresses himself in the world. In this way, the community of faith anticipates the "restitution and resocialization of politics and economic life to take place by way of the renewal of the Church as the primal order of creation." This takes place when "human beings are liberated from ... the idolization of what is politically or economically good, and are freed for the praise of God, the Creator, Redeemer, and Perfecter."[20]

Nevin's "Catholicity," moreover, complemented well the broader missiological tone of the Mercersburg theology, echoing the words of Schaff's 1844 "Inaugural," where, in the closing summary, 112 theses are offered. Concerning the mission of the church, it was proposed,

> It is the mission of the Church to purify the world in its different spheres of Science, Art, Government, and Social life, with the

---

19. Appel, *Life and Work*, 380. These paragraphs echo Nevin's earlier words in *Antichrist*, 49, namely that "Science, art, politics, and social life, are, for the genuine Sectarian, always more or less profane. His Gnostic Christ dooms him to perpetual imprisonment, gloomy and sad, in the labyrinth of a Manichean world."

20. Wannenwetsch, *Political Worship*, 63.

purifying power of her own divine life; to formally organize it as the Kingdom of God; which must invoke the absolute identity of Church and State, Theology and Philosophy, Worship and Art, Religion and Morality; and to renovate the whole earth, in which Christianity shall become completely the same with humanity, and God Himself shall be All in all.[21]

With Schaff, Nevin believed that the incarnate Christ, because he represents and encompasses the general life of mankind, must also have the power to subsume and transform all institutions which constitute man's natural existence. Christianity, after all, is not law or bare doctrine, but a living, organic constitution. It comprises the first idea of the world and forms the ground of all other spheres of human life. As the foundation of this constitution, the Incarnation is the only power that can elevate the progress of human life to unity and perfection in God.[22]

Nevin's theology demonstrates agreement with the best of his Reformation predecessors in the belief that social and political ethics is inherently related to the life of the church, just as the position of the father of a household and the office of the prince hinge on the ministry of preaching.[23] For example, in an address on the theme of Christian ministry, Nevin explained,

> The institution of the Christian Ministry stands foremost in point of importance, among all the arrangements on which the welfare of life, in its proper civilized form, is found to depend. No other enters so deeply and steadily into the inward moral economy of society; none links itself more vitally with all the radical interests of the individual and all the primary necessities of the State ... The agency of the pulpit, under this view, is of more might by far than the agency of the Senate chamber.[24]

In sum, no wedge can be driven between worship and mission. The church's mission, as the very extension of the incarnate Christ in the history of the world, is, first and foremost, to worship in spirit and in truth, in word and in sacrament. The implications of such an approach are characterized well by theologian and ethicist Bernd Wannenwetsch:

---

21. Schaff, *Principle of Protestantism*, in Appel, *Life and Work*, 206–7.
22. Nevin, "Trench's Lectures," 608, 610–11; also Nevin "New Creation,"11. See DiPuccio, *Interior Sense*, 28.
23. Wannenwetsch, *Political Worship*, 63.
24. Appel, *Life and Work*, 108–9.

> As an eschatological enterprise, worship . . . refuses to abide by the separation between knowing and doing which so largely determines political theory and practice. It does not proclaim the universal plausibility of its ethical directives as the premises of its public relevance and the subsequent translation of these worship directives into practice which is the logical consequence. Worship's universal claim depends precisely on its particularity, its special, unmistakable and irreplaceable experience. It is this which makes it the touchstone for every ethical concept and practice.[25]

The implications of this scheme, Wannenwetsch suggests, are reminiscent of Dietrich Bonhoeffer's notion of "qualified silence," which denotes the challenge of the church to be articulate and expressive even in silence, thus positioning itself for bold proclamation.[26] In this paradigm, not only is cultural mandate an inevitable byproduct of the church's orthodoxy and worship, but it is fundamental to the church's catholic identity and eschatological role. At this basic level, notwithstanding the inherent differences between Nevin and Bonhoeffer, there is a great deal of commonality.

The view towards catholicity which governs Nevin's understanding of history in relation to Christ and his body, the church, therefore obviates the application of popular "Christ and Culture" terminology. Hence, scholars' attempts to apply this typology to his theology have resulted in rather muddled interpretations.[27] Nevin would agree that Christ "transforms" culture, but for him, such a notion refers to the supernatural revelation of the Incarnation and the organic relation with humanity therein. Revelation, in this sense, is holistic and organically related to the living experience of the culture.[28] "Each sphere passes unto the next . . . only as it is caught up and assimilated by a force descending into it from a superior sphere . . . It is a transformation

---

25. Wannenwetsch, *Political Worship*, 103–4. Here, Wannenwetsch is critiquing William Temple's social ethic. Temple shares a number of values with Nevin by virtue of a modified Hegelianism, but his system lacks the Christocentrism upon which Nevin so greatly insists.

26. Bonhoeffer, *Sanctorum Communio*, 251. Cited by Wannenwetsch, *Political Worship*, 102.

27. As noted in the introduction to this study, see Bratt, "Antebellum Culture Wars," 14.

28. Layman, "Holistic Supernaturalism," 193.

from above which," according to Nevin, "adumbrates the salvation and perfection of humanity in God."[29]

To offer theology which implicates Christ for the sole purpose of "rescuing" man from the world and its institutions is to fundamentally misunderstand the Incarnation and what is meant by the "life" of man. For Nevin, the life of mankind is not based on his physical body alone, but upon all that informs who he is in history. Christ's mission—indeed the church's mission—is to redeem the life of man, not as a mere entity, but as one in relation with the history and institutions of the world. In this way, Christ's church extends its sacramental power to mankind so that all of creation might find its perfection in the life of God.

---

29. DiPuccio, *Interior Sense*, 38.

Conclusion: The Legacy of John Williamson Nevin and the Mercersburg Theology

NEVIN'S THEOLOGICAL PROJECT IS, of course, rather difficult for the post-enlightenment Christian to grasp. Indoctrinated with the signs, symbols, and values of modernity and postmodernity, the Christian of the twenty-first century, in order to appreciate Nevin's theology, must drastically rethink his or her presuppositions about the church, the sacraments, and the church's relationship to "secular" society (and not least the assumption that there is such a neutral space). Perhaps most fundamentally, this reorientation begins with rethinking the relationship between public and private life. The Enlightenment's privatization of religion, accommodated by revivalism and sectarianism, instilled within the American conscience the notion that religion is essentially a matter of the individual's experience and expression of faith.

A meaningful engagement with Nevin's theology thus begins with the admission that the modern world has profoundly shaped the individual in ways that should not be so easily accepted at face value. It begins with the acknowledgement that cultural symbols are inherently instructive and indoctrinating, enculturating the individual with a new language and narrative. The indoctrination takes place in the form of a "secular" liturgy that casts its own vision of the kingdom and citizenship therein. As James Smith writes, "Secular liturgies capture our hearts by capturing our imaginations and drawing us into ritual practices that 'teach' us to love something very different from the kingdom of God."[1] The American flag, for example, along with patriotic songs and depictions of American historical narrative, not only evokes certain memories and emotions, but also prompts efforts and actions that sustain a number of American values, principles, and ideologies.[2] Only when one recognizes this type of daily enculturation and inculcation of values can

1. Smith, *Desiring*, 88.
2. Leithart, *Against Christianity*, 86.

they begin to critically rethink the nature and the profound influence of sign, symbol, and "secular" liturgy.

Nevin understood this phenomenon. He took seriously the way in which American history and society were being shaped by the "secular" liturgies of privatization and sectarianism. These liturgies promoted a particular way of life that resulted in a mechanized, materialistic society that does not see the greater whole of reality beyond itself. It is a liturgy in which the "people's work," that is, their liturgical participation, is governed by social contract, voluntarism, and intellectual assent. In sum, Nevin saw a liturgy that was subverting the liturgy of Christ's catholic kingdom.[3] In response, he sought a liturgy that captured the sacramental and objective nature of the church, one which stood over and against those principles of the Enlightenment which tended to assume an anti-sacramental, subjectivist, flattened-out version of reality. In this way, Nevin saw very clearly what many recent Christian theologians have had to seemingly discover for the first time, namely that the church and its sacraments tell us who we are, not the other way around. As one theologian describes it, "to be converted into a faith is not to discover something within us, but rather to be subsumed into a new culture, to take up a new language that changes what is within us."[4]

In the midst of nineteenth-century revivalism, which championed a "save the individual, save the world" mentality, Nevin believed that reforming and strengthening the church catholic was to have the greatest "bearings" on the surrounding world. Consequently, it cannot be stressed enough that, for Nevin, praxis or "application" is not primarily something the church does in the world in addition to its worship; it is the inherent, organic manifestation of the liturgy beyond the walls of the church. Rather than seeking to acquire political clout and cultural "relevance," he would have the church refocus on its pursuit of unity and purity in the body of Christ. Peter Leithart captures this sentiment well: "... the really big kingdom activity—the act that radically changes the world—is the gathering of the people of God on the Lord's day at the heavenly banquet

---

3. Smith puts it well: "Implicit in the liturgies of American nationalism is a particular vision of human flourishing as material prosperity and ownership, as well as a particular take on intersubjectivity, beginning from a negative notion of liberty and thus fostering a generally libertarian view of human relationships that stresses noninterference... The vision of a kingdom implicit in this liturgy is antithetical to the vision of the kingdom implicit in Christian worship." Smith, *Desiring*, 107.

4. Willimon, *Pastor*, 208.

table, when God's people hear His Word, offer humble petitions to the King, and feast on the flesh and blood of Jesus."[5] Rather than spending time and energy on devising ways to "fix" culture by flexing political muscle, Nevin's approach suggests that the reconciling of culture back to God begins in worship by flexing liturgical and sacramental muscle.

Insofar as the church is reoriented towards its objectivity, catholicity, and liturgical identity, it reclaims its role as the society-shaping institution for which it was created. It reaffirms for itself and for the world that Christ is indeed Lord and does in fact have all authority under his feet. It reminds the world that the worship of the triune God is never irrelevant. It is, simply put, the church being the church. Rich Lusk's notion of "Re-Politicizing Ecclesiology" is reminiscent of this approach:

> Rather the church is political because in the very act of being the church—doing Word and Sacrament, in ministering in Word and deed, in binding and loosing—she's announcing and embodying the truth that the world has a new King, the crucified and risen Messiah of Israel. By these means, she is serving and shaping and reordering civilization as a whole. She is creating a new way of doing politics and a new way of structuring and organizing human community.[6]

The church's effort toward this end constitutes its fundamental mission as a liturgical community. Particularly in the way of political and social engagement, the task of the worshiping community is to delineate the way in which the liturgy of God's politics and socialization in worship relates to life beyond the walls of the *ekklesia*. It requires, as Hauerwas rightly points out, recognition that the sacraments are "the essential rituals of our politics . . . Instead of being motives or causes for effective social work on the part of Christian people, these liturgies are our effective social work. For if the Church *is* rather than has a social ethic, these actions are our most important social witness."[7] No less articulately, Nevin explains in his preface to *The Mystical Presence*,

> The visible Church may be imperfect, corrupt, false to its own conception and calling; but still an actual, continuously visible Church there must always be in the world, if Christianity is to have either truth or reality in the form of a new creation. A purely

5. Leithart, *Kingdom and the Power*, 212–13.
6. Lusk, "On Being the Church," 13.
7. Hauerwas, *Peaceable Kingdom*, 108.

> invisible Church has been well denominated a *contradictio in adjecto*; since the very idea of a Church implies the manifestation of the religious life, as something social and common. The whole conception that the externalization of the Christian life is something accidental only to the constitution of this life itself—a sort of mechanical machinery, to help it forward in an outward way—is exceedingly derogatory to the Church, and injurious in its bearings on religion. An outward Church is the necessary form of the new creation in Christ Jesus, in its very nature; and must continue to be so, not only through all time, but through all eternity likewise. Outward social worship, which implies, of course, forms for the purpose, is to be regarded as something essential to piety itself.[8]

Such was Nevin's unwavering passion for Christ and his church. Despite the church's flaws, deficiencies, limitations, and struggles with sin, Nevin fought tirelessly for its life, not only for its own sake but indeed for the sake of the world. If Christ truly is alive, he believed, and if the church is truly united to him, then the church must be the source of life for its members and subsequently for all mankind. This view proceeded from the conviction that God incarnate is neither a convenient metaphor nor an object of mere metaphysical speculation. The Incarnation is a living constitution, exhibited and communicated in the liturgy and wrought into the history of the world, thus posing the very possibility of the world's redemption and the promise of new creation.

---

8. Nevin, *Mystical Presence*, 5.

Bibliography

Acton, Baron John Emerich Edward Dahlberg. *The History of Freedom and Other Essays.* London: Macmillan, 1907.
Ahlstrom, Sydney. *A Religious History of the American People.* New Haven: Yale University Press, 2004.
———, ed. *Theology in America: The Major Protestant Voices from Puritanism to neo-Orthodoxy.* Indianapolis: Hackett, 1967.
Alexander, Archibald. *Evidences of the Authenticity, Inspiration, and Canonical Authority of the Holy Scriptures.* Philadelphia: Presbyterian Board of Publications, 1836.
Amos, Scott. "The Reformation as a Revolution in Worldview." In *Revolutions in Worldview*, edited by Andrew Hoffecker, 206-39. Phillipsburg, NJ: Presbyterian and Reformed, 2007.
Appel, Theodore. *The Life and Work of John Williamson Nevin, D.D., LL.D.* Philadelphia: Reformed Church Publication House, 1889.
Atkinson, Brooks, ed. *The Essential Writings of Ralph Waldo Emerson.* New York: Modern Library, 2000.
Barnes, Howard A. *Horace Bushnell and the Virtuous Republic.* Philadelphia: American Theological Library, 1925.
Baumgarth, William P., and Richard J. Regan, eds. *Aquinas: On Law, Morality, and Politics.* Indianapolis: Hackett, 2002.
Beecher, Lyman. *The Autobiography of Lyman Beecher.* Edited by Barbara M. Cross. 2 vols. Cambridge: Belknap Press of Harvard University Press, 1961.
Binkley, Luther J. *The Mercersburg Theology.* Manheim, PA: Sentinel, 1953.
Boersma, Hans. "On the Rejection of Boundaries: Radical Orthodoxy's Appropriation of St. Augustine." *Pro Ecclesia* 15, no. 4 (Fall 2006) 418-47.
Bonhoeffer, Dietrich. *Sanctorum Communio: A Dogmatic Enquiry into the Sociology of the Church.* London: Collins, 1963.
Bonomo, Jonathan G. *Incarnation and Sacrament: The Eucharist Controversy between Charles Hodge and John Williamson Nevin.* Eugene, OR: Wipf and Stock, 2010.
Bowden, Henry W. "Civil Authority and Religious Freedom." In *A Century of Church History: The Legacy of Philip Schaff*, edited by Henry W. Bowden, 148-67. Carbondale, IL: Southern Illinois University Press, 1988.
Bradstock, Andrew. "The Reformation." In *The Blackwell Companion to Political Theology*, edited by Peter Scott and William T. Cavanaugh, 62-75. Oxford: Blackwell, 2004.
Bratt, James D. "Christian Reformed History in German Mirrors." *Calvin Theological Journal* 42, no. 1 (April 2007) 9-32.
———. "Nevin and the Antebellum Culture Wars." In *Reformed Confessionalism in Nineteenth-Century America: Essays on the Thought of John Williamson Nevin*, edited by Sam Hamstra Jr. and Arie J. Griffioen, 1-22. ATLA Monograph Series 38. Lanham, MD, and London: ATLA and Scarecrow, 1995.

Bria, Ion, "The Liturgy after the Liturgy." In *The Ecumenical Movement: An Anthology of Key Texts and Voice*, edited by Michael Kinnamon and Brian E. Cope, 365–67. Grand Rapids: Eerdmans 1997.

Brownson, Orestes Augustus. *The American Republic: Its Constitution, Tendencies, and Destiny*. New York: P. O'Shea, 1866.

———. "Channing on Social Reform, Article I." In *The Works of Orestes A. Brownson*, edited by Henry F. Brownson, 10: 137–68. Detroit: Thorndike Nourse, 1884.

———. "Origin and Ground of Government." *The United States Magazine and Democratic Review* 15 (Sept 1843) 258.

Burns, James Henderson, and Mark Goldie. *The Cambridge History of Political Thought, 1450–1700*. Cambridge: Cambridge University Press, 1995.

Bushnell, Horace. *Christian Nurture*. New York: Scribner, 1861. Reprint, Grand Rapids: Baker, 1979.

———. "The Founders, Great in Their Unconsciousness." In *The New England Society Orations*, edited by Cephas Brainerd and Eveline Warner Brainerd, 2:81–120. New York: The New England Society, 1901.

———. "Native Quality Essential to the Greatness of a People." In *A Library of American Literature from Earliest Settlement to the Present*, edited by Ellen Mackay Hutchison and Edmund Clarence Stedman, 6:93–98. New York: Jenkins and McCowan, 1884.

———. *Nature and the Supernatural as Together Constituting the One System of God*. New York: Scribner, 1863.

———. "Our Obligations to the Dead." In *Building Eras in Religion*, 319–55. New York: Scribner, 1881.

———. "Unconscious Influence." In *Sermons for the New Life*, 186–205. New York: Scribner, 1858.

———. *Views of Christian Nurture and of Subjects Adjacent Thereto*. 2nd ed. Hartford: Edwin Hunt, 1848.

Calvin, John. *Institutes of the Christian Religion*. Edited by *John* T. Mitchell and translated by Ford Lewis *Battles*. Library of Christian Classics 21. Philadelphia: Westminster, 1960.

Carey, Patrick W. *Orestes A. Brownson: American Religious Weathervane*. Grand Rapids: Eerdmans, 2004.

Carwardine, Richard. *Evangelicals and Politics in Antebellum America*. New Haven: Yale University Press, 1993.

———. "The Politics of Charles Hodge." In *Charles Hodge Revisited: A Critical Appraisal of His Life and Work*, edited by John W. Stewart and James Moorhead, 247–97. Grand Rapids: Eerdmans, 2002.

Cavanaugh, William T. "The Body of Christ: The Eucharist and Politics." *Word and World* 22, no. 2 (Spring 2002) 170–77.

———. "The City: Beyond Secular Parodies." In *Radical Orthodoxy: A New Theology*, edited by Milbank et al., 182–200. London: Routledge, 1999.

———. "God is Not Religious." In *God Is Not: Religious, Nice, One of Us, an American, a Capitalist*, edited by D. Brent Laytham, 97–116. Grand Rapids: Brazos, 2004.

———. "The Liturgies of Church and State." *Liturgy* 20, no. 1 (2005) 25–30.

Cherry, Conrad. "The Structure of Organic Thinking: Horace Bushnell's Approach to Language, Nature, and Nation." *Journal of the American Academy of Religion* 40 (March 1972) 3–20.

Clapp, Rodney. *Border Crossings: Christian Trespasses on Popular Culture and Public Affairs.* Grand Rapids: Brazos, 2000.

Collins-Jones, Scott. "First-Fruits and Foretaste of the Kingdom: A Foray into the Sacramental Theologies of John Williamson Nevin and Lesslie Newbigin." Paper presented to the Reformed Theology and History Group of the American Academy of Religion, November 2001.

Conforti, Joseph A. *Imagining New England.* Chapel Hill, NC: University of North Carolina Press, 2001.

Cross, Anthony. *Baptist Sacramentalism.* Eugene, OR: Wipf & Stock, 2009.

DeBie, Linden J. *Speculative Theology and Common-Sense Religion: Mercersburg and the Conservative Roots of American Religion.* Eugene, OR: Pickwick, 2008.

DiPuccio, William. "The Dynamic Realism of Mercersburg Theology: The Romantic Pursuit of the Ideal in the Actual." PhD diss., Marquette University, 1994.

———. *The Interior Sense of Scripture: The Sacred Hermeneutics of John W. Nevin.* Macon, GA: Mercer University Press, 1998.

———. "Nevin's Idealistic Philosophy." In *Reformed Confessionalism in Nineteenth-Century America: Essays on the Thought of John Williamson Nevin*, edited by Sam Hamstra Jr. and Arie J. Griffioen, 44–54. ATLA Monograph Series 38. Lanham, MD, and London: ATLA and Scarecrow, 1995.

———. Review of *John Williamson Nevin: American Theologian*, by Richard D. Wentz. *Theology Today* (April 1999) 152–53.

Dorner, Isaak. *The Liturgical Conflict in the Reformed Church in North America, with Special Reference to Fundamental Evangelical Doctrines.* Translated by JHA Bomberger. Philadelphia: Loag, 1868.

Dorrien, Gary J. *The Making of American Liberal Theology.* Louisville, KY: Westminster John Knox Press, 2003.

Douglass, Ann. *The Feminization of American Culture.* New York: Macmillan, 1998.

Erb, William, ed. *Dr. Nevin's Theology, Based on Manuscript Class Room Lectures.* Reading, PA: I.M. Beaver, 1913.

Evans, William Borden. *Imputation and Impartation: Union with Christ in American Reformed Theology.* Milton Keynes: Paternoster, 2008.

Frost, Bryan-Paul. "Religion, Nature, and Disobedience in the Thought of Ralph Waldo Emerson and Henry David Thoreau." In *History of American Political Thought*, edited by Bryan-Paul Frost and Jeffrey Sikkenga, 355–85. Lanham, MD: Lexington, 2003.

Gamble, Richard C., ed. *Calvin's Thought on Economic and Social Issues and the Relationship of Church and State.* New York: Garland, 1992.

Gienapp, William E. "Politics Seem to Enter into Everything: Political Culture in the North, 1840–1860." In *Essays on American Antebellum Politics 1840–1860*, edited by William E. Gienapp, et al., 114–69. College Station: Texas A&M University Press, 1982.

Gougeon, Len. "Politics and Economics." In *Oxford Handbook of Transcendentalism*, edited by Joel Myerson et al., 136–52. Oxford: Oxford University Press, 2010.

Grabill, Stephen J. *Rediscovering the Natural Law in Reformed Theological Ethics.* Grand Rapids: Eerdmans, 2006.

Haddorff, David Wayne, ed. *Dependence and Freedom: The Moral Thought of Horace Bushnell.* Lanham, MD: University Press of America, 1994.

Hamstra, Sam, Jr. "Nevin on the Pastoral Office." In *Reformed Confessionalism in Nineteenth-Century America: Essays on the Thought of John Williamson Nevin*, edited by Sam Hamstra Jr. and Arie J. Griffioen, 169–92. ATLA Monograph Series 38. Lanham, MD, and London: ATLA and Scarecrow, 1995.

——— and Arie J. Griffioen, eds. *Reformed Confessionalism in Nineteenth-Century America: Essays on the Thought of John Williamson Nevin*. ATLA Monograph Series 38. Lanham, MD, and London: ATLA and Scarecrow, 1995.

Hankins, Barry. *The Second Great Awakening and the Transcendentalists*. Santa Barbara, CA: Greenwood, 2004.

Harrison, Jennifer. "Lane Seminary Debates (1834)." In *Encyclopedia of Antislavery and Abolition*, edited by Peter P. Hinks, et al., 403–404. Westport, CT: Greenwood, 2007.

Hart, D.G. *John Williamson Nevin: High Church Calvinist*. Phillipsburg, NJ: Presbyterian and Reformed, 2005.

Harvey, Barry. "Re-Membering the Body: Baptism, Eucharist and the Politics of Disestablishment." In *Baptist Sacramentalism*, edited by Anthony R. Cross and Philip E. Thompson, 96–116. Studies in Baptist History and Thought 5. Carlisle, Cumbria: Paternoster, 2003.

Hatch, Nathan O. *The Democratization of American Christianity*. New Haven: Yale University Press, 1989.

Hauerwas, Stanley. *The Peaceable Kingdom: A Primer in Christian Ethics*. Notre Dame: University of Notre Dame Press, 1983.

Helm, Paul. "Calvin and Natural Law." *Scottish Bulletin of Evangelical Theology* 2 (1984) 5–22.

Helseth, Paul. "Moral Character and Moral Certainty: The Subjective State of the Soul and J. G. Machen's Critique of Theological Liberalism." PhD diss., Marquette University, 1996.

Hewitt, Glenn A. *Regeneration and Morality: A Study of Charles Finney, Charles Hodge, John W. Nevin, and Horace Bushnell*. Brooklyn: Carlson, 1991.

Hodge, A. A. *The Life of Charles Hodge, D.D. LL.D*. New York: Scribner, 1880.

Hodge, Charles. "The Church and the Country." *Biblical Repertory and Princeton Review* 23, no. 2 (April 1861) 333.

———. *Discussions in Church Polity*. New York: Scribner, 1878.

———. "President Lincoln." *Biblical Repertory and Princeton Review* 37 (July 1865) 439–40.

———. "The Relation of Church and State." *Biblical Repertory Princeton Review* 35, no. 4 (October 1863) 691–93.

———. "Sunday Laws." *Biblical Repertory Princeton Review* 36 (Oct. 1859) 734–42.

———. *Systematic Theology*. Vol. 1. New York: Scribner, 1872–73. Reprint, Grand Rapids: Eerdmans, 1981.

Hoelzl, Michael, and Graham Ward. *Religion and Political Thought*. London: Continuum International, 2006.

Hoffecker, Andrew W., ed. *Revolutions in Worldview*. Phillipsburg, NJ: Presbyterian and Reformed, 2007.

Holcomb, Justin S. "Being Bound to God: Participation and Covenant Revisited." In *Radical Orthodoxy and the Reformed Tradition: Creation, Covenant, and Participation*, edited by James K.A. Smith and James H. Olthuis, 243–62. Grand Rapids: Baker Academic, 2005.

Holifield, E. Brooks. *Theology in America: Christian Thought from the Age of the Puritans to the Civil War.* New Haven: Yale University Press, 2003.

Hopfl, Harro. *Luther and Calvin on Secular Authority.* Cambridge: Cambridge University Press, 1991.

Horton, Michael S. "Participation and Covenant." In *Radical Orthodoxy and the Reformed Tradition: Creation, Covenant, and Participation,* edited by James K.A. Smith and James H. Olthuis, 107–32. Grand Rapids: Baker Academic, 2005.

Hutchison, William R. *The Transcendentalist Ministers: Church Reform in the New England Renaissance.* New Haven: Yale University Press, 2005.

Johnson, Matthew Raphael. "Nation, State and the Incarnation in the Political Writings of Vladimir Solov'yev: The Transfiguration of Politics." *Religion, State & Society* 30, no. 4 (2002) 347–55.

Kelley, Robert L. *The Cultural Pattern in American Politics: The First Century.* New York: Knopf, 1979.

Kelly, John E. "The Influence of Aquinas' Natural Law Theory on the Principle of 'Corporatism' in the Thought of Leo XIII and Pius XI." In *Things Old and New: Catholic Social Teaching Revisited,* edited by Francis P. McHugh and Samuel M. Natale, 104–43. Lanham, MD: University Press of America, 1993.

Kieffer, Moses. "Church and State." *Mercersburg Review* 1 (1849) 569–83.

Kilick, Bruce. *Churchmen and Philosophers: From Jonathan Edwards to John Dewey.* New Haven: Yale University Press, 1985.

Larson, Wayne A. "Philip Schaff's Idea of Historical Progress and Its Critique of the Church in 19th Century America." Unpublished Paper, 2001.

Layman, David Wayne. "Holistic Supernaturalism." In *Reformed Confessionalism in Nineteenth-Century America: Essays on the Thought of John Williamson Nevin,* edited by Sam Hamstra Jr. and Arie J. Griffioen, 193–208. ATLA Monograph Series 38. Lanham, MD, and London: ATLA and Scarecrow, 1995.

Leithart, Peter. *Against Christianity.* Moscow, ID: Canon, 2003.

———. *Defending Constantine: The Twilight of an Empire and the Dawn of Christendom.* Downers Grove, IL: InterVarsity Press, 2010.

———. *The Kingdom and the Power.* Phillipsburg, NJ: Presbyterian and Reformed, 1993.

———. "Medieval Theology and the Roots of Modernity." In *Revolutions in Worldview,* edited by Andrew Hoffecker, 140–77. Phillipsburg, NJ: Presbyterian and Reformed, 2007.

Lincoln, C. Eric, and Lawrence H. Mamiya. *The Black Church in the African American Experience.* Durham: Duke University Press, 1990.

Lints, Richard. "Imaging and Idolatry: The Sociality of Personhood in the Canon." In *Personal Identity in Theological Perspective,* edited by Michael S. Horton and Mark R. Talbot, 204–25. Grand Rapids: Eerdmans, 2006.

Littlejohn, W. Bradford. *The Mercersburg Theology and the Quest for Reformed Catholicity.* Eugene, OR: Wipf and Stock, 2009.

Livingston, James C., and Francis Schüssler Fiorenza. *Modern Christian Thought: The Enlightenment and the Nineteenth Century.* 2nd ed. Minneapolis: Fortress, 2006.

Lotz, David. "Philip Schaff and Church History." In *A Century of Church History: The Legacy of Philip Schaff,* edited by Henry W. Bowden, 1–35. Carbondale, IL: Southern Illinois University Press, 1988.

Luebke, Frederick C., ed. *Ethnic Voters and the Election of Lincoln*. Lincoln: University of Nebraska Press, 1971.

Lusk, Rich W. "On Being the Church in America." Unpublished Paper, 2007.

Luther, Martin. "The Blessed Sacrament of the Holy and True Body of Christ, and the Brotherhoods." In *D. Martin Luther's Werke: Kritische Gesamtausgabe*, edited by Weimarer Ausgabe, 2:742–758. Weimar: Böhlau, 1883.

———. "The German Mass and Order of Service." In *Luther's Works*, edited by Ulrich S. Leupold, 53:61–90. Philadelphia: Fortress, 1965.

———. "Secular Authority: To What Extent It Should Be Obeyed." In *Martin Luther: Selections from His Writings*, edited by John Dillenberger, 268–369. New York: Anchor, 1961.

Marsden, George. *Fundamentalism and American Culture*. Oxford: Oxford University Press, 2006.

———. *The Soul of the American University: From Protestant Establishment to Established Nonbelief*. Oxford: Oxford University Press, 1994.

Martinez, German. *Signs of Freedom: Theology of the Christian Sacraments*. New York: Paulist, 2003.

Mascall, Eric Lionel. *Corpus Christi*. London: Longmans, 1965.

McConnel, Tim. "The Old Princeton Apologetics: Common Sense or Reformed?" *Journal of the Evangelical Theological Society* 46, no. 4 (Dec 2003) 647–72.

McCormick, Richard P. *The Second American Party System: Party Formation in the Jacksonian Era*. Chapel Hill: University of North Carolina Press, 1966.

McDonald, Forrest and Ellen Shapiro McDonald. "Ethnic Origins of the American People." *William and Mary Quarterly* 37, no. 2 (April 1980) 179–99.

Milbank, John. *Being Reconciled*. London: Routledge, 2003.

———. "An Essay Against Secular Order." *The Journal of Religious Ethics* 15, no. 2 (Fall 1987) 199–224.

———. "Postmodern Critical Augustinianism: A Short Summa in Forty-two Responses to Unasked Questions." In *The Postmodern God: A Theological Reader*, edited by Graham Ward, 265–78. Malden, MA: Blackwell, 1997.

———. *Theology and Social Theory: Beyond Secular Reason*. Oxford: Blackwell, 1990.

———, and Catherine Pickstock. *Truth in Aquinas*. London: Routledge, 2001.

———, Catherine Pickstock, and Graham Ward. *Radical Orthodoxy: A New Theology*. London: Routledge, 1999.

Mueller, Franz H. "Principle of Subsidiarity in the Christian Tradition." *American Catholic Sociological Review* 4, no. 3 (Oct 1943) 144–57.

Murphy, Nancey. *Beyond Liberalism and Fundamentalism*. Valley Forge, PA: Trinity Press International, 1996.

Nevin, John Williamson. *AntiChrist: or the Spirit of Sect and Schism*. New York: John S. Taylor, 1848.

———. *Anxious Bench, AntiChrist, and the Sermon on Catholic Unity*. Edited by Augustine Thompson. Eugene, OR: Wipf and Stock, 2000.

———. "The Apostles' Creed" (3 articles). *Mercersburg Review* 1 (1849). "Article I: "Outward History of the Creed," 105–127. "Article II: Its Inward Constitution and Form," 201–221. "Article III: Its Material Structure and Organism," 313–347.

———. "Bible Anthropology." *Mercersburg Review* 24 (1877) 363–64.

———. "The Bread of Life: A Communion Sermon." *Mercersburg Review* 26 (1879) 14–47.

Bibliography

———. "Brownson's Quarterly Review." *Mercersburg Review* 2 (1850) 33–80.
———. "Catholic Unity." Reprinted in *The Mercersburg Theology*, edited by James H. Nichols, 36-39. New York: Oxford University Press, 1966.
———. "Catholicism." *Mercersburg Review* 3 (1851) 1–26.
———. "The Christian Ministry." *Mercersburg Review* 7 (1855) 68–115.
———. "Christianity and Humanity." *Mercersburg Review* 20 (1873) 469–86.
———. *The Church: a sermon preached at the opening of the Synod of the German Reformed Church at Carlisle, October 1846*. Chambersburg: German Reformed, 1847.
———. "The Church Year." *Mercersburg Review* 8 (1856) 456–78.
———. "Doctrine of the Reformed Church on the Lord's Supper." *Mercersburg Review* 2 (1850) 421–548.
———. "Dorner's History of Protestant Theology." *Mercersburg Review* 15 (1868) 262.
———. "Early Christianity." *Mercersburg Review* 3 (1851) 461–89.
———. "Early Christianity, Article III." *Mercersburg Review* 4 (1852) 1–54.
———. "Educational Religion." *Weekly Messenger* 12 (7 July 1847) 24–58.
———. "Faith, Reverence, and Freedom." *Mercersburg Review* 2 (1850) 97–116.
———. "German Character." In *The Life and Work of John Williamson Nevin, D.D., LL.D.*, edited by Theodore Appel, 111–16. Philadelphia: Reformed Church Publication House, 1889.
———. *The German Language*. Chambersburg, PA: Publication Office of the German Reformed Church, 1842.
———. "Historical Development." *Mercersburg Review* 1 (1849) 512–14.
———. "Human Freedom." *The American Review: a Whig journal devoted to politics and literature* 7 (April 1848) 406–18. Reprinted in *Human freedom, and A Plea for Philosophy, 2 essays*. Mercersburg: P.A. Rice, 1850.
———. "Lancaster Commencement Address." Lancaster: S.R. Driver, 1867. In *The Life and Work of John Williamson Nevin, D.D., LL.D.*, edited by Theodore Appel, 634–54. Philadelphia: Reformed Church Publication House, 1889.
———. "Lectures on History." In *The Life and Work of John Williamson Nevin, D.D., LL.D.*, edited by Theodore Appel, 590–602. Philadelphia: Reformed Church Publication House, 1889.
———. "Letter to Dr. Henry Harbaugh." In *Catholic and Reformed: Selected Theological Writings of John Williamson Nevin*, edited by Charles Yrigoyen Jr. and George H. Bricker, 407–11. Eugene, OR: Pickwick, 1978.
———. "Man's True Destiny: A Baccalaureate Address to the First Graduating Class of Franklin and Marshall College." Lancaster, PA, August 31, 1853. Reprinted as, "First Baccalaureate Address." In *The Life and Work of John Williamson Nevin, D.D., LL.D.*, edited by Theodore Appel, 454–61. Philadelphia: Reformed Church Publication House, 1889.
———. "The Moral Order of Sex." *Mercersburg Review* 2 (1850) 549–72.
———. "My Own Life." *Reformed Church Messenger* 36, no. 24 (June 15, 1870).
———. *The Mystical Presence: The Reformed or Calvinistic Doctrine of the Holy Eucharist*. Philadelphia: J.B. Lippincott, 1846. Reprint, Philadelphia: S.R. Fisher, 1867.
———. "The Nation's Second Birth." *German Reformed Messenger* 30, no. 47 (July 26, 1865) 1.
———. "The Natural and Supernatural." *Mercersburg Review* 11 (1850) 176–210.
———. "The New Creation in Christ." *Mercersburg Review* 2 (1850) 1–11.

———. *Party Spirit: An Address Delivered before the Literary Societies of Washington College, Washington Pa. on the Evening of September 24th 1839.* Chambersburg, PA: Publication Office of the German Reformed Church, 1840.

———. "Philosophy of History III: History as Particular." *College Days* (March 1873).

———. Review of *Psychology*, by F.A. Rauch. *Weekly Messenger of the German Reformed Church* 5 (June 10, 1840). Reprinted in *The Life and Work of John Williamson Nevin, D.D., LL.D.*, edited by Theodore Appel, 100–107. Philadelphia: Reformed Church Publication House, 1889.

———. "The Sect System." *Mercersburg Review* 1 (1849) 482–507; 521–38.

———. *A Summary of Biblical Antiquities.* Philadelphia: American Sunday School Union, 1829–30.

———. "Theology of the New Liturgy," *Mercersburg Review* 14 (1867) 23–66.

———. "Trench's Lectures." *Mercersburg Review* 2 (1850) 604–19.

———. "Undying Life in Christ." In *The Life and Work of John Williamson Nevin, D.D., LL.D.*, edited by Theodore Appel, 607–27. Philadelphia: Reformed Church Publication House, 1889.

———. *A Vindication of the Revised Liturgy, Historical and Theological.* Philadelphia: Rodgers, 1867. Reprinted as "Theological Vindication of the New Liturgy." In *Catholic and Reformed: Selected Theological Writings of John Williamson Nevin*, edited by Charles Yrigoyen Jr. and George H. Bricker, 313–403. Eugene, OR: Pickwick, 1978.

———. "Wilberforce on the Incarnation." *Mercersburg Review* 2 (1850) 164–96.

———. "The Wonderful Nature of Man." *Mercersburg Review* 11 (1859) 317–37. In *The Life and Work of John Williamson Nevin, D.D., LL.D.*, edited by Theodore Appel, 512–28. Philadelphia: Reformed Church Publication House, 1889.

———. "The Year 1848." *Mercersburg Review* 1 (1849) 10–44.

Nichols, James Hastings, ed. *The Mercersburg Theology.* New York: Oxford University Press, 1966.

———. *Romanticism in American Theology: Nevin and Schaff at Mercersburg.* Chicago: University of Chicago Press, 1961.

Niebuhr, Reinhold. *Moral Man and Immoral Society: A Study in Ethics and Politics.* New York: Scribner, 1947.

Noll, Mark. *America's God: From Jonathan Edwards to Abraham Lincoln.* Oxford: Oxford University Press, 2002.

———. "'Both . . . pray to the Same God': The Singularity of Lincoln's Faith in the Era of the Civil War." *Journal of the Abraham Lincoln Association* 18, no. 1 (Winter 1997). Online: http://www.historycooperative.org/journals/jala/18.1/noll.html.

———. *The Civil War as a Theological Crisis.* Chapel Hill: University of North Carolina Press, 2006.

O'Donovan, Oliver. *The Desire of the Nations: Rediscovering the Roots of Political Theology.* Cambridge: Cambridge University Press, 1999.

Papnikolaou, Aristotle. "Orthodox Christianity." In *The Encyclopedia of Christianity*, edited by Erwin Fahlbusch and Geoffrey William Bromiley, 5:414–18. Grand Rapids: Eerdmans, 2008.

Payne, John B. "Nevin on Baptism." In *Reformed Confessionalism in Nineteenth-Century America: Essays on the Thought of John Williamson Nevin*, edited by Sam Hamstra Jr. and Arie J. Griffioen, 125–52. ATLA Monograph Series 38. Lanham, MD, and London: ATLA and Scarecrow, 1995.

Peterson, John. *Aquinas: A New Introduction*. Lanham, MD: University Press of America, 2008.

Schaff, David Schley. *The Life of Philip Schaff*. New York: Scribner, 1897.

Schaff, Philip. *America: A sketch of the political, social, and religious character*. New York: Scribner, 1855.

———. *Church and State in the United States, or, The American idea of religious liberty and its practical effects: with official documents*. New York: Putnam, 1888. Reprint, Madison: Schaff and Scribner, 1889.

———. *The Civil War and Religious Life in the United States*. Berlin: Wiegandt und Grieben, 1866.

———. *History of the Apostolic Church*. New York: Scribner, 1853.

———. *History of the Christian Church*. Vol 7. New York: Scribner, 1892.

———. *The Principle of Protestantism*. Edited by Bard Thompson and George H. Bricker. Lancaster Series on the Mercersburg Theology. Philadelphia: United Church Press, 1964.

———. *What is Church History? A Vindication of the Idea of Historical Development*. Philadelphia: J.B. Lippincott, 1846.

Scheiber, Harry N. "American Federalism and Diffusion of Power: Historical and Contemporary Perspectives." *University of Toledo Law Review* 9 (1978) 619–80.

Schlesinger, Arthur M., Sr. "A Critical Period in American Religion, 1875–1900." *Massachusetts Historical Society Proceedings* 64 (1930–32). Reprinted in *Religion in American History: Interpretive Essays*, edited by John M. Mulder and John F. Wilson, 302–17. Englewood Cliffs, NJ: Prentice-Hall, 1978.

Schmidt, Jean Miller. *Souls or the Social Order*. Brooklyn: Carlson, 1991.

Scott, Peter, and William T. Cavanaugh, eds. *The Blackwell Companion to Political Theology*. Oxford: Blackwell, 2004.

Senn, Frank. *The People's Work: A Social History of the Liturgy*. Minneapolis: Fortress, 2006.

Shade, William G. "Pennsylvania Politics in the Jacksonian Period: A Case Study, Northampton County, 1824–1844." *Pennsylvania History* 39 (July 1972) 313–33.

———. "Political Pluralism and Party Development: The Creation of a Modern Party System, 1815–1852." In *Evolution of American Electoral Systems*, edited by Kleppner et al., 77–112. Ann Arbor: University of Michigan Press, 1981.

Sibley, Joel H., *The Partisan Imperative: The Dynamics of American Politics Before the Civil War*. New York: Oxford University Press, 1985.

Skillen, James. *Introduction to Abraham Kuyper: The Problem of Poverty*. Grand Rapids: Baker Academic, 1991.

Smith, James K.A. *Desiring the Kingdom: Worship, Worldview, and Cultural Formation*. Grand Rapids: Baker, 2009.

———. *Introducing Radical Orthodoxy: Mapping a Post-Secular Theology*. Grand Rapids: Baker Academic, 2004.

———. "The Spirit, Religions and the World as Sacrament: A Response to Amos Yong's Pneumatological Assist." *Journal of Pentecostal Theology* 15, no.2 (2007) 251–61.

———, and James H. Olthuis. *Radical Orthodoxy and the Reformed Tradition: Creation, Covenant, and Participation*. Grand Rapids: Baker Academic, 2005.

Smith, Timothy L. *Revivalism and Social Reform*. New York: Abingdon, 1957.

Solovyov, Vladimir. *Lectures on Divine Humanity*. New York: Lindisfarne, 1995.

———. "Law and Morality." In *Politics, Law and Morality*, edited by Vladimir Wozniuk, 131–213. New Haven: Yale University Press, 2000.

———. "Morality and Politics." In *Politics, Law and Morality*, edited by Vladimir Wozniuk, 6–19. New Haven: Yale University Press, 2000.

Stackhouse, Max. Preface to *Religion, Pluralism, and Public Life: Abraham Kuyper's Legacy for the Twenty-First Century*, edited by Luis Lugo, xi-xviii. Grand Rapids: Eerdmans, 2000.

Steuer, Daniel. "Nature." In *Encyclopedia of the Romantic Era, 1760–1850*, edited by Christopher John Murray, 2:792–94. New York and London: Taylor and Francis, 2004.

Taylor, William R. *Cavalier and Yankee: The Old South and American National Character*. New York: George Braziller, 1961.

Thomas, George. *Revivalism and Cultural Change: Christianity, Nation Building, and the Market in the Nineteenth-Century United States*. Chicago: University of Chicago Press, 1989.

Thompson, Ernest Trice. *Presbyterians in South, Vol. I: 1607–1861*. Richmond, VA: John Knox Press, 1963.

Torbett, David. *Theology and Slavery: Charles Hodge and Horace Bushnell*. Macon, GA: Mercer University Press, 2006.

Toulouse, Mark G. and James O. Duke. *Makers of Christian Theology in America*. Nashville: Abingdon, 1997.

Tully, Alan W. "Ethnicity, Religion and Politics in Early America." *Pennsylvania Magazine of History and Biography* 107, no. 4 (Oct. 1983) 491–536.

Turner, James. *Without God, Without Creed: The Origins of Unbelief in America*. Baltimore: Johns Hopkins University Press, 1985.

Valliere, Paul. *Modern Russian Theology: Bukharev, Soloviev, Bulgakov*. Grand Rapids: Eerdmans, 2000.

Vander Stelt, John. *Philosophy and Scripture: A Study in Old Princeton and Westminster Theology*. Marlton, NJ: Mack, 1978.

VanDrunen, David. *Natural Law and the Two Kingdoms: A Study in the Development of Reformed Social Thought*. Grand Rapids: Eerdmans, 2010.

Van Til, Kent. "Subsidiarity and Sphere-Sovereignty: A Match Made in . . ." *Theological Studies* 69 (2008) 610–36.

Van Til, Henry. *The Calvinistic Concept of Culture*. Grand Rapids: Baker, 1959, 2001.

Wallace, Robert M. *Hegel's Philosophy of Reality, Freedom, and God*. Cambridge: Cambridge University Press, 2005.

Wallace, Ronald S. *Calvin, Geneva, and the Reformation: A Study of Calvin as Social Worker, Churchman, Pastor and Theologian*. Grand Rapids: Baker, 1988.

Wannenwetsch, Bernd. "Liturgy." In *The Blackwell Companion to Political Theology*, edited by Peter Scott and William T. Cavanaugh, 76–90. Oxford: Blackwell, 2004.

———. *Political Worship*. Oxford: Oxford University Press, 2009.

Ward, Graham. *Cities of God*. London: Routledge, 2001.

Wentz, Richard E. *John Williamson Nevin: American Theologian*. Oxford: Oxford University Press, 1997.

Williamson, Gerald Irvin. *Westminster Confession of Faith: For Study Classes*. Phillipsburg, NJ: Presbyterian and Reformed, 1964.

Willimon, William H. *Pastor: The Theology and Practice of Ordained Ministry*. Nashville: Abingdon, 2002.

Winebrenner, John. *History of All the Religious Denominations in the United States.* Harrisburg: Winebrenner, 1848.

Witte, John. *God's Joust, God's Justice: Law and Religion in the Western Tradition.* Grand Rapids: Eerdmans, 2006.

Yong, Amos. "Radically Orthodox, Reformed, and Pentecostal: Rethinking the Intersection of Post/Modernity and the Religions in Conversation with James K.A. Smith." *Journal of Pentecostal Theology* 15, no. 2 (2007) 233–50.

Yrigoyen, Charles, Jr., and George H. Bricker, eds. *Catholic and Reformed: Selected Theological Writings of John Williamson Nevin.* Eugene, OR: Pickwick, 1978.

Ziegler, Howard J. B. *Frederick Augustus Rauch: American Hegelian.* Manheim: Sentinel, 1953.

Index

Adam, 24, 88, 94, 95n19, 98, 102, 103, 107–10, 118n19, 143
Alexander, Archibald, 62n11
America, 36, 38n72, 39n77
American Revolution, 43, 76
analogia entis (analogy of being), 4, 135, 139
antebellum politics, 40
anthropology, 33, 48, 59–88, 110
Anxious Bench, 20, 21, 75n20, 107n54 (*see also* new measures and revivalism)
Appel, Theodore, 2, 16n4, 42n4, 45n13, 46, 49n25, 53, 57n56, 70n41, 71n43, 79n78, 80n81, 81n82, 83n88, 91n6, 103, 107n54, 116n15, 123n35, 146n62, 149, 151n5, 157n19, 158
Apostles' Creed, 82n85, 87n105
Apostles/Apostolic, xiv, 52, 68, 69, 98
Aquinas, Thomas, 94, 111, 116, 124–26
Arminianism, 21
ascension, 94, 149–60
atonement, 21, 67n30, 93, 94
Augustine, 7, 90, 118, 120, 134, 142

baptism, 40, 89, 102–7, 118n19
Baconian method, 61
Barth, Karl, 8
Benevolent Empire, 18, 44n9, 49, 60, 69
Binkley, Luther, 67n28, 81, 82, 103n43
Bonomo, Jonathan G., xviii, xix, 11, 97, 99, 107n54
Bratt, James D., 1n2, 8–9, 42n4, 46n16, 47, 52, 55n50, 75n62, 126, 127, 150n3, 159n27
Brownson, Orestes, 2, 33–36, 69, 83n90
Buchanan, James, 42–43

Bushnell, Horace, 2, 11, 12, 29–33, 34, 37, 40, 102–5, 107, 145

Calvin, John, 95n19, 98–100, 113–23, 128, 134, 148
Calvinism, xvii, 21
Carwardine, Richard, xvii, 17, 23, 43, 44n9, 45
"Catholic Unity," 71n42
"Catholicism," 81, 83n88, 99n33, 101n38, 141n38, 151n5
catholicity, xiii, 10, 56, 57, 114, 127, 155, 157, 159, 163
Cavanaugh, William T., 136n21, 140–44, 153, 154n12
Chalmers, Thomas, 17
Christ: benefits of, 93–95, 100; divinity and humanity of, 64, 71–73, 88, 123, 130; life of, 76, 86–88, 92, 93, 95n19, 96, 98, 100, 105; person of, 98, 131; union with, 57, 58, 65, 75, 84, 86, 91–95, 98, 99, 107n53, 108, 135n19 (*see also*, incarnation, Christology)
Christian Nurture, 30, 103, 104, 105, 107
Christology, xiii, 67n30
Church: divinity/humanity of, 91–92; ideal/actual, 89, 91, 92, 102, 110, 118n19, 122, 138; polity, 90, 151; and state, 2, 7, 13, 24–26, 30, 31, 34, 36–39, 44n9, 48, 49, 54–56, 90n4, 100–102, 118n18, 119, 120–24, 126, 128, 133, 141, 142, 144n52, 147, 151; unity of, 3, 6, 58, 64–65; visible/invisible, 5, 65, 89, 90, 91, 92 112n3, 117, 118n18, 119, 121, 124, 135, 163, 164

Index

Church Fathers, xiii, 52, 68, 94, 97, 98, 129, 130, 141; Athanasius, 129; Cappadocians, 129; Cyprian, 129; Irenaeus, 129
church history, 65–68, 98
church question, xiii, 9, 58, 150n2, 151, 155
Civil War, 15, 16, 26, 40n79, 48–49, 74n59, 150n2, 150n4, 155n15
Coleridge, S. T., 138
Common Nationality, 70–71
Common Sense Realism, 24, 26, 27, 61, 62, 64, 72, 112, 137, 139, 151
Constitution, 36, 39, 40, 42, 52
Cooke, Henry, 17
creation, 28, 30, 49, 57, 58, 69n39, 72, 82n85, 84–87, 90, 93–96, 101, 103, 115, 125, 127, 128, 134, 136–40

democratization, xviii, 1, 11, 16, 20, 22, 60
DiPuccio, William E., 143n44, 158n22, 160n29, 4, 5, 10–11, 15n1, 61, 62n11, 64n17, 72, 73n56, 75n63, 86, 87, 91n7, 101n39, 109n59, 115, 116n13, 137–39
disestablishment, 11, 20
Dorner, Isaak, 65n21, 67, 129n1
dualism, 75–76, 103, 132, 133, 138

"Early Christianity," 12, 52, 97, 101n36, 121n30, 146n62, 128n55, 141n39
ecclesiology, xiii, xiv, xvii, 10, 11, 52, 55, 65n20, 75n63, 89, 90, 91n7, 96, 112, 140, 141, 163 (*see also*, church)
Edwards, Jonathan, xvii, 137, 138
Emerson, Ralph Waldo, 27–28
empiricism, 30, 64, 137
Enlightenment 7, 24, 26, 33, 48, 52, 60, 74, 138, 140, 142n40, 152–54, 161–62
epistemology, 72, 138
eschatology, 117, 124, 128
Eucharist, 5, 6, 35, 95–100, 102, 106, 112, 113, 141–42
Evans, William B., 107n53, 110n61

faith, 67, 77, 82–88, 92, 93, 95, 97, 98–105, 107, 125, 140, 146, 151n5, 156, 157, 161, 162
Fall, the, 5, 36, 94, 102–4, 109, 115, 147, 154
family, 37, 41, 42, 46, 53n42, 81, 103, 104, 105, 125–127
Federalists, 20n14
Fichte, Johann, 63
Finney, Charles, 20, 21, 62n10, 65n20

German idealism, 44n1, 62, 64, 74, 75, 112, 130, 133, 137
German Reformed Church, 44, 45, 65, 111
German theology, 67
government (American), 39
Great Awakening, Second, 21

Hart, Darryl G., 43n6, 46n15, 149, 150
Hatch, Nathan, 16n5, 20n13, 65n20
Hauerwas, Stanley, 8, 163
Hegel, G. W. F., 63, 65, 67, 71, 117, 122, 126, 130, 133, 140
Hegelianism, 65, 159n25
hermeneutics, 1, 10, 11, 148
historical continuity, 69, 153
historical development, 15, 51, 58, 68, 69, 70, 71, 92, 155n16
history, xiv, xv, xvii, 3, 5, 9, 11, 12, 15, 16, 22, 25, 26, 28, 31, 32, 36, 37, 39, 40, 47, 48–52, 54, 56, 58, 64–73, 89–101, 114, 116, 130–33, 140, 146, 148, 149, 150n2, 153–55, 158–60, 162, 164
Hodge, Charles, xviii, 1n1, 2, 11, 12 22–26, 31–33, 40, 44n9, 61n8, 75n61, 90, 102, 108, 109, 112, 135, 143, 146, 152
Holifield, E. Brooks, xvii, 63, 65n21, 69n38, 83n90, 88n109, 92, 103n44, 155n16
Holy Spirit, 70, 81, 118n19, 156
Humanity xiv, 5, 9, 21, 28, 34–36, 39, 50, 59, 64, 69–88, 92, 93–95, 99, 101n40, 102, 104, 107, 108, 117, 122, 124, 125, 127n51, 130, 131, 136, 143–45, 154, 157–60 (*see also*, anthropology)

Index

Hume, David, 56, 74

idealism, 27, 41n1, 49, 62, 63–64, 65n21, 69, 74, 75, 112, 124, 130, 133, 137, 139, 153
image of God (*imago Dei*), 5, 76, 87, 99
imputation, 90, 102–10, 135
incarnation, xiii, xviii, 3, 5, 6, 9–12, 15, 16, 34, 35, 63, 64–73, 81–84, 88, 89–101, 103, 197n54, 113, 114, 123, 124, 129–33, 136–40, 141–47, 153, 158–60, 164
individualism, xiv, 6, 22, 23, 30, 47, 54, 63, 65n20, 74, 112n3, 142, 155
infant baptism, 106, 107n53

Jackson, Andrew, 23; Jacksonianism, 16n5, 18n8, 24, 42n6, 43
justification, 67n30, 107, 109, 112

Kant, Immanuel, 60, 116, 126, 137
Keiffer, Moses, 122–23
Kuyper, Abraham, 126–28, 134

Lincoln, 45, 26n32
Littlejohn, W. Bradford, xix, 11, 12, 90n3, 92n9, 106n49, 111n1, 129
liturgy, 20n13, 89, 97n25, 106, 107, 111–14, 136n20, 142, 151, 153, 156–60, 161–164
Locke, John, xviin1, 27n35, 30, 61, 152
Log Cabin Campaign, 53
Luther, Martin, 67n30, 112n4, 113, 114, 117–21, 128
Lutheran, 112, 113, 119, 121

Medieval church, 112
"Man's True Destiny," 4, 84, 85n99, 86n103, 87n90
Manifest Destiny, xiv, 50–51
Materialism, 54, 91n7, 130, 131, 139
Mercersburg Review, 55, 65n20, 68, 122, 154
Mercersburg Theology, xvii, xviii, 2, 13, 40, 67n28, 72, 81n84, 82n86, 103n43, 129, 154, 157, 161–64
metaphysics, 137, 34
Methodism, 21
Mexican War, 48, 50

Milbank, John, 140–45
Mystical Presence, The, xvii, 52, 72n47, 73n54, 88n109, 92n10, 93n14, 95n18, 97, 98n28, 99n32, 100n35, 101n37, 108n55, 109n60, 139n30, 142n41, 163, 164n8
mystical union, 94, 99, 107, 135n19

nationalism, xiv, xv, 33n54, 48, 51, 130, 131, 162n3
natural law, 62, 115–117, 125n41, 126
nature, 24, 28, 34, 35, 54, 57, 59, 61n9, 63, 66, 69, 70, 72, 75, 76, 79, 80, 83–88, 89
nature vs. grace, 75
Neander, J. A. W., 65n21, 66, 67, 94
new creation, 72, 84, 87, 90, 92–95, 128, 146, 158, 163, 164
New Measures, 20–21, 62n10, 65n20 (*see also* Anxious Bench; revivalism)
New School Presbyterianism, 43, 44n9, 46n17, 53
Nichols, James H., 129n1
Noll, Mark, 17n7, 20, 22n18, 33n54, 40n79, 59–60, 74n59
nominalism, 60, 61, 74, 153

objectivity, 7, 16n5, 20n14, 71, 80, 97, 103, 137, 138, 146, 151n5, 155, 163
O'Donovan, Oliver, 123
Old School Presbyterianism, 44n9, 53, 123
ontology, 13, 24, 32, 33n55, 63, 64, 73–76, 85, 91n7, 123–25, 129, 134–37, 140, 142–44, 147
organicism, 65, 69, 119, 128
Orthodoxy, Eastern, 111, 129, 130, 156

pantheism, 65, 69n39, 75, 93
para-church, 17
participation, 129, 134, 135, 136, 138, 144, 148; in Adam, 108; in Christ, 77, 87, 93, 95, 99, 124, 125, 134n18, 136, 143; Eucharistic, 113; liturgical, 162; ontological, 125, 136, 147; sacramental, 125, 156; as *theosis*, 129

Index

Party Spirit, 80, 114, 131, 137, 138n29, 141n38, 142n42
personality, 59, 76, 78–80, 81
philosophy, 80, 123, 126, 130, 134, 137, 138, 141, 143, 149, 152, 154, 158
Pickstock, Catherine, 124n40, 139
Platonism, 136–139
politics, xvii, 2, 5–6, 7–8, 9, 11–13, 16 17n6, 18, 19, 22, 23, 29–36, 40, 42, 48, 54–57, 127, 130–34, 136, 140, 141, 155–57, 163
political theology, 1–2, 7, 111, 118n19, 123, 128
Presbyterian schism, 44
Princeton Theological Seminary, 66, 75, 108, 109
"Principle of Protestantism, The," 67n30, 68n33, 83n89, 158n21
private judgment, xiv, 68, 78, 83
privatization, 37, 83, 141, 142n42, 157, 161–62
Protestantism, 16n5, 22, 36, 67–69, 97,
Protestantism, American, xiv, 20, 60, 64–65, 83, 97, 149n2, 150n4, 151
Puritanism, 49, 52, 65n20

Radical Orthodoxy, 2, 13, 111, 134–37, 139, 140, 142n43, 143–148
rationalism, 60, 116, 130, 153
Rauch, Frederick A., 63–64, 138,
reconciliation, 6, 33, 79, 80, 85, 88, 92, 96, 100, 113, 146, 157
Reformation/Reformers, xiii, 2, 12, 38, 64, 67n30, 68, 96, 97, 110, 111–14, 119n22, 120n26, 121, 124, 128, 150n4, 156, 158
Reformed Theology, 97, 102, 106, 107n53, 109, 110, 111–18, 121–23, 126–29, 134–36, 139, 140, 141n40, 144, 145, 147, 148
Reid, Thomas, 61
regeneration, 107n53, 27
Republicanism, 16n5, 43, 59, 60, 74, 114, 151, 154
resurrection, 4, 87, 96–98
revelation, 4, 39, 61, 82n85, 85, 86, 92, 122, 137n26, 159

revivalism, xiv, xv, 1, 10, 11, 19–22, 27, 43, 80, 153, 161, 162
Roman Catholicism, 68, 91, 121, 138
Romanticism, 27, 129n1

sacramentology, 1, 11, 12, 17, 101
sacraments, xiii, xiv, 3, 5, 6, 8, 12, 35, 57, 89, 97, 100, 102n40, 106, 110, 112, 125, 135, 161–163 (*see also* baptism, Eucharist)
Schaff, Philip, xiii, xvii, 2, 11, 36–40, 64–68, 83, 90, 91, 119n23, 120n23, 157, 158
Schelling, Friedric, 63, 65, 130
Schleiermacher, Friedrich D. E., 65n21, 108n54
Scholasticism, Reformed, 112
Scotch-Irish, 2, 41, 43, 48
Scripture, 10, 67n30, 75, 148
Second Party System, 16–20, 44
Sect System, 2, 6, 12, 55, 56, 65, 68, 74n60, 141n39
sectarianism, 3, 5, 37, 51, 54–58, 68, 74, 80, 105, 142, 153, 157, 161, 162
Senn, Frank C., 112–13
Simeon, Charles, 17
slavery, 11, 12, 18, 21n17, 22, 24–26, 30, 39, 45–47
Smith, James K. A., 134n15
Social Contract, 34, 60–61, 153, 162
social principle, 53, 80–83, 93, 126, 141
Solovyov, Vladimir Sergeevich, 2, 13, 129–33
spheres, 5, 7, 24, 25, 29, 35–39, 53, 155–58
soteriology, 12, 59, 82, 89, 110

Temple, William, 8, 159n25
theosis, 129
Thoreau, David, 27–28
Transcendentalism, 27–29, 93
Trinity, 81–82, 100
Two Kingdoms, 117–24

voluntarism, 18, 21, 37, 38, 69, 74, 82, 143, 151, 153, 162
Voluntary Societies, 17, 23, 149

Wannenwetsch, Bernd, 7, 8, 100, 113n6, 152n7, 157n20, 158–59
Ward, Graham, 143–45
Wayland, Francis, 62
Wentz, Richard H., 1n2, 2, 3, 8, 10, 49, 50n28, 51, 52n32, 66n27, 99n33, 101n38, 128n54

Western Seminary, 45
Whig, 18, 22, 23, 43, 44, 48, 206
Wilberforce, Robert, 17, 92n11
Winebrenner, John, 65n20
Witherspoon, John, 61

"Year 1848, The," 50, 51, 70n40, 148n67

www.ingramcontent.com/pod-product-compliance
Lightning Source LLC
Chambersburg PA
CBHW062000220426
43662CB00011B/1762